HOME PAINTING, WALLPAPERING and DECORATING

Materials, tools and techniques for all kinds of painting, finishing and decorating

1952

WM. H. WISE & CO., INC.

NEW YORK

9524

Printed in the United States of America

INTRODUCTION

The man who takes pride in his home wants to preserve and beautify it—both inside and out—by keeping it well painted. The prerequisites of good painting are knowledge and skill, and the purpose of this book is to provide you with the information you need to master this craft. Instructions for maintenance work are also included in this book.

Once you have the necessary knowledge of methods and materials, skill in your work will naturally follow. Applying the knowledge successfully is principally a matter of care and patience. If you are willing to spend a little extra time, you'll see that it's possible for you to do as keen a job as a professional painter. We don't mean to imply that professional painters are not competent, but it is possible that they may be less interested in spending additional time on your house than you are.

Added to the satisfaction of knowing that you're doing the best job possible is the knowledge that the job is being accomplished at cost — an important factor these days. Labor is the largest single expenditure in any painting work, representing approximately seventy per cent of the total bill. You eliminate this major expense by doing the job yourself, and you have fun doing it and a great sense of satisfaction when it's done.

The terms used in this book are the regular terms of the painting and decoration trades.

As for materials, you already know that many manufacturers and distributors of painting materials dilute their products to working consistency or otherwise prepare them for immediate use. Hardware and variety stores usually carry these "ready-to-use" products, while the trade paint stores stock only the standard strength used in the trade. If you have any doubts, don't neglect to ask the advice of a competent sales person.

In a trade paint store, for example, you will find shellac labeled "5 lb. cut." This means that five pounds of dry shellac have been dissolved in one gallon of denatured alcohol. This mixture, which would be much too heavy to apply, must be thinned to a working consistency before it can be used. Although this system may appear to be unnecessarily complicated, it is practical because you will need shellac of varying consistencies. The first coats of shellac should be thin, and later coats should be heavier. By adding the correct amount of denatured alcohol to "5 lb. cut" shellac, you can thin it to the desired consistency.

The home painter and decorator has many reliable sources of information in these fields. Paint manufacturers, and paint and hardware stores have an abundance of free literature on the subjects that will keep you posted on current developments. It is to your advantage to make use of this service. Local paint dealers are also an excellent source of information on particular local conditions and the best way to handle them.

The editors wish to express their sincere appreciation for the assistance of Miss Lonore Kent, and Mr. George G. Sward, of the National Paint, Varnish, and Lacquer Association, who read the book in proof and gave much helpful technical advice.

ACKNOWLEDGMENTS: We wish to express our appreciation to the National Paint, Varnish and Lacquer Association, Inc. for reviewing the text and for their many helpful suggestions. We wish to express our thanks also to the illustrators of this book: Carl T. Sigman; William J. Ward, Jr.; Jane Vincil; Elaine White; Walter J. Karl; Carl R. Kinscherf; William A. Patrick; and Fergus Retrum.

CONTENTS

CHAPTER 1

PAINTS AND HOW TO USE THEM

The purpose of this chapter is to give you a quick over-all view of painting so that you can get on with a job and save yourself both time and money doing it. In order to do this you should familiarize yourself with the materials, tools, and methods which will do the best job with the least expenditure of money and the most efficient use of your time. Only straight simple jobs that the average home owner will run into are described in this chapter. Later on in the book you will find the specialized and more complicated jobs. If the condition of the surface on which you are going to paint appears to be different from the way it is described in this chapter, look for further information in the chapter covering that type of work in fuller detail.

Planning

As you know, planning your work is just as important as doing the work well, if you are to save time and money. A few moments—not more than fifteen minutes—can provide you with the necessary information to buy the right amount of paint, the right tools, and the other necessary items to do your job in the least time and with the maximum efficiency and economy in materials.

Look at the surfaces you are going to paint, note their condition and measure their areas. From this information you can determine the way you are going to do the painting and the quantity of paint and the tools required.

Why Paint?

There are various reasons for painting. Some people want to improve the appearance of a surface, others to change its appearance, and all get pleasure out of the colors used. Painting is closely allied to cleanliness. A newly painted surface always looks and is clean. But the principal reason for painting is to preserve the surface. Properly painted and maintained surfaces will last almost indefinitely in any climate. If you lived in a perfectly dry climate, you would not need to paint, but there is no such place except in a laboratory.

It is the moisture always in the air and rain that are the basic cause of the disintegration of woods, metals, and other common building materials. Moisture causes wood to swell, and the drying which follows causes a shrinkage. This alternate swelling and shrinking leads to the formation of fine cracks known as checking or to larger openings known as cracks or splits. If you can prevent the entrance into the wood of most of the moisture, you can reduce the amount of this checking or cracking. Paint will provide the necessary barrier to the passage of the moisture. Metals can be protected in the same way. By painting you prevent the moisture from getting to the metal surface and consequently prevent the chemical action commonly described as rusting. Other methods, such as galvanizing, do the same thing on iron and steel. The principle is the same. Protect the surface from the moisture with a material which is not affected by the moisture.

In climates where the temperature falls below freezing, the necessity for keeping water out of wood is even more important since the water in the wood can freeze. When it freezes,

Fig. 1. Various uses of paint.

it expands and further opens the checks or cracks. Again, the application of paint can prevent this condition by keeping the water out.

Limitations

However, it is impossible with ordinary paint materials to make the surface as waterproof as we would like. Paint must be a liquid in order to apply it, and it must dry to a smooth, good-looking surface. Within these limitations the manufacturers of paint have done very well. They are making great strides in the formulation of better paints all the time, but it is impossible to avoid some penetration of moisture when the underlying surface is as absorbent as wood. This moisture causes the wood to swell. The paint which is on the wood has to swell at the same rate or it will come loose from the surface. In order to achieve this, the binders (oils that bind the pigments to the surface) in the paint must remain slightly elastic, and so far nothing which has been invented will remain elastic indefinitely. This is one of the principal reasons for repainting at reasonable intervals.

The principal materials which have been used as binders are vegetable in nature. Oils like linseed, soya, and tung come from various seeds; as such they are liable to attack by bacteria and fungus, and they can be destroyed by these attacks and lose their usefulness as binders in the paint. Today great strides are being made in the use of plastics which are less affected by these two enemies of paints. In warm humid climates they are a serious problem and are usually combated by the inclusion in the paint of one of the strong fungicides and antiseptics. In the cooler climates, mildew is one of the chief problems affecting exterior paints; it discolors and breaks down the paint's protective surface. This difficulty can be minimized by coating unpainted surfaces with a copper-naphthenate solution and by adding a quarter-teaspoon of mildew-preventing concentrate to each gallon of paint.

In addition to natural causes of decay, paint frequently has to stand a great deal of wear or abrasion. It is used on floors, handrails, and other woodwork which is handled. In this case both the binders and the pigment must resist the wear. All in all, you will have to agree paint has many jobs to do and the better quality of paints do them very well.

Fig. 2. Paint manufacturers maintain testing laboratories to insure quality.

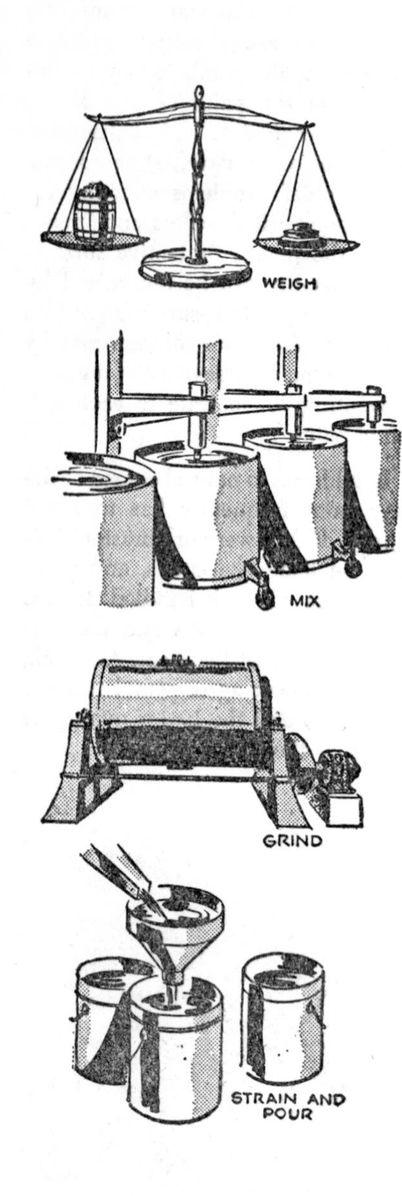

Fig. 3. Simplified steps in making packaged paints, showing the weighing, mixing, grinding, straining, and canning.

COMPOSITION OF PAINT

It is impossible to tell what is in a can of paint by looking at it, but the reliable manufacturers print this information on the label. It is generally listed under the heading of "Analysis" or "Formula." The contents usually fall into two groups: pigment and vehicle. The pigment includes all the solid materials in the paint and the vehicle all the liquids. The solid materials are generally in the form of powders before they are mixed into the paint. The proportions of these two materials will vary according to the type of paint. Wall flats—paints whose primary purpose is to cover the surface in the smallest number of coats and still have a reasonably durable surface—will contain about sixty per cent pigment and forty per cent vehicle. Enamels will usually reverse these percentages. Paints made for specialized purposes may vary considerably. Most modern paints are made of several pigments and several resins. The combination of these elements gives better wearing qualities to the paint. Whitewash is one of the exceptions; in it, the pigment is slaked lime and the vehicle water. However, anyone who has used whitewash knows that it is one of the least durable of paints. It has advantages of low cost and ease of application for some purposes but it provides little more than cleanliness and a high light reflection.

Calcimine is another simple paint. It is composed of whiting and glue and makes a good one-coat clean up job or ceiling paint.

Pigment

Most of the paint sold is made with a white pigment base. If the paint is not white, it is tinted by the addition of a color pigment. The white pigment used most frequently and in the largest amounts in manufactured paints is lithopone a synthetic pigment developed by chemists. This is cheapest of the good white pigments and is perfectly satisfactory when used for interior paints or in small amounts in exterior paints. Titanium dioxide is another of the newer white pigments which is being used. During the war it was in short supply, but nowadays, as it becomes available, you will find it listed in the formulas for exterior paints more and more often. Mixed with other pigments it is excellent. The older white-lead and zinc-oxide pigments are still used, but rarely alone. For one reason, they have become too expensive, and, further, chemists have found that if used in combination with other pigments, the over-all quality of the paint will be greatly improved. For a further discussion of this subject in greater detail see Chapter 9.

Color

The color in paint is provided by the addition to or the substitution for the white pigment of one of the color pigments. Light or pastel colored paints are made with one or more white pigments plus color pigment. If you have ever driven through one of the red clay sections of the country, you have seen a low grade of one of the color pigments.

Fig. 4. Adding tint coloring to a flat white paint.

Most of the brighter colors are made chemically. The common earth colors are raw sienna, ochre, and raw umber. Raw sienna and ochre are tan in color and can be changed to a fine brick red by calcining, that is, by heating them in a large furnace. And raw umber can be changed to a beautiful chocolate brown by the same process. These earth colors have the particular advantage of fastness to sunlight.

The bright colors are chemically made, and great strides have been made in their color fastness. However, it is still reasonably safe to say that the brighter chemical colors will fade upon exposure to sunlight. For a further discussion of this subject see Chapter 9, page 142.

Extenders

In addition to the pigments, there are solid materials known as extenders that are added to ready-mixed paints. When they are added to paint in the correct amounts they

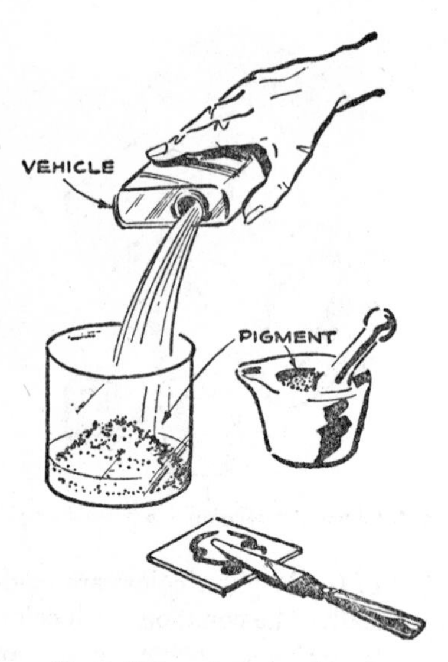

Fig. 5. Mixing pigment and binder.

are very beneficial. But when added in larger amounts they usually make the paint heavier and reduce its ability to cover an area properly. For the most part they are cheaper than the proper pigments and the temptation to reduce the manufacturing cost by their excessive use is great. In addition, painters and the public in general have come to associate weight with quality in paint due to the longtime use of white lead as a pigment. Your protection lies in understanding the proper use of extenders and in dependence upon reliable manufacturers.

Silica or sand—one of the extenders—in very small amounts is of definite benefit in an exterior paint as it increases its tooth. Tooth, or roughness, in the dried paint film is necessary for the proper adhesion of the next coat. However, it takes only a very little of this silica to the gallon to do the job. More than this simply makes the paint heavier in weight but poorer in covering power, since the silica remains nearly transparent. The extenders barytes, fibrous talc and China clay are added to manufactured paint for much the same reasons. In small amounts they are useful, but in larger quantities they are nothing more than cheapening adulterants. In addition to these relatively coarse crystalline materials, there are the fine smooth types such as alumina and talc. These are added to paint principally to keep the heavier pigments in suspension.

It is impossible to state a definite percentage for extenders as the most that should be found in a paint, but you should regard with a critical eye any paint which admits to more than ten per cent of the total pigment as extenders. This is not true of the tinting colors since many of them are composed principally of one or another of these extenders. And it does not hold for paints containing any substantial amount of titanium dioxide.

The Vehicle

The vehicles which make it possible to brush or spread paint are not as simple as they used to be. The modern vehicle generally contains a vegetable oil like linseed, a resin, either natural or synthetic, a thinner or several thinners, and a drier. The more complicated modern vehicle is an improvement over the older, simpler mixture, which was simply a mixture of linseed oil, turpentine, and drier. The purposes of these parts of the vehicle are as follows: Oil serves to bind the pigment to the surface, resin to harden the dried oil, thinners to make it possible to brush or spray the paint and to make it flow to a smooth surface, and driers to speed up the drying action so that it takes place in a reasonably short time, which ranges from a few hours to a day or two, depending on the paint or finish and the weather conditions.

Usually the oil and the resin are blended in large kettles. Then the pigment is ground into this mixture, and finally the thinners and driers are added. The purpose of grinding instead of simply mixing is to wet the pigment thoroughly. Pigments have a very rough surface and it is necessary to push the oil into the indentations. If this is not done, the air caught on each particle of pigment may make it float to the surface of the paint as it dries and there is no uniform strength throughout the thickness of the dried film.

Fig. 6. Linseed oil was once cooked in large kettles over open fires.

Oils

The oils which are used in paint are generally vegetable types. Mineral oils like lubricating oil would be useless; they will not dry. Linseed oil, which is pressed from flaxseed, is one of the most widely used types. It is relatively clear in color, can be made to dry in twelve to twenty-four hours by the addition of driers, and remains somewhat elastic after drying. It is this last characteristic which distinguishes it from many other paint oils. The elasticity allows the dried paint to expand and contract with the surface upon which it has been put. Other oils – such as those that come from soybean, sunflower, tung nut, castor bean, and fish – have different desirable characteristics, such as greater resistance to heat or moisture or harder drying qualities; these oils may be used either alone or mixed.

Resins

The strength or toughness of paint is generally supplied by the resins.

The natural resins which are used in paint are actually the dried sap of pine trees. The various names of the different resins–copal, kauri, and so on–simply indicate the port or part of the world from which they come. They vary somewhat in their characteristics, and these variations are taken into consideration in compounding the paint or varnish.

Synthetic resins have replaced the natural ones to a large extent. They are made from the same materials as plastics. As our knowledge of plastics increases and more and more compounds are developed, no doubt we will have even greater flexibility in the qualities and characteristics of paint than can be found at present. The synthetics are either substituted for the natural resins or added to them.

Thinners

Thinners used in paint serve two main purposes: to reduce the thickness of the liquid so that you can apply it with a brush or spray gun, and to help the paint to flow to a smooth surface once it has been applied. If you add too much thinner, the paint will become so thin that it will not cover the surface as intended by the manufacturer. If this happens, you can leave the can of paint uncovered overnight and the excess thinner will evaporate, restoring the paint to its proper consistency. A little additional thinner should be added to most paints if the temperature goes below about 70 degrees. You do this to bring the paint to the same consistency it would have if the temperature were warmer and that is the only reason. When using a manufactured paint, follow the thinning directions on the can to the letter. At the factory each type is tested on very accurate apparatus and the recommendations for thinning are made on the basis of those tests. Sometimes a paint is made with oils or resins which require unusual thinners, though manufacturers try to avoid this added complication for the consumer. If some such thinner is recommended, you should use it; ordinary thinners will not work as well or they would have been recommended.

Kinds of Thinners

The most popular is turpentine. It is a very satisfactory material. It evaporates completely from the paint when it dries but it does not evaporate too rapidly. And it is a good solvent for nearly all the oils and resins used in paint since it does not affect their desirable characteristics. Many oils and resins are dissolved by such thinners as benzine, naphtha, and mineral spirits, but a few are not.

The petroleum industry supplies us with mineral spirits and benzine. The former is available in fast- to slow-drying kinds, making it an excellent thinner, except that in some cases it evaporates too rapidly for brush application. The paint may not flow properly and dries with a ropy appearance. Benzol and naphtha, from the coal tar industry, are frequently used by the painter to make his paint more penetrating when working on excessively sappy woods.

Do not turn down a can of paint which lists mineral spirits as the only thinner contained in the vehicle; if the manufacturer is reliable, you can be sure that they will not harm the paint.

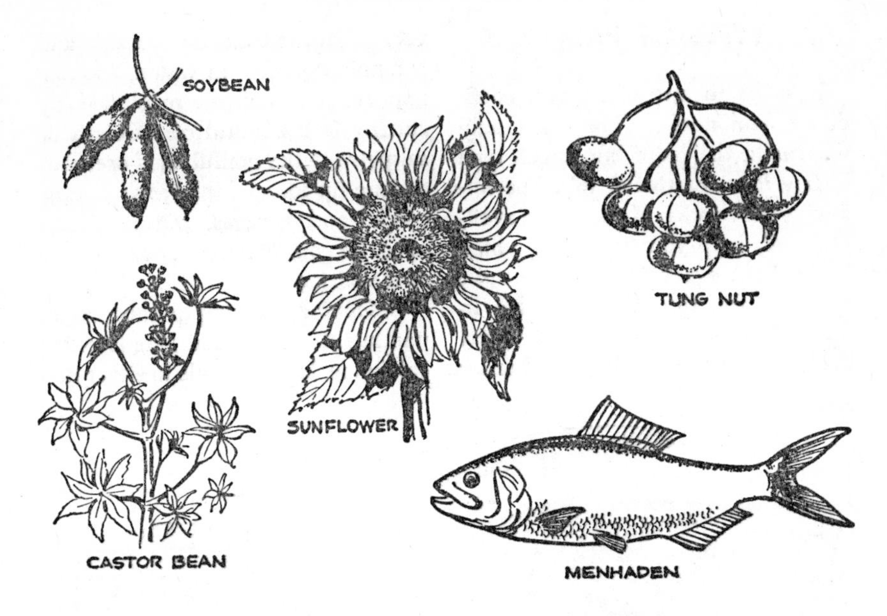

Fig. 7. Sources of oil used for binder in paint.

Some modern paints made with special oils and resins and the old-fashioned glue-binder paints use water as the thinner. In each case the manufacturer has determined the correct amount of water to add to the paint for thinning. Follow his directions carefully. Use an ordinary eight-ounce drinking glass or a measuring cup for accuracy.

For a detailed discussion of the use and nature of thinners, see page 20.

Driers

Driers are metallic salts, dissolved in a thin vehicle. The principal metals used are manganese, lead, and cobalt. The name "Japan" appended to most driers has no real significance.

The driers in paint are only put there to make the paint dry in a reasonably quick time. They do this by absorbing more oxygen from the air than they can use. The extra oxygen combines with the oil and makes it dry quickly. However, there is a limit to the speed with which the oil can absorb the oxygen, and the addition of drier beyond this point will not shorten the drying time any further. So, if you are mixing your own paint, add only as much drier as is recommended. Similarily, if you are using manufactured paint, it is useless and may possibly do damage to add extra drier. Boiled linseed oil, by the way, is never boiled, although in the old days it was cooked to speed up its drying characteristics. But nowadays the simple addition of a chemical or synthetic drier to the linseed oil does the same thing with less waste.

TYPES OF PAINT

In order to buy paint with confidence, you need to know not only what is in the paint but which type to buy for a particular job. The following description of the paints available will help you to decide which is the least expensive and the most practical for the job you have in mind. You can consult your local dealer for advice. Also, mail-order houses carry reliable lines of standard-specification paints for all household uses.

Water Paints

The simplest of the paints are the water paints.

Whitewash. This is a simple mixture of slaked lime and water. It is very cheap, but it is not durable and it remains soluble in water. You can improve its moisture-resistance by stirring in a handful of rock salt or saltpetre to the pailful. It is useful as a clean-up for such places as cellars, coops, and garages, but it should never be considered as a preservative of the surface.

Calcimine. A simple mixture of whiting and powdered glue is called calcimine. It is available in either hot-water or cold-water types. The name indicates which kind of water is required to dissolve tne glue. To mix for use, add water to the calcimine in a pail and break up the lumps with your hands. After this, the glue must be given an opportunity to jell.

The jelling generally takes overnight. Stand the pail of calcimine in a

Fig. 8. Casein paints are good for clean-up work and seasonal outdoor use. You often see them used for carnival colors.

bathtub or laundry tub half full of cold water and the mixture will be ready for straining and using the next morning. Warm water would cause the paint to sour, and any container much smaller than a laundry tub would let the water warm up to room temperature too quickly. You have to apply calcimine with a large brush—called a calcimine brush—because the paint sets so quickly that only fast work will prevent laps showing in your job. Laps are the marks or streaks which show up when you put wet paint on dry. Calcimine has been used frequently on ceilings and, if properly applied, makes a fine flat, or matte, finish. But you should first prime or size any plaster surface to prepare it for calcimine.

Casein Paint. Casein paint is a water paint which dries to a reasonably moisture-proof condition. The binder in the paint is casein glue, the pigment is generally whiting or one of the other cheap whites. This paint is very useful for clean-up work since it requires no preparation on new surfaces and only washing on old ones, and it covers in one coat. Use a large brush and work in short enough stretches to avoid laps. A stretch is the area you paint before moving on to the next area.

Water-Soluble Synthetics. These are a relatively new type of paint. They are made of a variety of pigments and water-soluble resins. Their principal advantages are that they cover in one coat and there is no odor. Their possibilities will no doubt be greatly improved as manufacturers continue to develop them. Even now they are very successful for quick and easy results, and you can clean up with merely a sponge and water when you have finished applying them. Be careful to clean your brush too, as the dried paint is very hard to get out of the bristles. While this paint is claimed to be entirely washable after it has dried several days, do not expect the washability you would find in an oil paint.

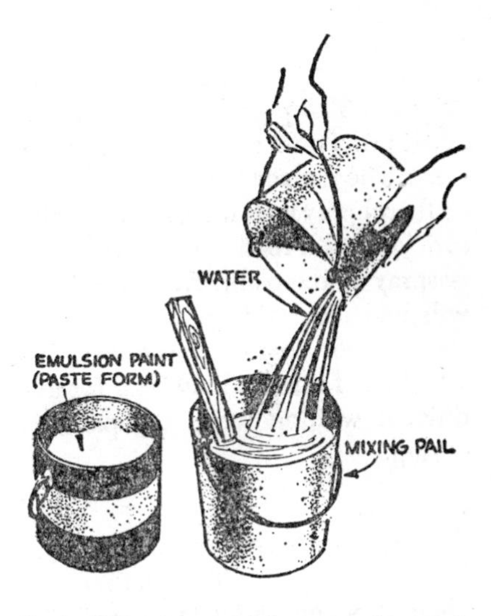

Fig. 9. Mixing water and the paste of an emulsion or water-soluble synthetic paint.

Texture Paint. All the water paints so far described flow to a smooth surface when they dry. Texture paint is intended to have a rough and definite surface. The binder is one of the hot- or cold-water soluble glues. Read the directions before you add the water. The pigment is usually fortified with a material like coarse sand or crushed oyster shell to add to the texture. Apply these paints with a large brush or trowel. Use anything from a whisk broom to a draftsman's triangle to create the surface texture you want. Naturally, this work must be done while the material is still wet. Most of these texture paints require a sized plaster wall, and all of them can be glazed to increase the effect of the texture. See Chapter 10, page 155, for further information on this technique.

Cement Paint. Stucco and cement walls and all other masonry surfaces can be painted with this simple type of paint. The pigment is any of the alkali-proof ones and the binder is cement. The surface to be painted must be thoroughly wet; use a hose to make sure you get it really wet. Then brush or spray on the paint. When it dries it will make a tight enough bond to stand exposure to the weather. Instructions for some kinds call for additional wetting while the paint is drying.

Oil Paints

The second large group of paints is known as oil paints, though they may contain no oil at all but an oil-like resin instead. For the sake of convenience, these paints are described in the order in which they would be used on a surface.

Primers

Plaster Primers. Plaster is a highly absorbent material and soaks up the oil from any paint put on it. In order to avoid the marks this absorption causes in the finished paint, it is customary to apply a coat of primer to new plaster first. These primers contain either enough oil to allow the plaster to absorb all it will hold or a very sticky varnish which will dry on the surface of the plaster but will not soak too deep into it. Both methods are satisfactory; the second is less expensive. Both types, if properly formulated, will dry to a non-absorbent surface with just the right amount of tooth for the next coat of paint. There is very little pigment in a primer, so do not expect it to cover like a coat of paint. If you are going to calcimine a ceiling, it is wise to prime it first. Then, when you have to wash it off preparatory to refinishing it, the calcimine will come off readily.

Wood Primers. Primers for wood serve the same purpose as those for plaster. They penetrate enough to stop the suction of the wood and provide a surface to support and hold the next coat of paint. Many manufacturers now make up wood primers as such, and nearly all put instructions on their cans of undercoater (see page 13) for the proper thinning to make a good wood primer. You can make your own primer out of white lead, linseed oil, turpentine, and driers, and for outside work nothing could be finer. Softwoods require more oil in the primer than hardwoods. You can determine which type you are dealing with by making up your paint and trying it out on a sample of the wood. If it is perfectly dull the next day, add some oil; if it has a high gloss, add some pigment and thinners. If it is slightly shiny in spots and dull in others, it is just right. The differences are due to the variations in the amount of sap.

The following formula is recommended for making your own white-lead primer:

White lead	100 lbs
Raw linseed oil	4 gals
Turpentine	2 gals
Japan drier	1 pt

This makes 9 and ⅝th gals of primer. Each gallon will cover 600 sq. ft. A one gallon formula is as follows:

White lead	11 lbs
Raw linseed oil	1¾ qts
Turpentine	⅞ qt
Japan drier	2 ozs

Metal Primers. Here we have a special problem not met with anywhere else. There is always a thin molecular film of moisture on metal which makes it very difficult for paint to stick to the surface. To overcome this difficulty the manufacturers of metal-priming paints include in the formula a chemical which enables the paint to penetrate to the metal and adhere properly. Job-mixed red lead and linseed oil make a good primer but the specially made primers are better. Zinc dust and zinc chromate are often used as pigments in primers. Chose the type made for the particular metal on which you are working and follow the instructions. Galvanized metal must be seasoned before paint will adhere to it properly or else it must be etched by the application of an acid, usually acetic acid.

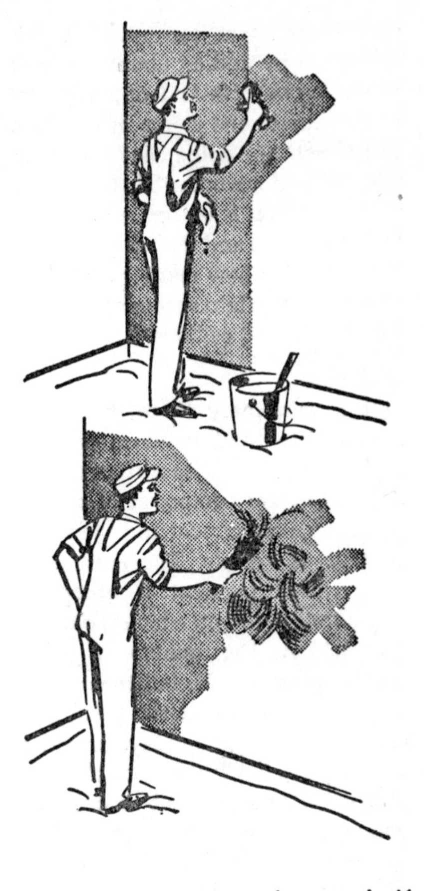

Fig. 10. Texture paints can be textured with almost any tool.

Undercoater

Following the application of a primer, it is best to apply at least one coat of undercoater, which is a paint that has high covering power and enough vehicle to dry to a hard non-absorbent finish. It is not intended for a finish coat and consequently does not necessarily dry to a perfectly even surface. If your job is a very small one, it hardly pays to buy extra undercoater—you can make a fair substitute by adding about one pint of mixing varnish and one-half pint of thinners to one gallon of wall flat. But if you are doing several rooms, you will find it worthwhile to buy the undercoater; it is less expensive than finishing paint and does a better job. To determine how many gallons you will need, take into account the walls, woodwork, and ceilings.

Wall Flats

It is customary to refer only to manufactured paints which dry to a perfectly dull or matte surface as wall flats. They are composed of a high percentage of pigment and a low percentage of vehicle. The most commonly used pigment is lithopone, a synthetic pigment, which is entirely satisfactory. The quality of these paints varies widely, but the competition is so keen that the price generally denotes the quality, provided the manufacturer is one of the reliable ones. As much as two dollars a gallon may separate the price of a low grade from a high grade. You can decide whether your job makes the higher price worthwhile. The better grades generally have more vehicle and consequently dry harder all the way through. This makes them more washable and more resistant to wear. As you increase the amount of vehicle, you must use a more expensive type of pigment to retain the same relative covering power, and this obviously increases the cost of the paint. Follow the manufacturer's instructions for thinning. Some manufacturers recommend the use of a special thinner because of the particular vehicle in their paint, but most suggest turpentine. Be careful not to add more than the recommended amount of thinner or the paint will not cover as well as expected.

These wall flats are available in both white and tints. You can readily add tinting color if you wish. Due to the relatively low percentage of vehicle in these paints, the undercoater should be non-absorbent or you may have dull areas where the paint chalks excessively.

White lead, mixing varnish, turpentine, and driers in the proper proportions make an excellent, though expensive, wall flat. When you buy a tub of white lead for the pigment, you will find instructions for mixing it into a flat paint on the can or on a slip under the lid of the can. This makes a very fine paint, as good as there is, although, of course, it requires more work than using a ready-made paint. The procedure is to break up the lead, mix in the varnish, tint it to the color you want, thin it, strain it. You will get about five to six gallons from a hundred-pound tub. If you expect to glaze the walls and woodwork (see Chapter 10, page 155), it is the best ground you can use.

Enamels

Paints whose proportion of vehicle is higher than that of the pigment are generally known as enamels. The obvious characteristic of enamels is their glossy surface when they are dry. The most important difference, however, is the large amount of vehicle. This means that the enamel dries with a high proportion of oil or resin throughout the thickness of the film, which makes it very hard and extremely resistant to washing or wear.

Enamels are classified according to the shine of the dried surface. Gloss enamels are very shiny, almost glass-like. Semi-gloss or semi-matte dry to a half-shine, and flat or matte enamels are nearly as dull as wall flats when they are dry. The gloss enamels will stand the most washing without showing any effects. The other two types tend to become more shiny from the polishing action of the abrasives used in cleaning them.

Exterior Enamels

These are made principally for porch floors, decks, concrete surfaces, and farm implements. The last mentioned kind is called implement paint; it covers unusually well in one coat. Generally they are made of a synthetic resin which is less penetrating and more impervious to water than other thinners. All enamels are improved by the use of an appropriate undercoat for satisfactory results.

Gloss Paints

Gloss paints are not enamels. They are made in the same way as wall flats, but the oil in the vehicle is especially treated so that it floats to the top when the paint dries and makes the surface shiny. Naturally, this does not contribute to the wearing quality of the paint, though it makes it look like an enamel to the casual glance. If you want the advantages of an enamel, do not accept a gloss paint—you will be sadly disappointed.

Interior Semi-Glosses

These are a relatively new type of paint. They are intermediate between enamels and wall flats. They are hard-drying, flow to a smooth surface, yet have a good covering quality. Their washability makes them desirable for all surfaces requiring such maintenance. They are frequently used for woodwork and service rooms like kitchens and bathrooms. They are made with an acceptable resin and a good grade of pigment properly proportioned. They are extremely durable and set to a final soft shine in about ten days. They are known variously as ivory tone or satin finish, as well as semi-gloss.

Exterior Oil Paints

Next to wall flats (see page 14) this type of paint is the most highly competitive, which leads to some of the most flagrant adulteration. Here —on the outside of your house—where the paint is exposed to extremes of temperature and moisture conditions, you would be wise to use only the best paint you can afford. This does not necessarily mean the most expensive on the market.

The climates to which the paint will be exposed vary so much throughout the country that there is no one perfect paint formula. In the northern section you cannot use too good a paint as the extremes of summer heat and winter cold test its endurance. The dry heat of the southwest hardly affects the paint film but it does make fading a problem. High humidity creates problems with mildew and fungus. Local paint dealers are usually very good authorities on the relative merits of various exterior paints for their areas. You will do well to talk with them; their experience in your area may save you money.

When you come to buying the paint, purchase it in the largest quantity you can use. Paint is always cheaper that way. A five-gallon can costs less per gallon than the single gallons and a thirty-gallon barrel is still cheaper. This may sound like a lot of paint, but if you plan a two- or three-coat job on a good-sized frame house, it won't be too much.

Job-Mixed and Ready-Mixed

Exterior paints are either job-mixed or ready-mixed. For the inexperienced painter it is probably better to buy the manufactured type. The paint is properly formulated for the finish coats and you will find instructions on the label for the addition of oil and thinners for the priming and undercoats. However, you can mix your own from white-lead paste, linseed oil, turpentine, and driers. All manufacturers of white-lead paste will be glad to supply you with the formulas for various coats.

Most manufacturers of ready-to-use exterior paints use a combination of pigments in order to get the benefits of each. They also add resins in order to improve the vehicle. They are now able to predict that the paint will chalk evenly and that the process will self-clean the surface. Not only does this self-cleaning maintain the appearance but it insures a good surface for repainting.

A paint which dries with a high enamel-like gloss is rarely a good investment on the exterior of a wood house. The film is too liable to check and crack.

Paints for Metal

After metal has been primed to eliminate the effects of moisture (see page 13), the primers are followed by the application of paints adapted to a particular use—heat resistant paints, reflective paints, or regular exterior paints, as the job requires.

Fire-Retardant Paints

Much experimentation has been done with this type of paint. No reliable manufacturer calls any of them fire-proofing. But there is little doubt of their effectiveness in retarding fire. Some work on the principle of smothering the fire, others depend on a glass-like ingredient which protects the undersurface from catching on fire. A third approach is a paint which puffs up when exposed to heat, thus providing an insulating blanket over the surface.

FINISHES

Clear Finishes

There are a variety of clear finishes to put on wood. The commonest of them are shellac, varnish, and lacquer.

Shellac

Shellac is a simple natural resin which is soluble in alcohol. You will usually buy shellac in "5 lb. cut." This means that five pounds of the resin have been dissolved in one gallon of alcohol. It is too heavy for use that way. For average use add another gallon of alcohol (use 190 proof denatured alcohol). This will then give you a two-pound cut. It is customary to use a two-pound cut for first coating and a three-pound cut for finishing coats.

Beware of shellac substitutes. The shortage of real shellac during the last war encouraged the development of the substitutes and some of them are perfectly satisfactory. There are also some very poor ones on the market. If you do buy a substitute, do it only on a money-back guarantee.

When dry, shellac is neither water- nor alcohol-proof. Water or moisture will cause bloom, a clouding of the surface, and alcohol will actually dissolve the shellac again. However, it is a good durable finish, is easily applied, and rubs to a good-looking, smooth, and polished surface. For furniture such as bookcases, chairs, and odd pieces upon which people are unlikely to stand beverage glasses, it makes an inexpensive finish.

Varnish

For greater durability there are the varnishes. These are mixtures of oils, resins, thinners, and driers. They are made for many different purposes and range from floor-finishing to baking types. For the average homeowner, three types are enough: floor varnish, cabinet rubbing varnish, and spar varnish.

The floor varnish is exactly what the name implies, a tough, hard-wearing, long-lasting material. It is obtainable either clear or stained. The clear kind will not add any color to the surface upon which it is applied. The stain varnish, as you would expect, contains a pigment or dye which will color the wood. Try out the material before you start a whole floor; you may find the color either too dark or too light. If it is too dark, add some clear varnish, if too light, return the can for one of a darker shade—ordinary tinting pigments are too coarse to add to this material. Keep the varnish well stirred, as the "color" has a tendency to settle out. And if the temperature is below 70

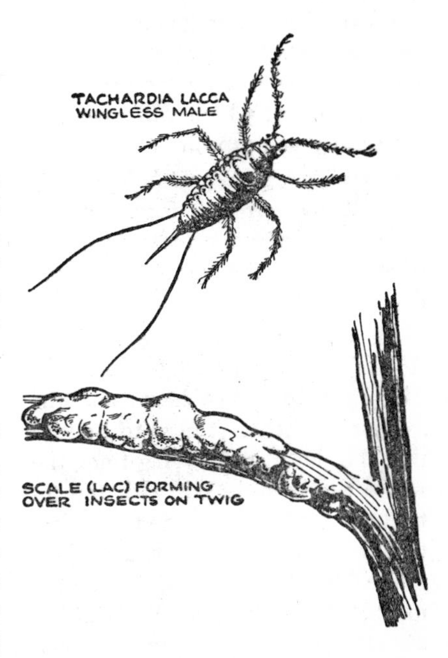

Fig. 11. Shellac is an insect secretion.

degrees, keep the can of varnish in a pail of water at about 100 degrees, or body temperature.

Cabinet rubbing varnish is a clear, hard-drying variety which can be sandpapered, rubbed with pumice stone, and polished to a very high lustre. Most modern varieties are made water- and alcohol-proof. Be sure that this is clearly stated on the label before you make a purchase. Like all varnishes, this kind should be applied only at normal temperature to get the best flowing qualities. For detailed information on the use of varnish in wood finishing, see Chapter 12, page 179.

Spar varnishes are made especially for exterior use. So far, no satisfactory substitutes have been found for the expensive ingredients used in making a good grade of this material. You will have to pay a good price for a spar varnish which will give you the service you expect.

Other Types of Varnish. There are also mixing varnishes for adding to job-mixed paint for extra lustre of hardness, and flat varnishes, which dry to a dull finish.

All these varnishes are made to dry in various time intervals. The shortest time is two hours and the longest two days. It used to be said that the shorter the drying time, the worse the varnish, but with the introduction of resins made from plastics, this is no longer true. Your best guide here is the reputation of the manufacturer. Nearly all varnishes are made to be thinned with turpentine; the exceptions will be noted on the label. The principal thing to remember is temperature; varnish will not flow to a smooth surface if the temperature is below normal.

Lacquer

The last of the group of clear finishes is lacquer. It dries very quickly and the only way to apply it successfully is with a spray gun. You can get wonderful finishes with it, but its use requires special skill and you should get careful on-the-job instructions before going ahead with any sizeable project.

Polishing

Polishing Oil and Wax. The polishing of shellacked or varnished surfaces is generally done with a polishing oil or wax. Polishing oils are very good if you rub them dry, otherwise they tend to collect dust.

Waxes are made in two types: the self-polishing and the "you" polish. The self-polishing type is not recommended for furniture if you are concerned about the underlying shellac or varnish, but it is perfectly satisfactory for floors, whether of composition or wood. Rubbing wax takes a little more effort but the high lustre is well worth it. Modern polishing waxes which contain some carnauba (a type of hard-drying wax) are the hardest drying and longest lasting.

Very recently silicone resins have been combined with waxes to make equally hard-drying polishes.

For full information on the finishing and polishing of wood surfaces see Chapter 12, page 179; and for full information on finishing floors, see Chapter 7, page 93.

Metallic Finishes

While it is true that all paints are metallic, the name is generally reserved for those paints which look like metal when they dry. Bronze and aluminum are the two metals most frequently used to obtain this effect. The various shades of bronze simulate gold and aluminum simulates silver. These metal powders are mixed with a suitable vehicle, and you simply brush them on. They are available in either paste or powder form and ready-mixed or in separate containers for mixing just before use. The two-container type, for mixing on the job, will dry to a more even finish than the ready-mixed. In it, the metal has already been mixed to a paste and it dissolves easily and evenly throughout the vehicle.

The vehicle used varies from asphaltum varnish to fine spar varnishes and is called "bronzing liquid." The metals are available in a wide range of colors.

In order to prevent the tarnishing of the metallic paint, it is necessary to coat it with shellac or varnish when dry. If you are going to use the paint on the outside of the house, make sure you get the type marked for exterior use.

Stains and Stain Finishes

The complex subject of staining and finishing is covered completely in Chapter 12, page 179. The subject of finishing floors is covered in Chapter 7, page 93. However, much of the staining we do is on fences, house exteriors, and the like, where the work is not of furniture quality, and the following brief summary covers such jobs.

Oil Stains. The simplest of stains is the oil type. This is merely a pigment or dye mixed in a thin vehicle. It is applied by brushing it on, and as soon

Fig. 12. If you have the equipment and skill, you can do a beautiful job of spraying furniture with lacquer.

as it has had an opportunity to soak into the wood—but before it has begun to dry out—the excess is wiped off with a rag. This stain is available in a wide variety of colors. But it is suggested that you try it out each time before proceeding with a particular job because woods vary in their ability to absorb and the more absorption which takes place, the darker the finish will be. It is easy to lighten a batch of stain by simply adding more thinner. However, do this carefully or the oil in the stain will become so thin that you will not be able to wipe to an even surface.

One class of oil stains is known as penetrating oil stains, which are exactly what the name states – they contain a thinner which aids the penetration of the pigment into the wood. You have to be a little more careful with this kind and wipe off the excess before it makes the wood too dark, especially if the wood is one of the soft varieties.

Wax Stains. Probably one of the handiest stains is the fortified wax stain. There are many brands on the market now. This product is simply a wax to which hardening gums have been added. To obtain colored varieties, a dye is also added. Apply a colored coat and let it soak in, then wipe off the excess. When dry, apply a clear-body coat of the same material in the same way, and follow this with polishing wax. These stains are not recommended for exterior use.

Exterior Stains. For outside purposes there are preservatives and stains of the copper naphthenate type. These are a mixture of a preservative and a stain in a water-thin liquid. You can apply this liquid by brushing or dipping. Dipping and soaking are recommended as being more thorough. A piece of oilcloth tacked in a simple wooden trough makes an excellent dipping tank. An old pail is fine for the bottoms of fence posts. Leave each post in as long as you can; two days is not too long a time.

There are many other materials, such as asphaltum, creosote, and old engine oil, which are often used, but none of them have the mildew-proofing and fungicidal action of the copper naphthenate type of preservative.

THINNERS

Thinners

There are three main classes of thinners: those for oil paint, those for shellac, and those for lacquer.

Turpentine. The safest type of thinner for oil paints is the standard turpentine. You will find that it varies somewhat in color and odor. But these differences are of no significance; they are caused by the way in which the turpentine was made. Turpentine is a distillate of the sap of pine trees, and in order to conserve the source, even the stumps of the trees are treated.

Benzine. Benzine, which is made from petroleum oil, is widely used as a paint thinner not only because of its cheapness but because it prevents some of the livering action of canned paints. The greatest objection to it is the fire hazard it creates. It catches fire at a lower temperature than any of the other common thinners. As a matter of fact, most city ordinances do not permit the storage of it. However, if its possession is not prohibited and you take extreme care, you can use it for cleaning brushes and pots and for wiping up. Most manufacturers list it on their paint labels as mineral spirits. "Benzine" may also refer to a highly volatile fraction of petroleum thinner; in this form it dries too rapidly to be used as a thinner in many paints.

Alcohol. Shellac is thinned with denatured alcohol. For this purpose you cannot use the anti-freeze type of alcohol, it may contain gasoline. The water would cause the shellac to bloom. The alcohol must be at least 190 proof denatured. All paint stores carry this kind, so there is no difficulty in getting it.

Lacquer Thinners. Lacquer is thinned with special thinners made for the purpose. Nothing else will do. There are standard, general lacquer thinners, but frequently you must use only the recommended thinner in order to obtain the best results with a particular lacquer.

CHAPTER 2

BRUSHES AND TOOLS, MATERIALS AND ESTIMATING

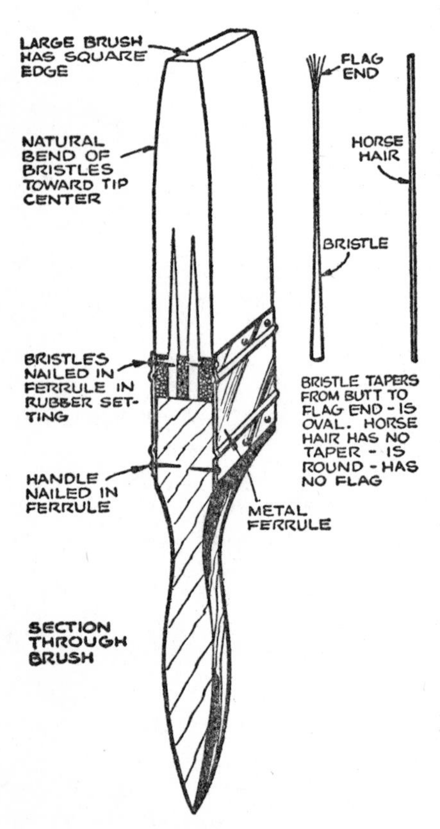

Fig. 1. Construction of a flat paint brush.

Selecting Brushes

Brushes are a painter's most impor-tant tools. They should be carefully selected and given the best care. The better brushes are made of Chinese black bristle. However, because of World War II and subsequent politi-cal changes in China, very little of this stock has been imported in recent years. Horsehair is a common substi-tute, but it has the disadvantages of being too coarse and of not with-standing water-soaking; when it has absorbed too much water, it becomes brittle and breaks off in short lengths.

Many other kinds of hair go into the manufacture of brushes for par-ticular uses. Expensive sable hair is used for artists' brushes, while goat's hair is used for mottling and bronz-ing brushes

The bristles are graded for length and thickness, and a wide selection of different lengths and weights is blended or mixed to make up a batch. This batch is then shaped for the fer-rule, and the butt ends of the bristles are set in rubber. The rubber is vul-canized to hold the bristles. After that the ferrule and handle are attached and the brush is finished. It sounds easy, but a great deal of care and skill go into this procedure.

Efforts are being made to use plastic filaments as a substitute for bristle. The manufacturers claim they are as good as the natural bristles. And there is no doubt they would be less affected by water and many of the solvents used in paint. But the test is in whether they will do as good a paint job. Opinions seem to vary on this point.

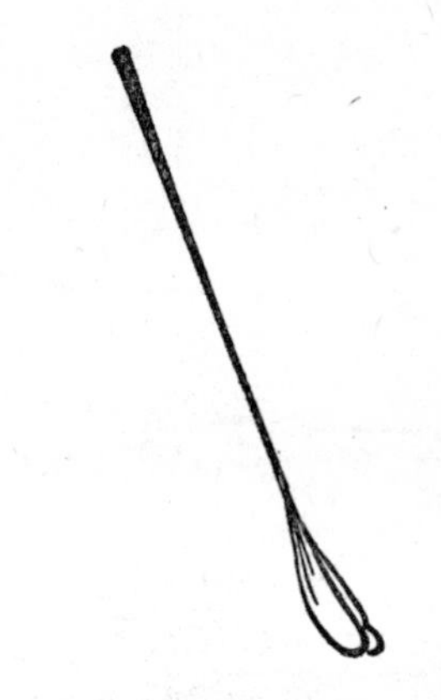

Fig. 2. Paint adhering to a brush bristle.

Brushes work on the simple principle of adhesion. When a brush is dipped into paint, the paint adheres to the surfaces of the bristles. When the loaded brush is placed in contact with a surface having greater adhesion for the paint, the paint flows off the bristles and coats that surface. The greater the amount of bristle surface, the greater the amount of paint the brush will hold.

Fig. 3. Flag ends.

The surface available for the paint to cling to is increased by the flag ends (see illustration) of each bristle. These also serve to give the brush greater flexibility at the tip. That is why a painter who knows brushes always examines the brush for its flags. If there are not enough of them – that is, less than 25 per cent flag-tipped bristles – or if they are not thin and tapered enough, he can reasonably assume that the brush is made of a substitute, usually horsehair.

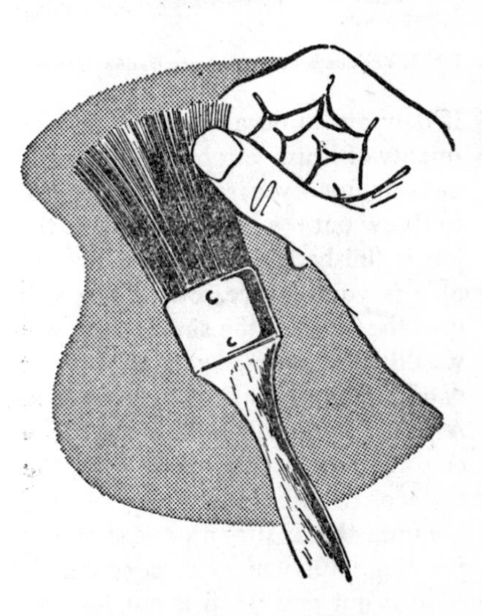

Fig. 4. Examine a brush for flags.

The brushes you buy should include a wall brush of four-inches width and a sash tool. You can get by with just these two brushes, but you must be prepared to keep them clean

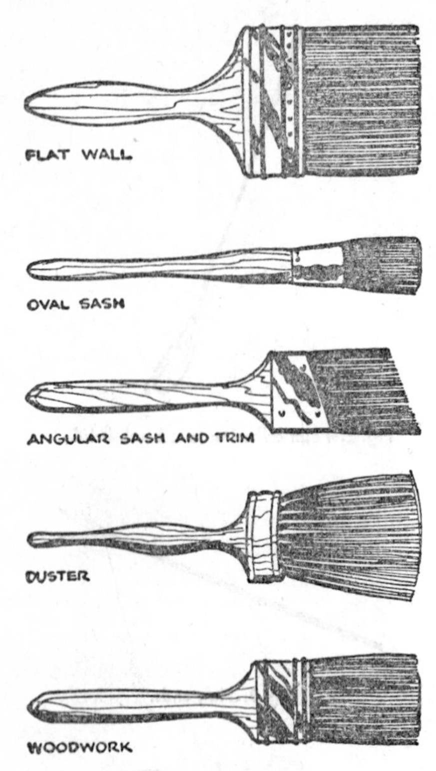

Fig. 5. Various brushes that are frequently used.

if they are to do all your work. The quality of brush you buy will depend entirely upon yourself. If you intend to throw out the brush as soon as the job is finished, the cheapest obtainable is your choice. But if you will give the brushes the simple care you would give your saw or plane, get good ones and you'll never regret it. A good brush will hold a maximum of paint and spread it evenly on the surface. It will retain its spring and life until the bristles are too short for painting. But you must consistently rinse it out and wash it out for any lengthy storage.

Types of Brushes

Flat Paint Brush. This is a metal-bound, rubber-set brush used for all ordinary painting. It is sometimes called a "wall brush." Select one having a chiseled edge.

They range from 3 to 6 inches in width. An experienced painter uses a 5-inch brush, but a beginner will usually find this width too tiring. For the beginner, a 4-inch brush is usually satisfactory. The bristle length ranges from 3 to 5¼ inches; the recommended length is 4 to 4½ inches.

Flat Varnish Brush. This is a metal-bound, rubber-set brush made for painting woodwork and for varnishing. Select one with a chiseled edge.

These brushes range from 1½ to 4 inches in width. A 3½-inch or 4-inch brush is standard for professionals, but it is difficult to use for cutting sharp lines; a beginner will usually find a 2½-inch or 3-inch brush satisfactory. The bristle length ranges from 2 to 4 inches; the recommended length is 3½ inches.

Round or Oval Sash Tool or Brush. This is a metal-bound, rubber-set brush having a long handle which is round or oval at the ferrule. It is used for painting window sashes or other small surfaces requiring extreme care and for mixing samples; in fact, you can use it for almost any job for which you don't wish to dirty a larger brush.

Buy several of these brushes in different sizes, and be sure they are chiseled. They range in size from number 1 to number 12. You will probably need a Size 6 and a Size 8; Size 10 is also recommended. The bristle length ranges from 1¼ to 2 inches. A 2-inch bristle is recommended. The size number does not indicate the actual size of the sash brush in inches, but is based on a complicated manufacturing formula. Size 6 or 8 is about one inch in diameter.

Flat Sash Tools. This brush is frequently used in place of the round or oval sash tool for cutting in window sashes; it has the advantage of thinness. It is available with either a square-cut or an angular-cut end. Square-cut brushes are usually chiseled while angular-cuts should be flat. They range from 1 to 2½ inches in width; 2 inches is the recommended width. The bristle length ranges from 1½ to 3⅛ inches; 2½ inches is the recommended bristle length.

Painter's Duster. This is a flat brush used for dusting off all surfaces before painting. While any old, clean brush may be used, a new painter will find it less expensive to buy one of the brushes made especially for this purpose. They are usually about 4 inches wide and made of horsehair or a hair mixture. The most expensive ones usually have white bristle. Select one which pleases you.

The trouble with using an old brush is that the bristles must have life in them, which may not be the case with an old brush. An old brush may also be stiff with paint in its heel.

Calcimine (Flat). This brush is used for applying calcimine and textured paint and is very good for glue-sizing walls. It is usually rubber-set and either galvanized or brass-bound. The

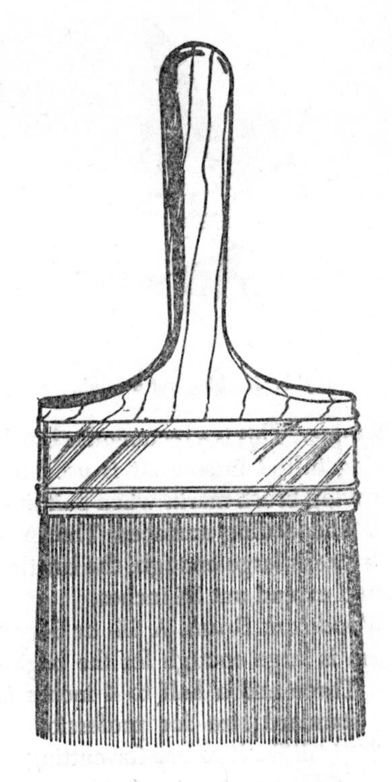

Fig. 6. A flat calcimine brush.

more expensive ones have an outside layer of light Russian bristle. They range from 7 to 8 inches in width; 7 inches is the recommended width. The bristle length is from 5 to 5¾ inches; 5 or 5½ inches is the recommended length.

Calcimine (Dutch). This brush is rectangular in shape and is available with the bristle set either in tufts or in continuous rows. The tufted type is somewhat easier to clean. They are generally about 7½ by 2½ inches. Select one which feels good in your hand, keeping in mind the fact that it will hold a lot of paint and will be heavy.

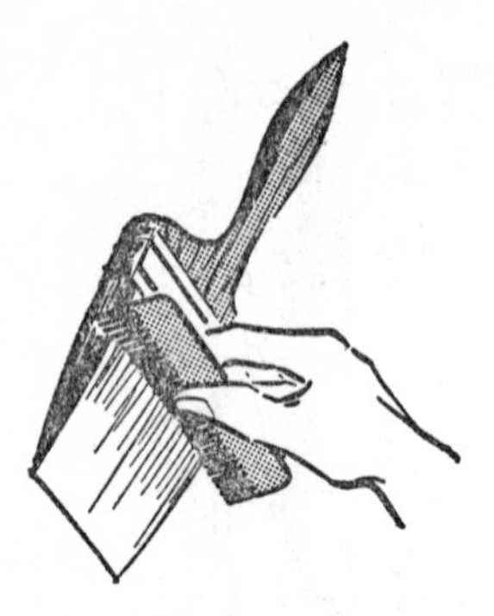

Fig. 7. Combing out a brush.

Stippler. This is a rectangular brush having tufted bristles. It is used for removing brush marks when painting wall and ceiling surfaces. The 8x3-inch size is large enough; the bristles should extend out 3½ inches.

Woodwork Brush. A 2½- or 3-inch brush is large enough for the beginner. Three and a half to 4 inches is the standard size for professionals, but it is difficult to use for cutting in sharp lines.

Other Brushes. The specialized brushes, such as sword stripers, broad liners, badger flowing brushes, stencil stipplers, and paperhanger's brushes, should not be acquired until you need them for the project they are intended for. Such special tools are discussed under the appropriate topics.

Care of Brushes

All new brushes shed a few bristles; it is nothing to be alarmed about. Before you begin to paint, bring out any loose bristles by spinning the brush between the palms of your hands, bristles down. When the loose bristles are seen extending beyond the others, pick them off.

Some painters soak new brushes in linseed oil for a day or two, and then rinse them in turpentine before using them.

Cleaning. Any brush that is used with glue, paste, or a water paint should be washed thoroughly with soap and water and rinsed as soon as the work is completed. Then the water should be shaken out and the bristles combed out straight with an ordinary hair comb. To dry the brush, hang it up by a string around the handle. Water remaining in any bristle harms it.

Brushes that have been used with shellac should be thoroughly rinsed in alcohol and then rinsed in a second bath of alcohol. Shape the brush between your fingers, and lay it on a flat surface to dry. If you intend to use the brush in shellac on the following day, do not wash it in water; it might not be entirely dry the next day and would cause your shellac to bloom.

Paint or varnish brushes which are going to be used the next day should be thoroughly rinsed in turpentine or benzine.

Be particularly careful to get the paint out of the heel of the brush. (The heel is the section of the brush where the bristles disappear under the metal ferrule). Use a comb to remove the paint. While it is still wet, lay the brush on a piece of paper and fold the paper in the same way as the wrapping in which the brush was delivered to you; this will keep the brush moist overnight.

If you have finished a paint job and will have no more use for the brush for some time, you must clean it more thoroughly. Rinse it out in turpentine or benzine. Comb out the paint. Rinse again. Then wash it thoroughly in soap and water. When its original black color has returned, rinse it in clear water. Then comb out the bristles again. Hang the brush up by a piece of string attached to the handle, and let it dry. When dry, wrap it in a piece of paper so as to preserve its shape and chisel. If you are going to store the brush for some time, place a few moth flakes inside the wrapping; moths will eat bristle.

Storing. There are on the market many containers for the overnight storage of brushes which are in constant use. Some of these have to be filled with a vaporizing solvent; the brushes are hung in the vapor, and a tight-fitting top prevents excessive vaporization. These devices are expensive and need to be refilled with solvent frequently. Although these containers will not substitute for a thorough rinsing when the day's work has been completed, they are useful and the amount of work saved may justify the cost.

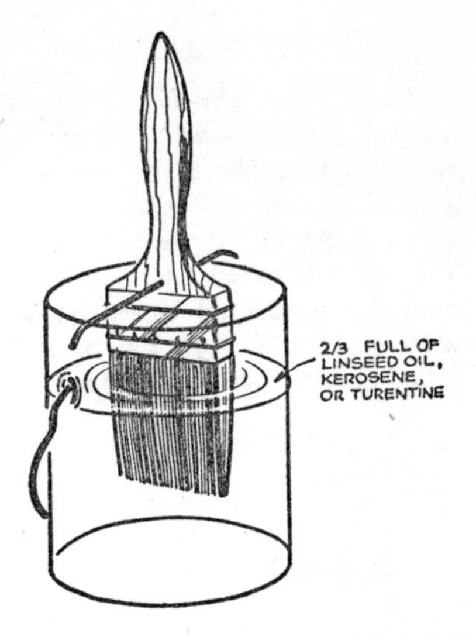

Fig. 9. Storing a brush in a pot of turpentine.

Fig. 8. Proper way to wrap a paint brush.

Another method is to rinse out your brushes in turpentine or benzine to remove all heavy paint from the bristle. Drill a hole in the handle just above the ferrule, pass a piece of stiff straight wire through the hole, and suspend the brush in a can or pot of turpentine with the end of the bristles just above the bottom of the can and the bottom of the ferrule below the surface of the turpentine. This is a good method, but it has the drawback of uncontrolled evaporation. When the thinner evaporates below the ferrule, it no longer keeps the brush soft. At a normal rate the turpentine will evaporate at the rate of about one-half inch overnight.

PAINT ROLLERS

Manual Feed. These are not paint brushes, but they serve very much the same purpose. There are two basic types. The manual-loading type requires that paint be placed in a pan. The roller is rolled back and forth until the surface becomes charged with paint, and then the paint is rolled onto the wall or ceiling.

Fig. 10. A mechanical paint roller.

Pressure Feed. The second type of roller is pressure-fed. Paint is placed in a tank, where it is put under pressure. This causes the paint to flow through a hose leading from the tank to the roller, and then through the roller.

For detailed information on the use and cleaning of paint rollers, see Chapter 6, page 91.

KNIVES

Broad Knife. This is a short, blunt-edged spatula which is used for spackling, patch-plastering, scraping off lumps, and so many other odd jobs that it would be impossible to list all of them. A 3½- or 4-inch flexible knife is good for all ordinary spackling or plaster-patching. Buy one which is made of the finest grade of steel that you can find; you will be repaid many times over for the small additional cost.

Putty Knife. This is a 1-inch version of the broad knife. It may have either a flexible or a stiff blade. A 1-inch stiff blade is best for all window puttying, and a 1-inch flexible knife is good for nail holes and for spackling small imperfections. It is recommended that you buy one of each; but if you want only one, select the flexible kind. Get the best steel you can find; cheap knives break easily.

PAINT POTS AND CANS

With the exception of brushes and knives, nearly all the equipment and tools you need to do the average paint job can be found around most homes. You need some sort of containers for the paint, some means of putting the paint on, some means of reaching the higher places, something to cover up floors and furniture, and a few rags.

The containers can be the cans in which the paint is bought. However, you will do well to have another pot into which to pour some of the paint for working—it is difficult to load a brush properly from a full pot. When you empty a gallon can of paint, trim off the lip with one of those can openers which leaves the top edge smooth. The lip interferes with proper loading of the brush. Pots with handles are more easily lifted and set than without. If you have a little paint left over at the end of a job, put it in a smaller can and clean up the big can for use on the next job. The left-over paint will keep better in the smaller can anyway—less skin will form.

The can in which you buy fifty pounds of white lead is probably as good a paint pot as you can get. It is sturdy, it has a handle, and the rolled top edge will help it to retain its roundness. The pots made for painters are also good. They are lighter in weight, and the rolled wire near the top helps them to keep their shape.

Fig. 11. A broad knife.

Cardboard paint pots are available and are useful when you do occasional painting. However, you will have to get one of the metal holders for them too.

Paint pots are probably a painter's greatest source of annoyance. They are always dirty. Keeping pots clean is a chore that should be done when the brushes are rinsed out. You can use the dirty turpentine or benzine to rinse down the pots, and then they will be in good shape for use on the following day. This consistent rinsing is by far the simplest and best way to keep your paint pots in good working order.

If, however, your paint pots should become encrusted with paint, you can remove the hardened paint with a solution of lye in water. Invert the pot in the solution (using any container that is large enough), and allow it to soak for a day or two.

Another method for removing paint crust is to burn it out. Place a small piece of newspaper in the pot, pour about one-half cupful of dirty turpentine or benzine over it, and set it on fire. This must be done out of doors. It is not a very satisfactory method, because the pot will need to be scraped, sanded, and shellacked before it can be used again.

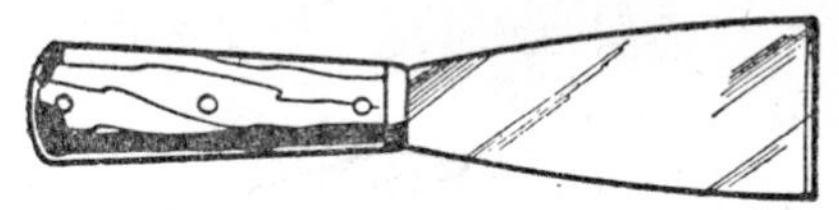

Fig. 12. A putty knife.

LADDERS, PLANKS, AND SCAFFOLDING

Ladders

Step Ladders. The flat steps of a step ladder are safe to stand on and are not tiring to the feet. A 6-foot step ladder is adequate for most work around a house. Five-foot step ladders are high enough to use for painting the interior of the average house. These ladders will be easier to keep clean if you varnish or shellac them, but this is, of course, by no means necessary.

Step ladders taller than six feet are, of course, available, but you may feel safer if you use trestles instead.

Good step ladders are made of Norway pine, Douglas fir, or spruce. The steps should have metal braces, and there should be a sturdy spreader between the front and back sections. For safety, the ratio for the spread between these sections should be 5½ inches for each foot of height. A folding platform, for holding a pot of paint, is a useful accessory. (Always remove the pot of paint before moving the ladder.)

Fig. 13. Step ladder.

Trestles. These are similar to step ladders, but they have rungs instead of steps. They are intended to support planks rather than to be worked from directly. A variation is an extension center ladder. With such a ladder, it is possible to place a plank as far as 10 feet above the ground or the floor. The trestles may be shellacked or varnished to keep them clean.

Straight Ladders. A 12- or 14-foot straight ladder will be adequate for exterior work on a single-story house. The sides, or rails, should be made of sound, knot-free spruce or fir. The rungs should be made of sound hickory or ash, and they should be mortised into the rails. Varnish or shellac the ladder if you wish – this will not only help to keep it clean but will also enable you to see any cracks or flaws that develop in the ladder. When the ladder is set against a wall, *the distance from the bottom of the ladder to the wall should be one-fourth of the height.*

Extension Ladders. Exterior work above the first floor will require the use of an extension ladder, which is an adaptation of the straight ladder. A rope and pulley permit one 12-foot straight ladder to be slid up over another one, making an extended length of 20 feet. Clamps are attached to the rails. These ladders can usually be rented. If you purchase your own, you can shellac or varnish it for the same reasons as mentioned for straight ladders.

An extension ladder should also be *set at a distance from the wall equal to one-fourth of its height.*

Extension ladders up to 40 feet in two sections and 50 feet in three sections are available. The longer they are, the heavier and more awkward to handle they become. A 32-foot ladder is adequate for most two-story houses. If you are going to work at any considerable height, you might well consider renting scaffolding.

When judging the length of ladders you need, remember that you will lose a little height because the foot of the ladder must be set away from the wall. A 20-foot ladder set 5 feet from a wall reaches to approximately 19 feet.

Fig. 14. A trestle for use with extension planks

Planks

Planks. You can buy or rent extension planks to use with trestles or ladders, but you will probably find it simpler and more economical to make your own planks for painting around the house. Twelve feet is a convenient length, though in your particular case you may find that a shorter length will serve all your purposes. The planks should be 2 inches thick. As for the width of the plank, the safety code recommends 20 inches. A plank of this size is heavy, expensive, and not always available, and most persons get along with something less. A 12-inch width will do, but it is better to use two 2x6's or 2x8's held together with two or three battens. Whatever you decide on, you should have a width to stand on that is at least equal to the length of your foot.

To make the planks, buy fir or spruce that is free of cracks and checks and with as few knots as possible. Sandpaper the corners to protect your fingers against splinters. For maximum safety, the planks should be dressed on all four sides and coated with boiled linseed oil. Most persons don't bother to do this, but it does have the advantage of allowing you to spot any cracks that may eventually appear in the wood. This practice will also, of course, help you to keep the planks clean and reduce the splinter hazard.

Extension Planks. An extension plank is comprised of a series of wooden strips which can be doubled over one another or opened out. Extension planks are safer than plain planks because they are wider, usually 18 to 20 inches. They are also far more convenient than plain planks; they can be collapsed to a length of six or eight feet, thus permitting easier transportation. However, they are also far more expensive. Coat them with oil, as paint would gum the slides.

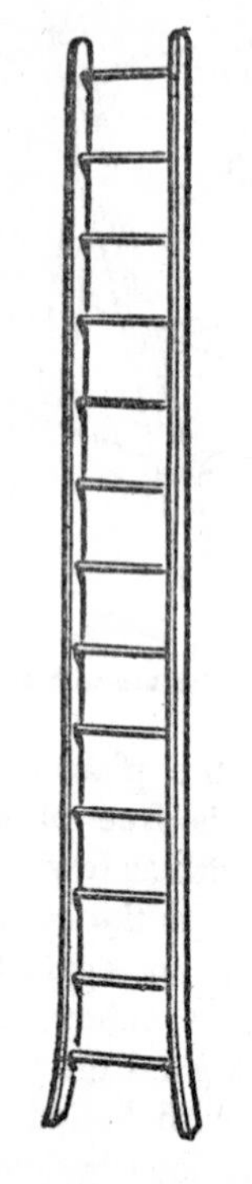

Fig. 15. Straight ladder.

Scaffolding and Stages

Scaffolding. For safety's sake, don't attempt to erect your own 2x4-inch scaffolding unless you have had building experience. You can have a scaffold for either interior or exterior use built by a competent carpenter. The principal objection to this is that you must purchase the lumber, and when you have finished with it, it has only second-hand value.

It is best to rent sectional unit scaffolding. This is erected and dismantled by the company from which you rent it. It is flexible and safe, being approved by even the strictest state safety codes.

Swing Stages. These platforms are supported by ropes which are attached to hooks on the roof. If you are not familiar with them, don't try to rig one. It is better to rent one from one of the many companies handling them and to let the company men rig it for you. Swing stages look very simple, but an improperly made blackwall hitch can cause one end of the scaffold to fall. And if the scaffold is not raised or lowered evenly, an improperly secured stirrup iron can come loose and let it drop.

Once rigged, swing stages are simple to handle if you carefully follow the rigger's instructions for raising and lowering.

Ladder Stages. There are several devices which can be attached to straight ladders to support a platform between them. If the ladders are properly set (a distance equal to one-quarter of their height away from the wall), and if the devices are securely attached to the ladders, they are relatively safe. Your paint dealer can provide you with literature and information on ladder stages. The most common types consist of iron braces that are set over the rungs of the ladder.

PLASTER, SPACKLE, AND PUTTY

Plaster

Plaster is used to fill cracks in plaster walls and ceilings only. It is simply mixed with water, troweled into the opening, and allowed to set. If you buy it packaged in the store, you can get patching plaster or plaster of Paris. The patching plaster will generally contain some lime and possibly some fine sand; it works and sets more slowly, but it does not dry to the hard shiny surface of the pure plaster of Paris.

Plaster does not stick very well to any level surface. When you open up a crack for patching, you must undercut it so that the plaster will hold. A beer-can opener will do the job very nicely. You must also wet the crack very thoroughly with water just before you mix up the plaster and apply it.

Do not mix more plaster than you can use in five minutes or it may set on you and have to be thrown out. An old pie plate makes a good container in which to mix it. Pour about ¼ inch of water into the plate. Take up some dry plaster on a broad knife and shake it off gently into the water. Keep adding plaster in this way until the water no longer wets it. Then pick up the wet plaster and work it on the palm of your hand with three or four strokes of the knife. The plaster is then ready to be put into the crack. (Half of a rubber ball is also very handy for mixing plaster in.)

If you add the plaster gently, as described, it will not harden as quickly as it will if you mix the water and plaster together with a spoon and knife.

The plaster may shrink in drying, and for large areas you will have to face up the opening to make it perfectly flat.

You should not attempt to smooth over rough areas with plaster. A material known as spackle is much better for this purpose. (See immediately below.)

Remove excess plaster from either side of the crack with a wet sponge.

Fig. 16. Extension ladder.

When the plaster is dry, sandpaper it lightly and then touch it up with either plaster primer or else wall flat thinned with oil and turpentine.

For New Plaster

When *newly* plastered walls are to be painted, a small bottle of phenolphthalein solution should always be added to your shopping list. Ask your druggist to mix ½ ounce of phenolphthalein in 4 ounces of denatured alcohol and to put the solution in a bottle with an eye-dropper stopper. Instruction for its use in detecting free alkali will be found in Chapter 3, page 47. If the test reveals the presence of free alkali, you will need enough zinc sulphate, at the rate of four pounds to the gallon, to wet the plaster. One gallon of this solution should wet about 700 square feet of wall surface.

The quantity of patching materials, such as plaster or spackle, that you will need is almost impossible to suggest, as it will depend upon the condition of the walls. However, it is difficult to imagine that a newly plastered room would require more than two or three pounds. Previously painted plaster walls in bad repair, especially in frame houses, may easily require as much as ten pounds.

For Composition Board

If the walls and ceilings are made of composition board, measure the joints in lineal feet. Purchase either the tape or the perforated metal which is recommended for covering the joints. Both types come in a package which also contains enough spackling material to smooth over the amount of tape in the roll. However, you will first have to fill any open joints with additional spackling material. If the joints are not more than ⅛ inch open, five pounds should be ample for the average room.

Spackle

Spackle is a mixture of whiting and glue. You can make your own very easily by soaking and thinning some glue and adding enough whiting to it to make a thick paste, but the packaged varieties cost so little that it does not pay to go to this trouble. Simply add to the powder in the package enough water to make a stiff paste and the spackle is ready for use. However, you must be sure there is paint on the surface upon which you are going to put the spackle. It will not stick to bare plaster or wood, only to a painted surface.

An improvement on ordinary spackle is called Swedish spackle. There is no precise formula for it, but most painters add about one-quarter by volume of white-lead paste to the mixed whiting and glue and some add a little varnish as well. Add the varnish sparingly or you may thin the mixture beyond the firm paste it must be if you are going to be able to knife it into place. Mix in the white lead and varnish thoroughly by knifing it back and forth on a board or an old piece of glass. Spackle will not set up—that is, harden—the way plaster does and extra mixing can do it no harm. When the spackle is dry, it should be sandpapered and then touched up with a primer as its surface is very absorbent. Swedish spackle will shrink less and dry much harder than ordinary spackle, but it takes longer to dry because of the oil in the white lead.

Putty

Putty is the right material for filling all holes or cracks in wood. It is a simple mixture of whiting, white lead, and linseed oil. Buying it is much easier than mixing it and there is less danger of your getting the white lead on your hands and perhaps into your mouth. White lead is enough of a hazard to have provoked many ordinances controlling its use. If you find that the putty is too hard in the can, simply knife in a little linseed oil; if it is too soft, knife in a little whiting. Knifing-in is best done on a board. You can do it and not get a single speck on your hands. Putty will only stick to a prepared surface. Make sure there is some paint or oil on any surface you are going to use it on. One of the commonest failures of putty—falling out of windows—is due to putting the putty on raw wood when the glass was set.

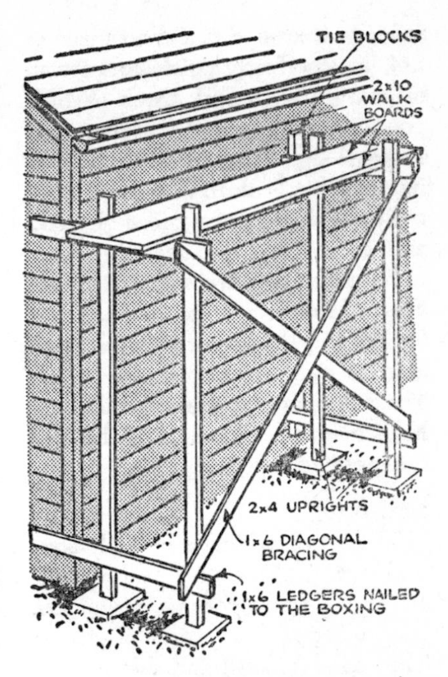

Fig. 17. Constructed scaffold.

SANDPAPER AND STEEL WOOL

Sandpaper

Once all the holes are filled in and the rough surfaces smoothed over, you will have to use sandpaper to complete the smoothing operation. Sandpaper is made in many grades, from very rough to very smooth, and, for painters' use, in two types, flint and garnet. Wood finishers use a third type known as wet-or-dry. The roughest grade is #3 and the finest #9/0. The best grades for ordinary painting are: #2, for tearing the nibs off lumpy areas; #0, for ordinary purposes; and #2/0, for finer work. The flint paper is the cheaper to buy but does not keep its cutting ability as long as the garnet. This is not too important if you are working on paint as the paint will clog the paper rapidly anyway.

Proper sanding is done with the paper wrapped around a block, but for simply taking the nibs off paint, you can do as well by simply folding a whole sheet into one-quarter of its original size and turning it to expose a new side when it clogs. Frequent slapping of the paper on your hand or a board will shake out a lot of the accumulated paint dust and give you more mileage on a sheet.

Sandpaper Blocks. The simplest type of block to use for wrapping sandpaper around is a short piece of 2x4. This perfectly satisfactory for all ordinary jobs. A cork block – which you can make yourself – that is 5 inches long, 3 inches wide, and 1½ inches thick, is ideal. It does not have the hard corners of a piece of wood and so will not accidentally gouge the surface you are sanding. There are also many manufactured devices for holding sandpaper that are available at paint and hardware stores. The advantage of these is that they have mechanical means of holding the sandpaper tight and firm.

Steel Wool

Steel wool, which is actually steel shavings, is also a very useful material to use for smoothing operations. It, too, comes in a variety of grades. The coarsest is #3 and the finest in common use is #3/0. It is particularly useful on curved surfaces where a piece of sandpaper would rub all the paint off the projecting edges. Again, use the coarser grades for the roughest surfaces and the finer for real smoothing. The common household steel wool used for cleaning pots and pans is #1 or #0. This will give you some idea of the other grades.

The finer grade, #3/0, is particularly useful in wood finishing. Simply dip a handful of the steel wool into some liquid or paste wax and rub the shellacked or varnished surface. Four or five strokes over the same area, in the direction of the grain, will smooth the surface and deposit enough wax so that you can polish it to a fine lustre when the wax has had several hours to dry.

PROTECTIVE COVERS

Paper

When painting inside, floors, fixtures, and pieces of furniture too heavy to move out of the room need protection from paint drippings. Outside the shrubbery may need protection, though most persons don't bother with this.

Fixtures should be loosened and moved away from the wall if possible, and then covered with cloth or heavy paper. Small pieces of furniture should be moved out of the room and the rest gathered in one convenient spot, if they can be moved. These large pieces of furniture and the floors should be covered with paper or cloth. Most people use newspapers. Five or six sheets will give enough protection unless a quantity of paint or water is spilled directly on them. If you have trouble with breezes, a few pieces of tape will hold the paper in place.

On new, unfinished floors, you may find it worthwhile to tape down building paper while finishing the ceiling and walls.

For the furniture, you may find it easier to use heavy wrapping paper taped in place than the newspapers. This method also works particularly well around sinks, tubs, and so on. An old sheet or old bedspread will often be enough for a simple job, particularly outdoors where paper can be so readily blown away.

Dropcloths

Professional painters use dropcloths to catch any paint drippings.

A new development in this line is the crêpe paper dropcloths. They come in a 9x12-foot size and are tough and resistant to paint and water. They cost a little less than two dollars and can be folded up and stored after any paint on them has dried.

Dropcloths of duck are frequently used by professionals, as you have undoubtedly noticed. They are too expensive an investment to be worthwhile for painting around the house. They also come in 9x12 size. And they need laundering every once in a while.

MISCELLANEOUS MATERIALS

Masking Tape

Masking tape is a most satisfactory method for protecting stationary fixtures, such as sinks, where they meet the surface that is to be painted. It is also a good solution to the problem of painting the window sash; to determine how many rolls of tape you will need for this, simply measure the distance around a single pane of glass and multiply this by the number of windows.

As you gain experience, you will find it easier and faster to paint sashes freehand without masking tape. What paint accidentally gets on the glass can be removed, after it dries, with a razor blade.

Masking tape is also a great help in achieving straight edges when painting borders, stripes, and so on. It is put along the edge to be protected and removed as soon as you have finished painting.

Strainer or Cheesecloth

If you are going to mix or tint your own paints, you will need either cheesecloth or a fine wire strainer. Cheesecloth will do a more thorough job, but it cannot be used for more than a day or two before the paint begins to harden in it. The best cheesecloth for this purpose has

Fig. 18. Ladder stage.

about a 30-by-40 thread count. The finer the thread count, the slower the paint will pass through but the better the straining. Allow about one yard for each room. You can prolong its usefulness by leaving it in water.

A wire strainer is simple to use and is easily kept clean. The best strainers have 18 to 24 wires to the inch and measure about six inches in diameter. These are considerably finer than the average kitchen strainer.

Ready-made paints should not need straining. But if they get lumpy you will have to strain them to avoid streaking. In this case, an old piece of (clean) wire screen may be enough to do the trick.

Rags

You will need a number of paint rags. You can, if you wish, provide a can with a hinged top for storing them; but by far the safest procedure for avoiding spontaneous combustion is simply to spread or hang the rags so that the heat of oxidation will be dissipated into the air.

For the sake of safety, remove all oily rags from the building each night.

Sponges

Sponges are good for general washing and cleaning up. The new cellulose sponges are very good. They are stronger than the natural type and a lot cheaper.

Hand Cream or Gloves. The painter who wishes to minimize the problem of cleaning his hands after work should use gloves or a hand cream. A good hand cream can be removed with water and will take all of the accumulated paint away with it. Hand creams work very well but most persons don't bother to use them.

Stirring Paddles

Pieces of wood 16 or 18 inches long, 2 inches wide, and ¼ inch thick are very useful for stirring paint. Many paint stores give them to you free when you buy paint. There is nothing elaborate about them and any stick that is clean enough, strong enough, and long enough will do.

Leftover Paint

Leftover paint should not present a serious problem if you have carefully estimated how much of each kind you will need. However, it is not unusual to find that some does accumulate. A simple method of handling it is to store all light colors in one pot and all dark colors in another. These mixtures can be used for painting bins in the cellar, floors, fence posts, or anything else that requires protection more than a decorative color. If this paint should dry to a very dull finish, its protective qualities can be considerably improved by the addition of about one pint of raw linseed oil or reinforcing oil to each gallon.

You must, however, keep separate the paints with different bases. The general rule is to keep oil paints and rubber-base paints apart. Water-base paints should be thrown out as they will not keep anyway.

ESTIMATING

While you are doing this cleaning, smoothing, and patching, or otherwise preparing to paint, you can be assembling the necessary information to estimate the amount of paint you will need. Very accurate information for this estimating will be found in the Appendix, but some "round number" methods will work satisfactorily.

Most paints cover about 400 square feet to the gallon. Primers may go a little further and finish coats not quite so far.

Finding the Area

To find the number of gallons you will need, you must first, of course, find out the number of square feet to be covered. To find the quantity of paint needed for a ceiling, simply multiply its length by its width in feet and divide the product by 400. To find the quantity for the walls of a room, if the opposing walls are parallel, measure the length of two adjacent walls, double this figure, multiply it by the height of the room, subtract the areas of any doors and large windows, and again divide by 400. If the walls are irregular, you will have to measure their length all the way around the room; then multiply by the height of the room and continue as before. The procedure for woodwork is much the same. Find the areas of the windows, doors, panelling, and so on. And don't forget there are two sides to a closet door. Be generous in your measurements here; woodwork usually includes mouldings, which take up more paint than a flat surface. When you have the total area of woodwork to be painted, again divide by 400.

The Number of Gallons

Always get your measurements in square feet. When you have divided by 400, you will know the number of gallons needed for *one coat*. Multiply this figure by the number of coats you are going to put on, and you will know the amount of paint that you will need.

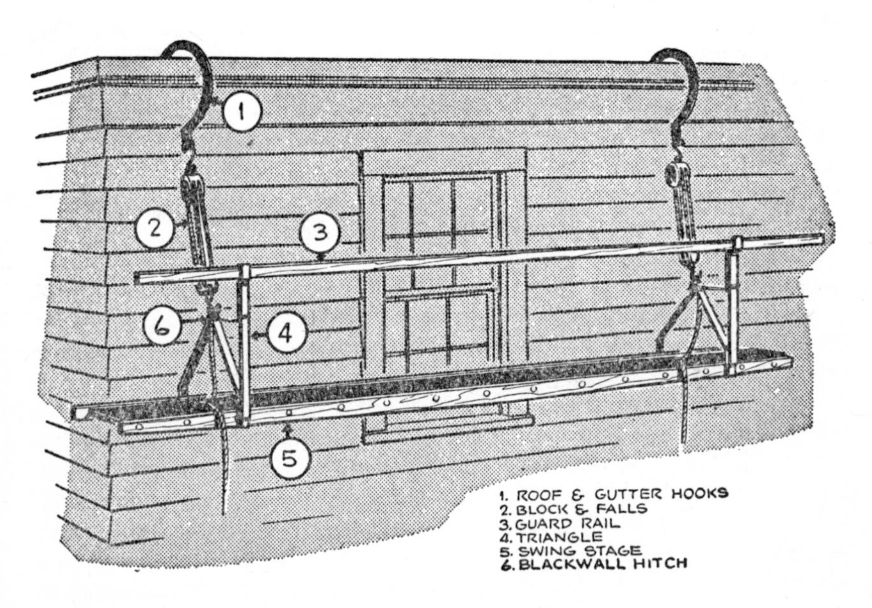

Fig. 19. Swing stage.

A Typical Example

As a typical example, take a bedroom 10′ x 14′ x 8′ with two windows, two doors, and one closet. The perimeter of the room is 48 feet and the height 8 feet. The total wall area is therefore 384 square feet. The area of each window is 16½ square feet, the total for the two windows, 33 square feet. The total area of the two doors is 42 square feet. The total area to subtract from the wall area is 75 square feet. This leaves 309 square feet. Divide this figure by 400—and we know that the walls will take ¾ gallon of paint per coat.

The area of the ceiling equals 140 square feet. This means you will need ⅓ gallon per coat. The woodwork is composed of two windows totaling 33 square feet and three sides of doors, each of which is 21 square feet; the total of all these is 96 square feet. If you allow one foot in height for the baseboard, which is probably 8 inches or less, you will have 48 square feet to add to the 96 and a total woodwork area of 144. This means ⅓ gallon of paint per coat.

Assuming that you are doing a two-coat job and that you will use the same wall flat for the ceiling and walls, you will need a total of 2 gallons and one quart (1½ gallons for the walls and ⅔ gallon for the ceiling). The best practice is to do the woodwork with one of the interior semi-glosses, and you will need ⅔ gallon for that. Buying a half-gallon and a quart is only slightly less expensive than buying a whole gallon, so you will probably do as well to buy the full gallon of semi-gloss.

By doing this estimating beforehand, you can buy the right amount of paint and have only a little left over for any touching up that may eventually become necessary.

CHAPTER 3

PREPARING TO PAINT NEW SURFACES

Intelligent planning is the keynote of successful work. By beginning your work on paper, you will be able to avoid wasting time and money. So before you begin to paint, assemble the pertinent information. For a very careful job, consult the tables on planning and estimating in the Appendix, page 238.

ASSEMBLING THE INFORMATION

The following guide will simplify the work of assembling the information you need for preparation and painting. Stained wood finishes and wallpaper are not mentioned, because the sections covering these subjects should be studied separately.

Walls and Ceilings

Materials. Determine whether the walls and ceilings are made of plaster, composition board, or plywood, or whether they are made of some other material which requires special treatment.

Surface Area. See page 39 for the methods of determining the size of the areas to be painted.

Condition. Check plaster for cracks, dents, loose pieces, free lime, hardness, dryness, and joints of plasterboard lath.

Check composition board for joints, nail heads, dents, bruises, absorbency, and grease or dirt.

Check plywood for joints, nail heads, dents, bruises, and dirt.

New surfaces will not need as thorough a check in these matters as old ones, but you should not overlook the possibility of their occurring. Having assembled this much information, you will be in a better position to decide what type of paint you want to use. Using this basic information in conjunction with the tables on pages 238 and 239, you will be able to estimate the amount of paint, as well as the amount of time, that you will need for each part of the job you are going to do.

Equipment, Time and Cost

Equipment. The condition of the surfaces will help you to determine what kind of supplies you might need in order to make any recommended repairs. See Chapter 2 and page 44 in this chapter.

Treatment and Time. Determine the type of paint and the number of coats that are best suited to the surface, and estimate the amount of time that will be required for each coat. Decide whether you want to do a quick job or a more thorough one. See Chapter 1 for types of paint and page 238 for estimating time.

Quantity and Cost. Determine how much paint you will need for each coat and how much it will cost. (See page 239.)

Reasonably careful preparation will simplify the assembling of materials and the organization of the work. If you are planning to work in your spare time—in the evenings and on weekends—your foresight will insure your assembling all of the necessary material beforehand and before the stores have closed. By scheduling the work, you can rule out the possibility of finding yourself with a half-painted ceiling at quitting time.

TYPES OF PAINT

Paint, as you know, is a liquid which is applied to various surfaces either to beautify or to preserve them, or both. For quick one- or two-coat jobs, the paint must be thick, adhesive, non-penetrating, and opaque. For more thorough and exacting work, paint should be thinner, penetrating, and somewhat less opaque. Between these extremes are found many variations. There is no ideal paint which satisfies all demands and uses. The manufactured paints are good. In fact, they are sometimes triumphs of chemistry; but none of them is suitable for every job. In choosing any paint, you must consider the factors of climate, the surface to be covered, the quality and cost of the paint, and how fine a job you think it is worthwhile to do. At one extreme you might choose a one-coat paint, although it is not as washable as other kinds. At the opposite extreme you might decide on a paint that dries to an extremely hard surface but is somewhat more liable to crack after a while. The differences are not as serious as might appear, but you should recognize them in making your choice of materials to be used.

If time is your most pressing concern, you will want to use a paint that covers with the least possible number of coats. Most distributors handle lines of one-coat and two-coat paints. A reliable dealer will help you to select one of the better grades, and you will do well to follow his advice. If you follow the instructions carefully, while using one of the better grades, you will be rewarded with a satisfactory job from the standpoints of both appearance and serviceability.

You will also have to decide between a ready-to-use paint and the more old-fashioned mixed-on-the-job variety The use of the latter type is somewhat more expensive and more time-consuming. Some experienced painters prefer to do their own mixing. It is possible to achieve a top-quality finish with either type of paint. The packaged paints are much safer for the beginner to use, because their preparation and application present no special problems.

As far as *materials* go, the difference between a makeshift job and a top-quality job is slight. Many *quick* jobs turn into a headache when the time for repainting arrives. But you are the best judge of your future painting needs, and you should consider the possibilities before deciding what kind of job you wish to do.

When you have estimated the amount of paint you will need, order it all at once. Some dealers will grant you a discount on a large order—that is, five gallons or more.

Paint should be thoroughly stirred before it is applied, and most dealers have electrical shakers to do this for you. If your dealer can't do it, you should box and stir the paint yourself —and do it thoroughly. If you should find that one can has not been shaken up thoroughly, you can replace the lid and return the can to your dealer for proper shaking up. If you cannot do this immediately, you can still proceed with the job, using another can.

Thinners

In addition to the basic paints, you will need thinners. Most manufac-

Fig. 1. A mixing table properly arranged.

turers recommend that not more than one pint of thinner be added to one gallon of paint. Allow for this possible thinning and also for the rinsing and cleaning of brushes and pots. About two gallons should do for a large job. You can use benzine for brushes and pots, but be very careful about the additional fire hazard. The fire department regulations of many cities prohibit your keeping more than one pint of benzine, and require that this be kept only in a special container. See page 20 for additional information on thinners.

MATERIALS AND EQUIPMENT

Workroom and Table

Once you have completed the initial planning and ordered your paint, it is time to select a workroom where you can assemble your equipment and do any mixing or tinting that may be necessary. Garages, cellars, and utility rooms are satisfactory. If you have a large job of mixing or tinting to do, the room should have good northern light. Protect the floor with newspapers. If your plans make a somewhat more permanent protection desirable, you can cover the floor with a good grade of building paper and paste the joints together to make a neat, professional job.

If you are planning to do any of your own mixing or tinting, you will need a table that will provide a convenient working level. A table consisting of several lightweight planks (about five feet long) and a set of two horses serves this purpose very well.

Lay down at least one extra thickness of paper where you are going to do your mixing or tinting.

Tinting colors, containers for the overnight storage of brushes, and stirring sticks are usually placed on the table. All other materials generally are kept on the floor.

Brushes and Tools

The brushes and tools you need will depend, of course, on the particular work you are planning to do. The four basic brushes for general painting are: the wallbrush, the woodwork brush, the sash tool or brush for windows and fine work, and the painter's duster for cleaning. For detailed information on all types of brushes, see Chapter 2, page 28.

The broad knife and the putty knife are the two basic tools you will need if you have to do patching, spackling, or repairing of imperfections. See Chapter 2, page 32.

Ladders and Planks

For interior work, step ladders or saw horses and planks will take care of your needs. In exceptional cases, it may be more convenient to use trestles and planks. Outside, you will need, in addition, straight or extension ladders or scaffolding for high work. See page 29.

Miscellaneous Equipment

Besides what has just been listed, the following are needed for general work: Sandpaper and a sandpaper block; masking tape, if you are very unskillful; rags and a sponge for cleaning up; newspapers to protect floors, furniture, and so on; possibly a stick to stir up the paint; and some pots or pails. One pot or pail is usually enough to hold the paint and let you thin it. If you are going to box the paint—that is, pour it back and forth to ensure an even mixture—you will, of course, need two pots. If you are mixing or tinting your own paint, you will need a pot for that too. For more details, see the chapter on equipment, page 22.

Miscellaneous Materials

Particular jobs call for special materials. For instance, testing and patching plaster (see pages 46 and 32), or spackling (see page 34), or tape for concealing the joints in composition board (see page 34). In any case, you will probably need putty for concealing nail holes, shellac for priming wood, and caulking compound for exterior work.

Primers

Priming is a necessary step in preparing all new surfaces for painting. Primers fall into three main classifications: plaster, wood, and metal. For full information on such of these as you may need, see page 12.

OUTLINE FOR PAINTING A NEW ROOM

When all preparations have been made, materials ordered, and work is ready to proceed, it is recommended that you do the work in the following order:

1. *Floors.* Sweep, scrape, stain if desired, and apply one coat of whatever type of finish is to be used. When dry, cover with newspapers or builder's paper, preferably pasted together. (See also Chapter 7, page 93.)

2. *Electrical Fixtures.* Loosen canopies or brackets and allow to hang free of the wall or ceiling. Cover with newspaper and tie with string.

3. *Radiators and Stoves.* Radiators can frequently be uncoupled and moved out of their recess or away from the wall. Stoves can be uncoupled after disconnecting gas or electric lines. Tubs, lavatories, and toilets should be covered. Masking tape and heavy wrapping paper make a neat job.

4. *Plaster Ceilings and Walls.* Test for free alkali with phenolphthalein solution (see page 47). Plaster-patch cracks, dents, or joints if the plastering was done on plaster board. Scrape or sandpaper lumps. Prime dull spots if necessary. Do this on ceiling and walls. Spackle any indentations.

Fig. 2. A painter's duster.

Touch up dry spackle with primer. The ceiling should be finished first. Paint plaster wall with first coat. Paint second, third, and fourth coats, depending upon number you intend to apply.

5. *Woodwork.* Prime-coat woodwork after priming plaster walls and ceiling. Putty nail holes. Spackle dents, bruises, or other imperfections. Sandpaper. Shellac, one coat (two-pound cut). Paint woodwork with one, two, or three coats; last coat after last coat on walls.

6. *Replacing Fixtures.* Remove paper and replace electric fixtures. Paint radiators or recesses. Replace radiators.

7. *Final Floor Finish.* Remove covering. Wipe up any paint spots with a turpentine rag. Apply last coat of floor finish. Wax and polish.

Fig. 3. Cover the floor with newspaper or building paper.

Now that you know the extent of your proposed work and the materials and equipment you will need, you will want exact instructions for each part of the work. The following instructions are in the same sequence as the above outline but in sufficient detail so that you will be able to complete the work satisfactorily. More detailed instructions for the specialized skills will be found in later chapters. Information on choosing colors, for instance, can be found in the chapter on color.

This chapter will cover the preparation of surfaces and the next chapter, page 53, will cover the application of the paint itself. Since new surfaces don't generally require any great amount of cleaning, smoothing or patching, you are referred for detailed information on these matters to the chapter on repainting, page 67.

READYING PLASTER FOR PAINT

If you are going to paint fresh plaster, you should first test to see that it is dry enough for painting, and to see that there is no free alkali present.

Testing for Dryness

Check the plaster for dryness by scraping your fingernail over the surface. A screeching sound means the new plaster is probably dry. If there is a dull sound, and some of the plaster scrapes off beneath your nail, it probably contains too much moisture to be safely painted. If you do not find this method accurate enough, or if you still have any doubts as to whether the plaster is dry enough, borrow an electric moisture-tester from your local building-supply dealer.

When you consider the fact that about a ton of water was contained in the original plaster mix for your room, it is not surprising that it takes some time for all of the water to evaporate.

Testing for Alkalinity

When you are satisfied that the plaster is dry enough, test it for alkalinity. Take your bottle of phenolphthalein solution (see page 34) and mix 20 to 30 drops of the solution with a gallon of water. Brush this diluted solution onto the wall. If it turns red or pink, the presence of free alkali is indicated.

Only specially prepared paints are fast in the presence of free alkali. Painting over it will cause most paints to crumble and their colors to bleach.

Neutralizing

The next step is to neutralize any free alkali that may be present. Mix 4 pounds of zinc sulphate (you can get this at your paint store) with a gallon of water, and brush a coat of the solution onto the wall. Retest with the phenolphthalein solution and, if pink still appears, apply a second coat of the zinc sulphate solution.

If any patching or repairing of the plaster is necessary, see page 32 for the proper procedure.

Priming

When your alkalinity test is satisfactory and the fresh plaster is dry,

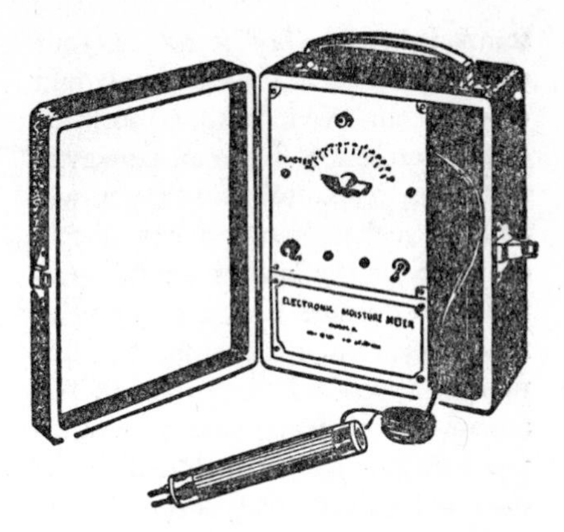

Fig. 4. An electric moisture-tester.

you are ready to apply a coat of plaster primer. Buy one of the prepared primers; they are compounded to penetrate just enough and to really seal the absorbent surface in one coat. If you expect to finish with only one coat of paint over it, you may wish to tint the primer lightly for color. Do not add more than eight ounces of tinting color to the gallon.

On the following day, spackle out any imperfections and check the primed surface for dull spots. If you find any dull spots, thin out a little primer and recoat them. When the spackle has dried, touch it up with primer, and your wall is ready for the first coat of paint. The first coat of paint will not adhere properly to most primers if they are permitted to dry for more than one or two days.

READYING COMPOSITION BOARD

Manufactured compressed board is made with varying degrees of absorbency. You should test a piece of scrap for this. Try some of your chosen paint. If it brushes freely and dries to an even finish, absorption doesn't present a problem. However, if it dries to a blotchy finish, you will have to seal the surface first. A thin oil-paint primer is best for this purpose. To prepare it, add one pint of raw linseed oil and one quart of turpentine to one gallon of wall flat. The advantage of using this primer in place of glue size or shellac is that it does not shrink upon drying. If the surface is still too absorbent, you can coat the dry priming coat with glue size or shellac (two-pound cut).

The joints of composition board are usually covered with wooden strips; these should be primed and shellacked before they are applied. Be sure that any nail holes are filled up with putty. The wood strips can be painted at the same time as the board.

Instead of being covered with wooden strips, the joints may be filled with spackling materials recommended by the manufacturer of the wallboard, and then sealed with tape. These joints will be reasonably satisfactory until there is a considerable change in humidity, at which time they will expand or contract so as to become noticeable. Some manufacturers have attempted to solve this problem by using tongue-and-groove or lock joints; these permit blind nailing and allow for expansion and contraction.

READYING PLYWOOD

The plywood used for walls and ceilings is usually made of fir. The rotary cutting method used to make the plies results in a very conspicuous pattern, which can be seen through most paint. The figure can be covered over by the use of one of the primers that are commercially prepared for this purpose.

Fill the nail holes with putty. Spackle the joints, and cover them with one of the patented tapes. This makes a very satisfactory joint covering. If you spackle the entire surface to a uniform smoothness, the joints will be very hard to detect. The surface will undoubtedly be too large for efficient use of a broad knife in this case, so you will have to use a plasterer's trowel.

Of course it will be necessary to seal the spackle, and a thin coat of 2-pound-cut shellac will do this well. After priming, spackling, and sealing, any of the regular wall paints can be used successfully.

PREPARING WOODWORK

Priming

Normally, trim, sash, frames, and cabinet work delivered to your home have already been primed and back-painted while siding and sheathing have not been. Priming means laying on the first coat preparatory to finishing, and it must be done at some time before any woodwork is installed. Priming, or painting, the back side will reduce to a minimum problems of swelling and shrinkage by helping to reduce moisture absorption.

The priming paint used for woodwork is a thin oil-and-pigment mixture. You can make your own according to the formula which follows. This is the formula recommended by the National Lead Company.

The amounts given in the first column are those upon which the formula is based, and those given in the second column are the amounts used to make one gallon of primer. If you need more or less than one gallon, vary the proportions accordingly. Each gallon will cover 700 square feet.

Ingredients	*For 8⅓ Gals*	*For 1 Gal*
White lead	100 lbs	12 lbs
Raw linseed oil	3 gals	1 qt, 18 ozs
Turpentine	2 gals	1 qt
Japan drier	1 pt	2 ozs

Puttying and Spackling

Both puttying and spackling must be done after the priming, because neither putty nor spackle will adhere to raw wood. Using either the ball of your thumb or your flexible putty knife, fill every nail hole with a standard white-lead-and-linseed-oil putty. Then knife-spackle over dents, bruises, and other imperfections. If this work is done carefully, it will be almost unnecessary to sandpaper.

If there is the slightest hint of a knot, or of discoloration of the priming coat by sap, it is best to shellac the woodwork. The shellac will seal in the excess sap or the resin from the knots. Use one coat of 2-pound-cut shellac for this purpose.

Preparation for Staining and Finishing

You will find stained and finished woodwork in many modern homes.

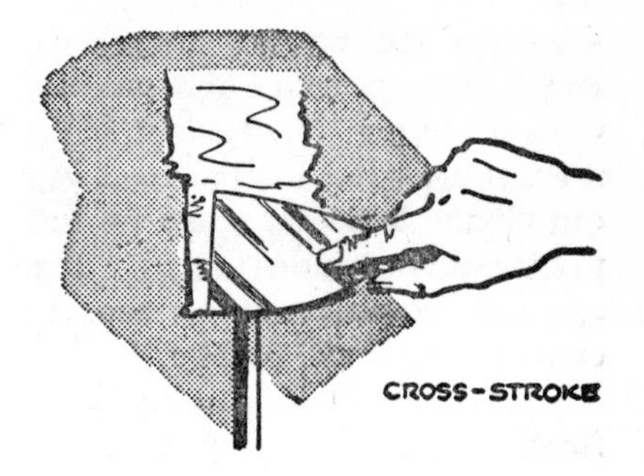

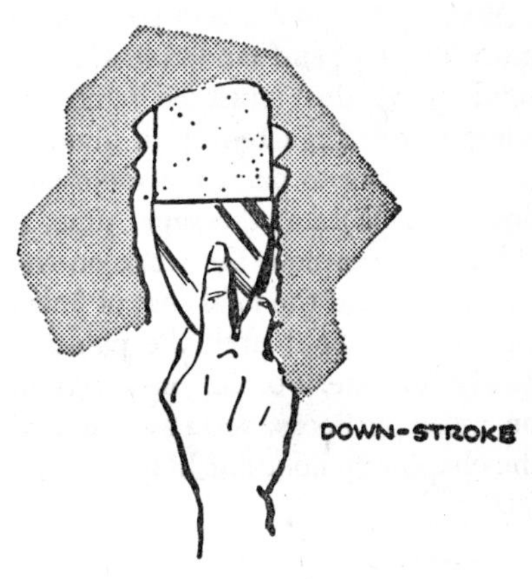

Fig. 5. How to apply spackle.

Often doors of the flush-type are faced with beautifully-grained wood, and sometimes entire walls are made of fine veneers. These woods should be finished so as to bring out all of their natural beauty and, if possible, be preserved by staining.

The preparation for either stained or plain finishing is the same. The wood surfaces must be free of all dirt and grease or the finish won't adhere properly. Usually you can remove the worst of this with some benzine or other so-called dry cleaner. Then the wood must be perfectly smooth and free of scratches. Sandpaper it with a

#0 paper until no scratches are visible. Follow this with a light sanding, using fine paper; #7/0 is best, but if it is not available, use the finest you can obtain. You cannot overdo this preparatory sandpapering. The smoother the surface at this step, the easier the work will be later.

Floors

Wood floors that are to be finished must be swept and sanded first. After sanding, all dust must be removed. Some woods then require a filler. If you are going to paint the room and finish the floors at the same time, it is best to complete the work on the floor except for the final coat of finish and then cover it until the painting has been done. For full information on finishing floors, see page 61 and the chapter on floor finishing on page 93.

PREPARING NEW EXTERIOR SURFACES

Exterior painting of new surfaces breaks into seven steps: estimating paint and labor; mildew-proofing; priming; setting up ladder and scaffolding; puttying and caulking; undercoating; and applying exterior finishing paint. The last two steps are treated in the next chapter, page 53, the others are taken up here in the order given.

Estimating Paint and Labor

Determine the number of square feet of each type of surface you intend to paint, including siding, trim, plywood siding, stained wood, shingles, masonry, metal (iron, copper, or bronze, galvanized iron), wooden porch floors, and fences. From this list decide the quantities of the various kinds of paint you will need. You can also determine about how long the job will take. Chapter 1 will help you decide on the paint, and the tables on page 238 and 239 will help you estimate quantities and time.

Mildew-Proofing

Dip, spray, or paint a coat of one of the copper naphthenate rot-and-mildew preventatives on all exposed wood. Dipping is the most effective method but is also the most cumbersome for large pieces. For long pieces of siding it requires constructing a tank large enough to hold them, then stacking them to permit drying. Brushing is the method most frequently used and is effective if a generous coat is applied. It is even more important to coat the backside of wood than the face. Do not neglect this. Mildew-proofing preparations do not leave a film on the surface of the wood and are not to be considered as priming.

If you live in a particularly humid area, add a small amount of a concentrate of mildew preventative to your paint.

Priming

Prime all surfaces of all exposed wood with a rich oil paint, preferably before the wood is erected.

You can buy manufactured exterior wood primers. Many paint authorities recommend them in preference to the job-mixed formula. Generally they are more heavily pigmented and give a solid paint cover sooner than a job-mixed primer.

If you prefer to mix your own, you will find the formula for it by referring to page 13.

Puttying and Caulking

After the primer is dry, putty all nail holes and caulk all possible openings around window or door trim—any opening through which water could penetrate.

With a nail set and hammer, drive all nail heads ⅛ inch below the surface. This will permit you to insert putty sufficient to hold in place firmly. If the next coat of paint is going to be tinted, you will do well to mix a little of the appropriate dry color with the putty. If you add too much and the putty becomes stiff and dry, work in a little linseed oil. Apply the putty to the nail holes with your thumb or with a flexible putty knife, being sure you fill the hole completely.

Use a gun made for the purpose for caulking. Several heads are available, from a round tube to a flat fishtail. Simply squeeze the trigger, pumping the caulking compound into the opening until full. At times the opening is too small for the stiff compound to penetrate. In this case press the compound in with the blade of your stiff putty knife.

Glazing

If you have to putty the glass in the window sashes, make certain that the sashes have been primed, especially where the glass is to go. Place a thin strip of putty about 1/16-inch thick on the moulding where the glass will rest. Gently press the glass into place until properly seated on the putty. Then tap in the glazier's points and finish puttying in the glass.

Porch Floors

If the tongue-and-groove flooring has been properly laid, there will be no joints to fill. But if shrinkage has occurred, prime with standard exterior wood priming, and then fill the joints with good putty. You will then be ready to proceed with the undercoater.

Fig. 6. How to putty nail holes.

PREPARING METAL SURFACES

Iron

Iron rails or other trim should be painted to prevent rusting. Wire-brush off any small rust spots and apply one coat of rust-inhibiting primer.

Copper and Bronze

These metals should be varnished to prevent green stains from forming on surrounding paint. Wipe clean with a turpentine rag and apply one coat of spar varnish.

Galvanized Iron

Allow the zinc to oxidize to a dull gray color. Then prime with zinc dust or chromate primer. Either adheres well to the metal. See also pages 13 and 66.

CHAPTER 4

PAINTING NEW SURFACES

The previous chapter explains the preparation of new surfaces, and you should consult it if you are in any doubt about what to do before you put on the paint itself. This chapter tells you how to finish the job, taking up the various surfaces in the following order: Painting ceilings and walls, wallpapering, finishing woodwork, finishing floors, doing service and utility areas, and exterior painting. For detailed information about kinds of paints, consult Chapter 1; for information on materials, equipment, and estimating, consult Chapter 2. If you are concerned with specialized work, such as glazing or graining, refer to the appropriate chapter giving specific instructions for what you want to do.

Fig. 1. A Dutch calcimine brush, one of the two types used for painting calcimine.

PAINTING CEILINGS

If you wish to finish the ceiling with a single coat of paint, you can use one of the oil or rubber-base paints made for that purpose. Finishing the ceiling with two coats (after the primer) will be more satisfactory for several reasons. For one thing, it will be easier to apply the paint, and any slight slips in the painting will be less likely to show. For another thing, a two-coat job gives a better holding surface for repainting later. Use an ordinary wall flat for the first coat on top of the primer. Finish with a second coat of the same wall flat. The cheaper wall flats will generally give you a duller finished surface but they are harder to apply evenly as they dry more rapidly.

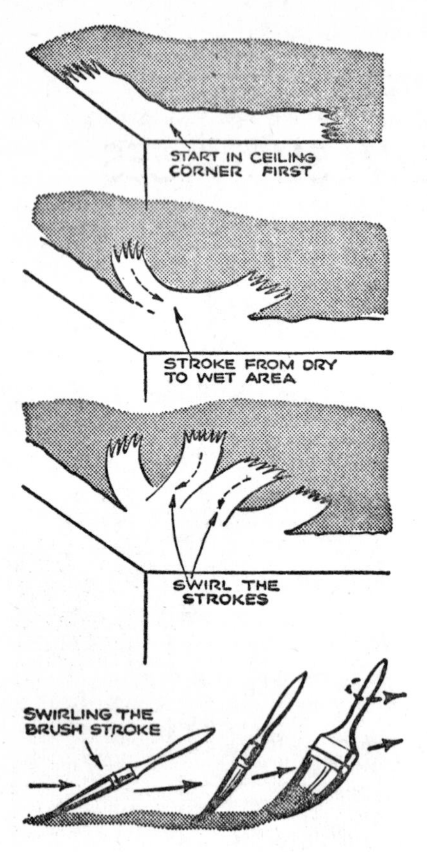

Fig. 2. Pointers in painting a ceiling.

One-Coat Paints

The paints that are intended to cover with one coat have a very thick consistency and very little "flow." If you are using a paint of this type, it must be applied with a very full brush in short, arcing strokes. The brush marks are apt to be obvious. If so, they can be smoothed out with one of the felt rollers made for this purpose or with a stippling brush.

Calcimine

Calcimine is not so widely used for ceilings as it used to be. It probably fell into disfavor because of occasional difficulties in washing it off to prepare for repainting. These difficulties arose because the painter had not properly primed the plaster. If, however, plaster has been thoroughly sealed, the old calcimine will wash off readily. (See page 47.)

If you are using calcimine for the ceiling, remember that the wet color is much darker than the dry color. Follow the directions on the bag, and use only dry colors for tinting. Test it by coating some on the ceiling or on a piece of paper and allowing it to dry.

Brush on the calcimine in arcing strokes, always starting and ending in a wet section. Apply it with a calcimine brush as smaller brushes do not apply evenly enough.

Application of Paint

Start the work with a dry brush, and do not dip more than two inches of the length of the bristles into the paint. This will reduce the amount of paint that will run down the handle. If the paint begins to run, scrape the excess off on the edge of the paint pot and wipe the handle and ferrule dry with a rag. Some painters prefer to tie a rag around the ferrule of the brush, but this seems to be a rather clumsy solution to a problem simply requiring careful work.

If the application is to be heavy enough to cover the surface of the ceiling, it is impossible to avoid splattering some paint. This splattering can cause considerable annoyance if you do not take some simple precautions. It is, for example, well to wear a hat or cap in order to save yourself the trouble of washing paint out of your hair.

Always apply the last coat to the ceiling before the last coat on the walls.

Ladders and Planks

In painting the ceiling of a room, you will always work across the width rather than the length. The reason for this is that the shorter the stretch of fresh paint, the less will be the likelihood of the edge's setting before you can move your ladders and plank forward. It is not advisable to try to paint more than two feet wide on any trip across the plank; this means that you must move the ladders more frequently, but it also insures against dry laps.

Place the ladders so that their backs or platform sides face a side wall of the room. Your plank should be of generous width and should extend at least a foot beyond the step on which it rests. This will provide you with good foot-space while you are working at the edges of the room. Always make sure that the side spreaders of the ladders are completely open and locked into position; this will minimize the possibility of the ladder's falling.

If you are painting a room with composition flooring, be careful to avoid denting the floor with the legs of the ladder. Avoid this possibility by nailing a three-inch strip of wood across the bottom of the legs, both front and back. A single nail through the board into each leg is sufficient and will make later removal of the strip easier.

When moving the ladders and plank, always remove the paint pots and other tools. It can be very discouraging to find the paint that was intended for the ceiling on the floor.

PAINTING WALLS

Paints

For the walls of the living room, bedrooms, and other living area of the house, it is recommended that you use the flattest drying paint available, in order to reduce glare and resulting eyestrain. See Chapter 3, page 41, for the proper preparation.

Wall flats are available in a wide range of qualities and types, but all of them have several qualities in common—high hiding power, a dull finish when dry, and low penetrating power. They vary widely in price, and

Fig. 3. Tre tles and planks are the most convenient support for painting a ceiling.

the price is not always a true indication of the quality. You will do well to depend upon the recommendations of a reliable paint dealer and to purchase only standard brands. Wall flats may be compounded with an excess of extenders and low-quality vehicles, which will result in a paint that does not withstand washing and that may not cover completely.

Follow the manufacturer's instructions for thinning paint. If you have not purchased the paint in the color you want to use, determine the necessary coloring matter you'll need. If you add tinting color, be sure to strain the paint afterwards in order to avoid streaking. For detailed information on the mixing of colors, refer to the appropriate chapter of this book, page 138.

Application of Paint

It is best to begin from the window wall and work back into the room so that the reflections on the wet paint will reveal any spots that have not been properly coated. Obviously, it is best to begin at a natural break in the wall, such as a corner.

Painting from ceiling to floor, adapt the width of the stretch to the paint and to your own convenience. If the paint is quick-setting, take narrower stretches to avoid dry laps.

Apply the paint in arc-like strokes, always starting and ending in wet paint. You can finish off with long, straight strokes, starting alternately at the ceiling and the baseboard and overlapping near the mid-point.

If the paint is slow-setting, watch carefully for sags; they can be disfiguring to a wall. You can, if you wish, even out the painted surface by stippling or by using a paint roller.

The number of coats to be applied will depend entirely upon yourself. The usual choice is either two or three. Less than two on top of the primer will give a very thin-looking job, and more than three is entirely unnecessary from the standpoint of wearing quality and solidity of appearance.

Painting Composition Board and Plywood

No special techniques are required for painting these materials; once the surfaces have been properly prepared, they are treated in much the same way as plaster. When painting plywood, spread the paint evenly and then finish off by taking long vertical strokes with the brush, by stippling, or by rolling.

When painting composition board, make the application heavy enough to cover, but keep it from being heavy enough to sag. Some composition boards have textured surfaces which eliminate the necessity of stippling or otherwise removing brush marks.

WALLPAPERING

Wallpaper can be used successfully over any of the ordinary wall materials. Plaster probably offers the fewest problems. But don't hesitate to use it over composition board or plywood. Finish painting the ceiling and woodwork before beginning to hang wallpaper. The following brief account of wallpapering will enable you to fit it into your plans for finishing off a whole room. For detailed instructions, see Chapter 8, page 108.

Preparation

Prepare the plaster surface for wallpaper just as you would for paint (see page 46), and be sure to do any necessary patching. Remember that paper cannot permanently conceal any imperfections in the wall. Then apply one of the prepared glue sizes, carefully following the instructions on the package.

The Lining Paper

It is advisable to hang a layer of lining paper before hanging the wallpaper. While this is not absolutely necessary, it will improve the appearance of the walls and will make the job of papering easier.

To determine the length for strips, measure the walls from baseboard to ceiling. To determine the number of strips you will need to cover the walls, measure from corner to corner. You do not have to trim the edges of lining paper as you do those of wallpaper. There is very little waste in the cutting of lining paper; a 10 per cent allowance for waste is ample.

For best results, purchase some prepared paperhanger's paste. It costs no more than making your own and it is much safer to use. Follow the directions on the package. Apply a generous coat to one side of the paper and then fold the paper in.

To hang, unfold the top of the folded-in sections and apply the paste side to the wall. Then unfold the bottom end and paste the rest of the strip to the wall. Butt all joints between strips, as lap joints would show on the finish paper.

Fig. 4. Make use of the light from a window to show you the paint coverage when painting a ceiling or wall.

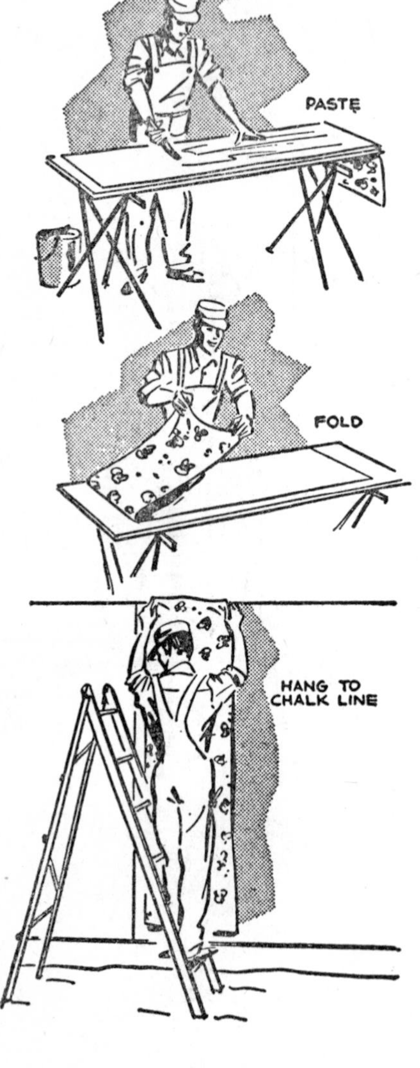

Fig. 5. Pasting and folding wall or lining paper.

Amount of Wallpaper

Measure the walls of the room to determine the total surface area. Add 10 to 15 per cent of this figure to allow for waste. (If the pattern in the paper is small, 10 per cent should be enough for cutting waste; large patterns may require 15 per cent or more.) Divide this total by 36, and you have the number of single rolls of wallpaper. When you buy the paper, ask the dealer if you may return leftover rolls, and don't hesitate to take a few extra rolls. The tendency seems to be to underestimate the quantity of paper needed.

Cutting and Hanging

Cutting. Unroll two rolls of paper and check them for the matching of the pattern. If they match straight from one strip to the next, simply cut enough strips (about 8 or 10 inches longer than the distance from baseboard to ceiling) to cover the walls. If the design is a drop figure, your cutting will be somewhat more complicated.

Hanging. Paste each strip of paper in the same way that you pasted the lining paper and fold the paper in. After pasting and folding, trim off the selvage along the markings printed on the paper.

Strike a vertical line with a chalked plumb-bob line at a convenient starting line on the wall. Hang the first strip of paper with one edge just touching the chalk line. Continue hanging strips around the room, carefully butting each joint to the other.

For more detailed instructions for paper hanging, see Chapter 8.

PAINTING INTERIOR WOODWORK

The woodwork gets more wear than any other surface in the house. It is advisable, therefore, to finish it with a paint that will stand considerable washing. The best paint for this purpose is a hard-drying, high-gloss enamel. But most persons don't like this type of finish in the living areas. Using one of the semi-gloss or lustre enamels is usually satisfactory. These semi-gloss finishes are best applied on an undercoat. See Chapter 3, page 41, for the proper preparation.

Fig. 6. How to strike a vertical line with a chalked plumb line.

Undercoating

There are on the market many very fine undercoat paints which cover well and provide a good, hard, toothy surface for the application of enamel or semi-gloss paint. Apply one or two coats of this undercoater over the primer or shellac. If one coat provides a solid surface, you are ready for the finish paint; but if there are dull areas, apply a second coat.

The finish coat will tend to sag and run if it is applied too heavily; the secret for avoiding this is proper loading of the brush. Use a well-worn brush if you have one; otherwise, do not overload the brush or you will get more than the proper thickness. The paint should be evenly distributed but not over-brushed. Excessive brushing interferes with the leveling qualities of the paint.

Fig. 7. Semi-gloss paint is excellent for interior woodwork.

Sequence of Painting

If you are finishing the woodwork with a single coat of paint, this is applied after the last coat of paint has been put on the walls, or before wallpaper is pasted up. All woodwork is painted from the inside toward the outside. The sequence for painting paneled doors is as follows: the panels, the mouldings around the panels, the rails (horizontal members), and finally the stiles (vertical members). For windows, the moulding next to the glass is first, then the sash, then the frame, and finally the trim.

Staining

A simple staining method is to use a prepared penetrating oil stain, carefully following the directions on the container. It is possible to make your own stain; however, the pigment will be considerably coarser than those used by manufacturers and, consequently, your work will appear muddier. When the stain has been applied, wiped, and permitted to dry, the surface is ready for finishing.

This is one of the easiest ways to stain wood, but it is not so satisfactory or durable as more careful methods. For a full discussion of all the ways to stain and finish wood, see Chapter 12, page 179.

Finishing

Apply one coat of 2-pound-cut shellac over either the raw or the stained surface and allow it to dry overnight. Then lightly sandpaper it with the finest sandpaper you can obtain; this will remove the nibs (the rough specks which can be felt when you run your hand over the surface). Dust off, and apply a generous coat of 3-pound-cut shellac. Allow this to dry overnight, and the surface is ready for steel-wooling and waxing.

Use number 3/0 steel wool. Take a bunch about the size of your fist, dip it into a pan of liquid wax (not the self-polishing type), and rub over the surface of the wood in the direction of the grain. Keep the steel-wool pad moist with wax. When you have smoothed the surface and spread the wax, allow it to dry. Then rub the surface to a good luster with either a scrubbing brush or a soft cloth. Don't use steel wool over electrical outlets.

If you wish to avoid the rubbing operation, you can substitute a coat of semi-matte or flat varnish for the second coat of shellac. However, the color will probably turn out to be darker and yellower than it would with the shellac. Gloss varnishes dry to a greasy finish which is not desirable for interior woodwork.

Quick Finishing

There are on the market quick two-coat finishes made of gums and waxes. These consist of first-coat stainers and second-coat finishers. They are good and serviceable finishes, but they do not have the depth of color or the richness of the shellacked finishes. It is well to test them on a small piece of wood before going ahead with the job.

These quick finishes are simple to apply. Brush on the stainer, let it penetrate for fifteen minutes, and wipe off the excess. On the following day, apply the finisher coat. Let this dry overnight, and on the third day rub it to a soft luster.

FLOORS

The following brief outline for the procedure in finishing floors will fit this subject into its place when painting the interior of a new room. For detailed instructions see the Chapter on Floor Finishing, page 93.

Preparation of Floors

Softwood Floors. A new softwood floor that is to be prepared for finishing, or an old one that is to be refinished, should be swept and then scraped with a sanding machine. You may, if you wish, rent a sanding machine and do the job yourself. You will also need a small edger for scraping near the baseboard. After scraping, even up the floor with coarse sandpaper and then finish with fine sandpaper. It is extremely important that you do all of this work with the grain of the wood. Sweep up, or better, use a vacuum cleaner on the dust, and the floor is ready for finishing.

Hardwood Floors. Hardwood floors are prepared in exactly the same way as softwood floors, except that the rough scraping is done either across the grain or at an angle of 45 degrees to the direction of the grain. (Finish sanding is always done with the grain.) You may wish to apply a coat of filler to even out the larger pores that occur in hardwoods.

Finishing

There are three methods of finishing floors to retain the natural color of the wood. Apply two coats of 3-pound-cut shellac, two coats of a good floor varnish, or two coats of a clear gum-wax preparation. Allow the first coat to dry thoroughly before applying the second. If you have applied a filler, be sure that it is dry before you apply shellac or varnish. Do not use a gum-wax preparation over a filler, because it will act as a remover, softening and raising the filler. Apply

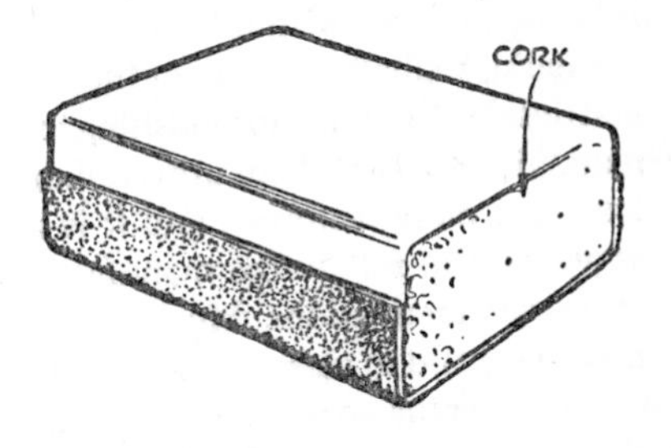

Fig. 8. A simple type of sandpaper block that is handy for finishing and other operations requiring sanding.

wax over the dried finish with a steel-wool pad, and polish on the following day. Many people think that two coats of varnish make the best possible finish for a floor.

Staining. If you choose to stain the floor, rather than to retain the natural color, allow the stain to dry and then apply two coats of shellac or varnish. Or simply use one of the colored gum-wax preparations. Apply wax after the finish has dried, and polish on the following day.

Finishing While Painting

Finishing while Painting. The dust created by the scraping process is so fine that it penetrates the dust bag of the sanding machine and settles on all of the exposed surfaces in the room, even the ceiling. If the floors are to be finished and the room is to be painted at the same time, it is best to complete the floors, except for the final coat of finish, before doing any painting. By so doing, you can avoid the possibility of dust's settling on fresh paint.

Composition Floors. Among the various materials included under the heading of "composition" flooring are linoleum, asphalt tile, rubber tile, and mastics. Instructions for finishing and maintaining all of them are available from the manufacturers, and it is always wise to follow the manufacturer's recommendations. Most of these floors respond to cleaning, with either dry cleaner or soap and water, and shining with self-polishing wax.

SERVICE ROOMS AND UTILITY AREAS

Kitchen and Bathroom

Finish the plaster and woodwork with a good grade of enamel in most cases. Refer to the index for reference to the treatment of the stained woodwork, painted brick walls, or other finishes required in some modern kitchens and bathrooms.

Use a good grade of prepared primer, checking it for dull spots when dry and spackling out any imperfections. Recoat with primer where necessary. Apply one coat of enamel undercoater. Then brush on one or two coats of enamel, either semi-gloss or gloss according to preference.

Before painting the woodwork, prime, putty, spackle, and retouch it. Then apply an undercoater and one or two coats of the same enamel as used on the plaster.

Paint in the same sequence as for the other rooms—ceiling first, walls second, and woodwork last. Spread paper or cloths where necessary.

In kitchens and bathrooms, the same kind of enamel is usually used for both walls and woodwork. It may be either a gloss or a semi-gloss enamel, depending upon your preference. For a new wall, you will need one coat of enamel undercoater on top of this primer and one or two coats of a good grade of enamel.

Cellars

A cellar should properly be waterproofed from the outside when the foundation is installed. If, however, this was not done, considerable benefit can be derived from the application of some one of the new waterproofing paints to previously unpainted cellar walls.

The sealing action of such a paint will improve the moisture condition and will also help to check the dusting of the cement walls. Apply it according to the directions on the label of the container.

Calcimine paint makes a good, easy, one-coat clean-up job for cellar walls and is frequently used in this way. (See page 10.)

There are on the market rubber-base paints made especially for cellar floors. A paint of this type will withstand wetting and reasonable wear. It will also completely control the dusting of the cement. For further details on painting the cellar see pages 78 and 101.

If you wish to convert the cellar into a playroom or make it part of the living area, give it a finished wall, woodwork, and ceiling comparable to that of a living room. Follow the instructions for such surfaces set forth earlier in this chapter.

Closets

Indoor closets are usually painted at the same time as the adjoining room. You do not have to be fussy about the job, but it should be as complete as the other areas. Many people tend to "skimp" a coat of paint when doing the closets; this is not a good practice, because the incomplete finish absorbs dirt very readily.

A variation frequently used is to paint the closet walls with one of the specially prepared paints containing the aromatic oil in red cedar. Its moth-preventive action lasts from one to two years. Its effectiveness can then be restored by the application of an additional coat. These cedar paints are water paints and usually come in powdered form. They need only to be mixed, allowed to soak for a few hours, and brushed on the walls and ceiling. One coat is enough.

Garages

The interiors of garages are rarely painted, although they could utilize the advantages of paint as well as any part of the house. The floor should be painted, preferably with one of the rubber-base paints, to allow for easy cleaning (see page 101). And the woodwork should receive one or two coats of paint for priming, to preserve the wood.

If the garage contains any built-in bins or racks, painting them will enable you to clean and maintain them more easily. Leftover paints are ideal for this purpose.

PAINTING NEW EXTERIOR WOODWORK

For the proper preparation of new exterior surfaces, see Chapter 3.

Undercoating

When the primer is dry, apply shellac to all knots in the wood. With puttying and caulking completed, apply one coat of undercoater. Modern manufacturers have compounded this to give maximum coverage with necessary adhesion. Use only the product of a reliable manufacturer recommended by your local paint dealer. Do not try to make the paint glossy by adding oil. This upsets the blend of pigment and vehicle, sometimes causing blistering or peeling of the finished surface. Add a second coat of undercoater if not satisfied with the appearance of the first.

Paints

You may choose from a wide variety of exterior finishing paints, from dull to glossy, in any color. If you expect to repaint in the future, select a paint which dries semi-matte, guaranteed to chalk properly. If the paint is so compounded that it will slowly weather away, it will self-clean and will present an ideal surface for repainting. This paint will last as long as the glossy types and is much less likely to check and crack.

Follow the manufacturer's instructions carefully in thinning and tinting. Generally the paint comes ready for use and should only be thinned if the temperature is below the ideal, about 70 degrees. Apply the paint generously, brushing out to an even coat. Press the brush to push the paint into irregularities of the surface, leaving a minimum of air and moisture between the surface and the paint film.

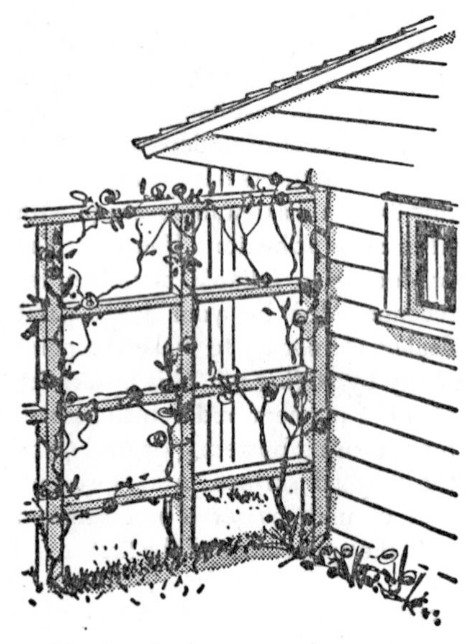

Fig. 9. Special paints are made for trim and trellis work.

Trim

If you are not painting the window trim, shutters, and other parts a separate color, paint them the same way as for the siding. If you are painting the trim a separate color and are using one of the intense colors, pick a "trim and trellis" paint. The manufacturers will have used tinting colors for the pigment. The reliable manufacturers will use the most non-fading colors obtainable, and knowing the oil absorbency of the various pigments, will be able to compound the paint much better than you could. Follow directions on thinning exactly, as well as instructions on whether the paint should be brushed out or flowed on.

Plywood Siding

The exterior type of plywood siding presents no serious problem in painting. Use one of the recommended nongrain-raising primers. From there on all operations and paints are the same as for solid wood construction.

Stained Wood

Modern architecture has introduced extensive use of stained and finished wood for exteriors. You can do as much or as little as you choose with this type of finish. Perhaps one of the simplest finishes is one thin coat of asphaltum varnish. The color will be a pleasant soft brown, but the protection will be limited.

For sturdier protection apply one coat of one of the copper naphthenate wood preservatives with stain added. This can be varnished when dry. Use exterior or spar varnish. Interior varnishes nearly all bloom when exposed to the weather.

Do not use linseed oil either as a sealer or stain. It may darken and change the color of the wood. If you use an oil stain, purchase one of the penetrating oil stains. Apply it according to directions and varnish when dry. Two generous coats of exterior or spar varnish applied in warm weather will leave a tough, glossy surface on most woods. Putty nail holes after applying the first coat of varnish, with putty tinted the approximate color of the stained wood. Wipe off excess putty with a turpentine-soaked rag before applying a second coat of varnish.

Shingles

Wood. Wood shingles are occasionally left untreated to turn a natural silver-gray color. But usually they are treated with creosote stain or painted. Staining or painting reduces warpage and erosion, lengthening the useful life of the shingles.

Apply creosote stain by dipping the shingles. Use one gallon of the stain to dip about 300 shingles. A second coat of stain can be applied after the shingles have been set in place.

You can paint shingles after they have been nailed in place but it is better to dip them. Rig up a drying rack where you can stand the shingles after dipping and draining. The first coat should be a regular exterior primer, the second coat a regular exterior undercoater. Brush on the final coat after the dipped shingles have been nailed in place. In general, however, painting shingles is not recommended. Once shingles have been painted they can only be repainted.

Asbestos. Paint shingles and siding made of asbestos and cement to minimize dust and moisture. Use paint specially made for the purpose, following the manufacturer's instructions to the letter.

Porch Floors

Lay on one or two coats of exterior undercoater. Finish with one liberal coat of floor and deck enamel.

Fences

A stain finish is most readily applied with one of the tinted copper naphthenates. These both preserve and color the wood. Dip posts in the solution, allowing them to soak as long as possible. Soaking two to three days permits thorough penetration. Because rails do not touch the ground they need only be brushed with the copper naphthenate solution.

Fig. 10. Dipping shingles.

Painted fences will last longer if treated with rot preventative before painting. After doing so, add priming, apply one coat of exterior undercoater, and finish with a good exterior paint. Make certain to paint the underside of rails or pickets, where moisture remains longest.

MASONRY AND METAL

Masonry and Brick

Only paints made especially for use on masonry are satisfactory for painting these materials. The pigments and vehicles used in these paints resist the free alkali in bricks and cement. Follow the label instructions exactly. These paints are good for cement, stucco, cement and cinder blocks, other masonry surfaces, and brick.

Metal

Iron. After removing rust and applying primer, apply one flowing coat of exterior enamel or implement paint.

Galvanized Iron. After proper oxidizing or etching, apply a coat of paint as described for iron.

Copper and Bronze. These metals are best finished, after cleaning with turpentine, by applying a coat of spar varnish.

Fig. 11. You must thoroughly wet the surface of masonry before applying cement paint.

CHAPTER 5

REPAINTING, INTERIOR AND EXTERIOR

The formerly painted house presents no unusual problems but it does require the exercise of good judgment. You should examine the existing surface and paint to determine its type and condition. This will prescribe many of the steps preparatory to painting.

PREPARATION FOR PAINTING

You should know that *the preparation is just as important as good paint and proper application.* It will generally take you about as long to prepare surfaces as it does to paint them. Usually it is a sheer waste of money and time to put a high-grade paint on a poorly prepared surface.

The recommendations for preparation are simple:

1. If the surface is dirty, clean it.
2. If the surface is rough, smooth it.
3. If the surface is cracked, patch it.

The materials for these jobs are cheap and readily available.

Cleaning

Nearly all painted surfaces should be washed before painting. This is essential in kitchens and bathrooms, and almost as much so in other living areas.

Cleaning will remove dust which would streak paint, and grease which would make it impossible for the paint to stick. Use soap and water when possible and rinse thoroughly. Use stronger washing materials like washing soda only when necessary. Wash from the bottom up so that the washing solution will not streak the present paint. Rinse thoroughly and allow enough time for the surface to

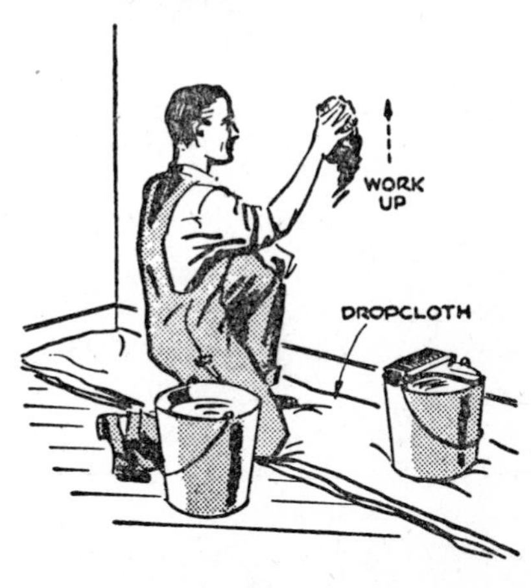

Fig. 1. Wash walls from the floor up to avoid streaking.

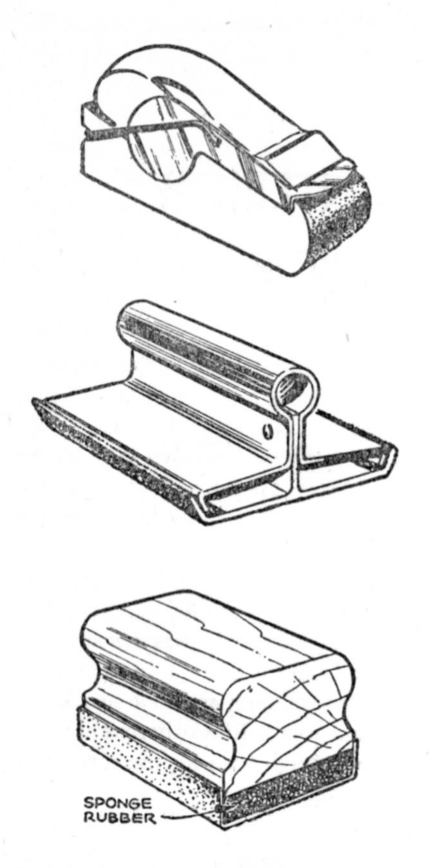

Fig. 2. Manufactured types of sandpaper blocks are particularly useful for any heavy sandpapering.

dry completely before painting. Even new work should be checked for smudges of dirt or grease. Exterior surfaces can generally be dusted, though hosing down is even better.

The only tools and equipment you will need for washing are a brush—a scrubbing brush will do—two pails, and either a sponge or an old dishtowel. Mix a handful of washing powder in a pail of warm water. Fill the other pail with clean water. Dip the brush into the soapy solution and spread it on, starting from the bottom. Do not cover more area than will stay wet until you rinse it. For walls, a stretch three feet wide from floor to ceiling is about right. Spread clean water over the washed surface and rinse it off with the sponge or dishtowel. Do the rinsing also from the bottom up. Wring out the sponge or dishtowel and, if necessary, go over the section just rinsed to pick up any excess water.

This method will prevent streaking and will thoroughly clean the surface. You should put something absorbent, like an old sheet, a piece of carpet, or burlap bags, along the baseboard to soak up the run off. It's a good idea to have a mop handy. Furniture should be covered before you start washing ceilings; small pieces can, of course, be removed altogether. It is impossible to avoid dripping but you can reduce it by using the sponge for putting on both the washing and rinsing solutions. Allow surfaces to dry before proceeding; under normal conditions they should be dry by the next day.

Smoothing

The recommendation to smooth the surface applies to all but purposely textured ones. Old paint which has chipped, cracked, or otherwise become rough should be wire-brushed or sandpapered. This will reduce the high spots and the indentations can be filled in with spackle.

As mentioned before, spackle will stick only to a painted surface; so if you have removed any of the paint to the bare undersurface, apply a coat of primer to those areas. When the primer is dry, trowel on the spackle. If necessary, give it a second going-over when the first coat has dried. Sandpaper this—and you should have a good smooth surface on which to apply a coat of plaster primer or wall flat thinned with both oil and turpentine. Even metals should be given a smoothing treatment if you want the paint to stay on and remain solid.

See page 34 for detailed information on spackle.

Patching

Surfaces which are cracked or have holes in them should be patched or puttied to prepare them for the paint.

Plaster. Cracks should be cut out, wetted, filled with plaster, smoothed off, and primed.

It is best to leave any small dents or rough spots to be smoothed with spackle later, because plaster tends to fall out of small irregularities. Smooth any lumps by scraping or sandpapering.

If the plaster was troweled on metal or wood lath, it is unlikely that any large cracks will have developed. But if the plastering was done over one of the many commercial plasterboards, you may find that the joints in the board have caused the plaster to crack. If there are bruises or dents, remove any loose pieces of plaster. They can then be faced over with plaster and broad knife. Splash enough water over the prepared surfaces to wet them thoroughly.

See page 33 for detailed instructions on preparing the plaster.

Wood. Cracks or holes should be filled with putty. Run a little thin paint or primer into them and allow them to become at least tacky before puttying. Putty will stick fairly well to the typical rough crack, but it shrinks a little on drying and the paint helps to hold it in place.

Fig. 3. Cutting out cracks in plaster. Be sure to undercut them.

On new wood you can frequently do a better job with plastic wood or woodpowder patching compound. Apply this material only to clean raw wood. Trowel to a slightly raised surface and sandpaper flat when dry. These materials dry harder and more rapidly than putty but they are considerably more expensive.

OUTLINE OF PROCEDURE FOR REPAINTING

Preparation of Interior Surfaces

General:

1. Measure room for quantities of paint
2. Remove furniture (if possible)
3. Loosen electric fixtures and drape paper over them
4. Remove hardware
5. Cover furniture and floor

Previously Painted Walls and Ceilings:

1. Wash calcimine from ceiling
2. Wash walls
3. Cut out cracks in walls and ceiling
4. Plaster patch and touch up when dry

Previously Papered Walls:

1. Soak and remove paper
2. Cut out cracks and plaster patch
3. Prime coat

Any New Plaster:

1. Test for hardness (scratch with finger nail, if it screeches, you can paint)
2. Patch with plaster if necessary
3. Prime coat

Previously Painted Composition Board and Plywood:

1. Wash
2. Spackle imperfections
3. Touch up spackle with primer

Any New Composition Board and Plywood:

1. Fill joints and tape
2. Prime coat
3. Spackle in nail holes and other imperfections
4. Touch up spackle with primer

Previously Painted Woodwork:

1. Wash
2. Putty holes and joints
3. Spackle, sandpaper, touch up with primer

Previously Enameled Woodwork:

1. Wash (use washing soda to cut gloss)
2. Putty holes and joints
3. Spackle, sandpaper, touch up with primer

Any New Wood:

1. Prime coat
2. Putty holes and joints
3. Shellac knots and sappy areas
4. Spackle, sandpaper, touch up with primer

Preparation of Exterior Surfaces

Previously Painted Wood:

1. Check for moisture conditions and repair
2. Remove paint which cannot be repainted
3. Wire-brush or sand down rough paint
4. Dust or hose down all surfaces
5. Set all nail heads
6. Putty all nail holes and cracks
7. Caulk around windows and any place water could enter
8. Touch up bare wood with primer

Any New Wood:

1. Set all nail heads
2. Prime coat all surfaces
3. Putty all nail holes and checks
4. Caulk around windows and any other places where water could enter.
5. Shellac all knots and any sappy areas

Painting

Interior Wall and Ceiling Surfaces:

1. Paint one coat of undercoater
2. Apply finish coat of paint
3. Even out the texture with a paint roller if necessary

Interior Woodwork:

1. Paint one coat of undercoater
2. Paint second coat of undercoater for more solid job
3. Paint one coat of interior semi-gloss

Exterior Woodwork:

1. Paint one coat of exterior undercoater
2. Paint finish coat

Clean Up

1. Wipe up floors with turpentine rag
2. Wax polish
3. Clean electric fixtures and replace
4. Clean hardware and replace
5. Rinse out paint brushes and wash clean
6. Rinse down all pots
7. Remove all paint rags and burn or otherwise dispose of them

Fig. 4. Protect shrubbery with a cloth when painting outside.

CEILINGS AND WALLS

General Preparations

The initial step in preparing a room for painting is to move heavy furniture to the center of the room and cover with cloths or paper. Remove all small or delicate pieces to another room or, if the floor is to be finished, remove all of the furniture from the room.

Protection of electrical fixtures is important. Remove the switch plates from the wall. Loosen canopy-type or bracket-type fixtures so that they hang free of the wall or ceiling. Tie newspaper around them with string.

All fixtures, such as lavatories, bath tubs, and toilets, should be covered. Heavy wrapping paper and masking tape make a neat job. Stoves can be uncoupled and moved after the gas or electrical supply lines have been disconnected. Radiators can usually be uncoupled and moved away from the wall. If you are planning to paint the radiators, it is best to do so after the walls have been painted and the fixtures replaced. Do this before applying the final coat of floor finish.

Assemble the necessary equipment, such as ladders, brushes and pails, just as instructed for the painting of new surfaces.

Ceilings

The principal problem in refinishing formerly painted ceilings is in the preparation. For many years it was the custom to finish ceilings with calcimine. It was a very satisfactory method and its only drawback was that you had to wash off all the old calcimine before you could go ahead and refinish. Today the manufacturers have developed oil-type paints which can be applied directly to this calcimine with some success.

Plaster. Ceilings made of plaster are readily washed off, though a few may prove stubborn, in which case generous wetting is necessary. Once cleaned, patch any cracks and imperfections. In the meantime, examine the ceiling to see if it was primed or sealed. You can tell by scratching it to see if some of the primer or sealer comes off under your fingernail and leaves a clean white streak of plaster. If it was, simply touch up the patches with plaster primer. If not, coat in the whole ceiling with a good plaster primer. Proceed with a coat of undercoater and finish with a coat of wall flat.

If you prefer the complete matteness of calcimine, you can use it on top of the coat of primer. You can also add about one pound of ground pipe clay to a gallon of wall flat. Stir *thoroughly,* and use this for the last coat. Use one of the cheaper wall flats — they dry to a very dull finish. Stippling or rolling the final coat also increases the matteness by giving it a slight pebbly texture. The final coat should be applied to the ceiling before either the wall or woodwork is finished.

Composition Board and Plywood. If the ceiling was constructed of composition board or plywood, simply sponge the surface dirt off. The amount of water necessary to thoroughly clean off the calcimine would probably harm these materials. When clean, patch the joints and coat with one of the paints made especially for painting on old calcimine.

Ceilings Painted with Oil Paints. Ceilings that were previously painted with an oil paint should be cleaned and repaired, if necessary. You can then apply an undercoater and a coat of oil paint for a good job or just a coat of the paint for an acceptable job.

Plaster Walls

If plaster walls were previously painted with a typical wall flat, wash them in preparation for repainting. Check the walls for plaster cracks. If you find any, plaster patch to a flush surface. This smooth surface may not match the rest of the wall in texture. If you wish to completely hide your repair, you will have to prime the raw plaster and when this is dry touch up the area with one coat of undercoater paint. Then give the undercoater the same texture as the surrounding paint by stippling, rolling, or brushing. If any spackling is necessary, it should be done on a painted surface. It does not matter whether it is new or old paint. When dry, touch it up with primer and texture if necessary.

When this preparatory work is complete, the wall is ready for painting. You can use either a one- or two-coat paint. The thinner two-coat paints are more durable and washable. The finish coat can be brushed, stippled, or rolled for texture.

Watercolor Paint. If the paint on the walls is watercolor, you will have to wash it off completely before you can repaint. Oil paints will not properly adhere to calcimine. Protect the floor with paper, wet the wall thoroughly, and sponge off the calcimine. When the calcimine is off, examine the plaster surface to see if a paint primer was applied before the calcimine. If none was used, you will have to apply it. But first cut out and repair all plaster cracks. When plaster patching is dry, apply the primer. When this is dry, apply one coat of interior undercoater. Finally apply the finish coat of wall flat.

Previously Papered Plaster Walls

If the walls were covered with wallpaper this will have to be removed before you can paint. It is true that several manufacturers advertise that their paints can be used on existing wallpaper. But this practice is considered a health hazard. The paste with which the paper was hung can be a fine culture medium for mildew if shut off from air and kept humid. This condition is encouraged underneath a film of paint.

Removing Wallpaper. Soak the paper thoroughly with water, making sure you protect the floor before you do it. You may have to repeat this soaking several times before the paper begins to loosen. When the paste loses its adhesion, the paper will come off in large sheets. Do not try to rush the process. Putting on water is a lot easier than scraping the paper off with a broad knife, and a lot less damaging to the wall. A few papers will prove particularly difficult and there are chemical softeners available at your paint dealer to speed up the work. However, remember that the main loosening agent is water.

It is unlikely that papered walls were primed with paint before papering. After you have cut out and repaired any cracks in the plaster and the patches are dry, you can apply a coat of plaster primer. When the primer is dry, do any necessary spackling. Touch up these areas with primer, and when dry, paint on one coat of undercoater. When this is dry, apply a coat of wall flat.

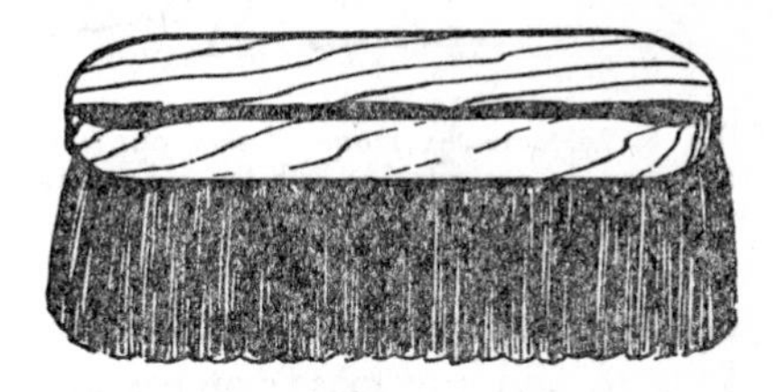

Fig. 5. A stippler for smoothing the paint surface.

Rehanging Paper

If on the other hand you wish to rehang with paper, check in some out of the way place for the number of layers of paper already on the wall. If you find more than two, you should remove all of the old paper.

It is considered safe practice to hang up to three layers of paper on a wall. More than this tends to pull itself loose because of the amount of adhesion. If the number of layers is

Fig. 6. Relocate the seams of new paper so that they do not coincide with the old seams.

not excessive, go over the paper carefully to find any loose patches and carefully paste them back. Hold them flat for a few minutes until the paste softens the paper and allows it to lie flat. Check the joints. If any of them are lapped or a bit open, sandpaper them smooth. When you are sure the existing paper is smooth and sound, you can safely repaper. But one more word of caution. Do not locate your new paper joints over the old ones. Strike a chalked plumb-bob line in the middle of one of the old strips and start hanging from that line. Detailed instructions will be found in Chapter 8, page 108.

Composition Board and Plywood

Repainting any walls made of composition board or plywood presents no serious problems. If buckling has occurred, you can do nothing to improve the condition with paint. You will have to remove the panel, install more wood grounds, and replace with a new panel.

The painting preparation simply amounts to a very gentle washing. Use a half-wet sponge for both application and rinsing. Spackle any open joints and touch up the spackling when dry. The walls are then ready for repainting. Either a one- or two-coat job will be satisfactory.

Previously Papered Walls. If walls constructed of composition board or old-fashioned plywood (made with water soluble glue) were previously papered, you will be wise not to attempt to remove the old paper. The composition board, with few exceptions, will not stand the wetting necessary to remove the paper. And the glue under the outer layer of the plywood may soften and the outer ply come loose. It would be better to compromise and hang new paper. With the great number of patterns and types of wallpaper available from the most fragile to strong, oilcloth-like materials, surely one of them will satisfy your requirements and tastes.

REPAINTING AND REFINISHING WOODWORK

Preparation for Repainting

Repainting woodwork presents no serious problems. The exercising of a little judgment in recognizing the previous paint, and knowledge of the method for applying the new paint will serve you well. If the old paint was an enamel, the surface must be broken so that the new paint will adhere properly. There are chemical washes made for this purpose. They require only light sponging. When dry, the surface is ready for repainting. Or you can use washing soda and water – a cupful of soda to the gallon of water is strong enough for any enamel. Rinse with clean water and let dry before proceeding with painting. However, in the kitchen and bathroom you should thoroughly wash the woodwork as well as the walls and ceiling to remove all accumulated grease.

Once clean and ready, you can scrape off all unsightly ridges of paint on panels and sandpaper off all sharp edges of chipped paint.

Windows and sills should receive particular attention as they are exposed to greater variations in temperature, more moisture, and direct sunlight. Scrape and sandpaper them until you have a smooth surface. Then prime, if necessary, and spackle to a perfectly smooth surface. When dry, touch up and proceed with painting.

Painting

Choose the paint which best suits your preferences. Enamels and semi-glosses are to be preferred for their wearing qualities and resistance to repeated washing. Apply one coat of undercoat paint. Follow this with a coat of enamel or semi-gloss.

Brushing out the paint is more necessary for windows and sills than for any other place as an excessively heavy coat here increases the likelihood of checking and cracking.

Refinishing

Stained woodwork may need refinishing. It may be restored to its stained appearance, refinished in a different stain, bleached, or painted. Brief instructions follow. You will find more detailed information on all sorts of staining and bleaching in Chapter 12, page 179. The brief instructions will be followed by more detailed directions for painting formerly stained woodwork.

Restaining the Same Color

Wash down the woodwork with turpentine or paint thinner (but not benzine – the fire hazard is too great).

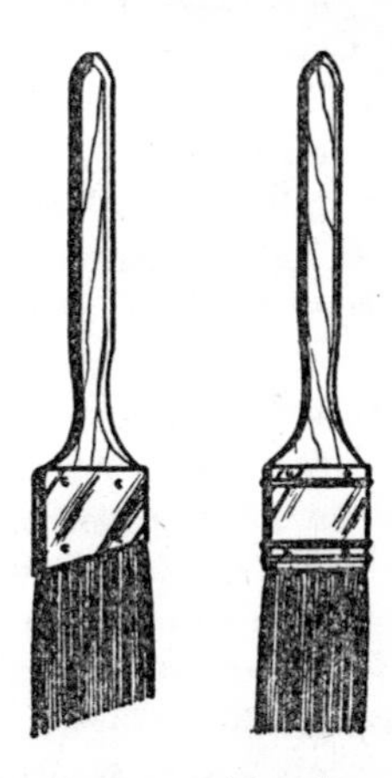

Fig. 7. Use a flat or angular sash tool for fine work when painting wood.

If necessary, use number 3/0 steel wool for this washing. When dry, the surface should squeak as a finger is drawn over it. Unless it is entirely clean of wax or polishing oils, shellac or varnish will not adhere to it. It also may not dry.

When the wood is clean, you can make up a little oil stain (see Chapter 12, page 179) and touch up the light, worn spots. Use a second dry brush to blend out the edges or you will have a dark ring around the touched-up area. When the touch-up is dry, shellac or varnish all of the woodwork. You can then wax-polish the shellac finish by dipping a pad of number 3/0 steel wool in some liquid wax (not the self-polishing type) and rubbing the coat of shellac. This will both rub the finish and apply the wax. When dry, polish to a lustre with a scrubbing brush or dry cloth.

Preparing to Refinish in Different Color

If you decide to finish the previously stained woodwork in a different color stain, you will have to remove both the old finish and probably most of the stain. Some old finishes respond well to mild removers, such as tri-sodium phosphate (available at paint stores). Others respond to the water-soluble combination removers and bleaches. These removers are particularly useful in that they reduce the operations to one. They were originally made for use on floors.

Mix exactly as directed and don't be afraid to use a second coat if the first one does not clean the finish enough. Protect the floor with enough paper. Scrub off the finish with No. 1 steel wool. Finally rinse with clean water. Vertical surfaces will generally take more applications than floors due to the run off. You can slow down the drying of the remover by the addition of about one cupful of paperhanger's paste to each gallon of solution. But you should be cautioned about the use of this type of remover on old-fashioned plywood as the amount of water necessary will almost certainly loosen the glue and the outer layer of veneer.

The second remover you can use is a standard paint-and-varnish remover. You cannot be cautioned too much about the fire hazard and the ill effects of prolonged exposure to the fumes of this material. The slow-drying types of these removers are somewhat better than the liquid form. The electric fuses leading to any outlet in the room in which you are working should be removed, so that every electric circuit is completely dead. Fires have frequently been started by the remover's flowing into a receptacle and being ignited by an electric spark. The windows should all be wide open and no open flame permitted in the room.

Apply generous coats of the remover as directed on the can and allow it to soak in. The softened-up finish can then be scraped or scrubbed off. Use a broad knife for the flat surfaces and No. 1 steel wool for the curved ones. Rinse the surface thoroughly with turpentine or denatured alcohol to remove any wax residue. The wood surface will now be ready for staining and refinishing.

Staining

The simplest stain is one of the tinted gum-wax preparations made for floor finishing. This comes in a good variety of colors and is simple to apply. Brush on as directed, allow to partially set. Then wipe off the excess. The next day apply a clear coat of full strength of the same material. When this is thoroughly dry, polish with a scrubbing brush, or for higher lustre apply a coat of polishing wax (not the self-polishing variety) and rub up.

You can also finish by applying a coat of one of the penetrating oil stains, also available in a wide variety of colors. Apply with a brush and wipe lighter to the desired depth with a rag. Be careful of the rags. They can ignite by spontaneous combustion; spread them out to dry. When the stain is dry, either shellac and wax the polish or apply one of the varnishes. You have your choice of gloss, semi-matte, or flat varnish.

Bleaching

If you wish to refinish in one of the modern bleached effects, you will have to be most thorough in cleaning off the old coatings. Then apply one of the two-stage bleaches described on page 190. Several applications may be necessary. When you are satisfied that your color is as light as you can make it, sandpaper smooth, using a fine grade of paper. Number 7/0 is the best. Use the finest you can get. To keep the finish as light as possible, it is best to use bleaching lacquer. However, all lacquers are very hard to apply with a brush—they dry too quickly. You can do almost as well by using two coats of banana oil. It will almost maintain the light color and is readily brushed. Then you can apply one thin coat of white, 2-pound-cut shellac. Wax polish this. The main thing is keep any of the common paint oils or waxes off the wood fibres. They all tend to yellow and darken the cellulose.

Painting over Stain or Finish

Painting stained and finished woodwork is simple if you observe two precautions. Remove all traces of wax or polishing oils, and roughen the surface. This is readily done with turpentine or strong washing-soda solutions. Use steel wool and scrub thoroughly. This will clean the surface and roughen it so that paint will adhere to it.

One quart of turpentine and one quart of interior varnish to one gallon of undercoater will make a good adhesive first coat. Check the adhesion when this binder coat is dry by scratching with the fingernail. If the undercoater comes off, remove with paint remover and apply a new coat of the same thinned undercoater. The second coat should be a full-bodied undercoater, followed by your choice of enamel or semi-gloss paint.

Painting Floors

Painting wood floors is frequently done, though it is not recommended because the paint wears more rapidly than other finishes. However, the procedure is simple. Clean up the existing floor by washing it. When dry, apply one or two coats of floor and deck enamel. For full information on finishing and refinishing floors, see Chapter 7, page 93.

REPAINTING CELLARS

Walls. When repainting a cellar, first examine the existing paint carefully. If the existing paint is calcimine, the next coat must be the same. It would be almost impossible to remove the old calcimine from the rough surfaces found in most cellars.

Woodwork. This can be washed and painted with any paint desired. Naturally the most durable paint will be the cheapest in the end.

If the floor is concrete, coat it with a rubber-base paint. If it is wood, paint it or apply a floor oil—either finish will make it easier to clean. See Chapter 7, page 101, for full details.

EXTERIOR REPAINTING

Begin your exterior repainting job on paper. Measure the surfaces to be repainted. Referring to the tables on page 238 will tell you the amount of paint and time required. Check the condition of the old paint and structural material; this will help you determine the various materials and equipment you will need.

Examining Old Surface

Scratch the old paint with your fingernail and rub the palm of your hand over it. If it is smooth and simply dusts off on your palm, it is in good condition. Dusting will make it ready for repainting.

If the paint chips off under your fingernail, or is checked, cracked, blistered, peeled, or crumbled, it must be removed. If the paint is peeling or blistered, look for moisture. This often spreads from a board in contact with the ground, loosening the paint as it travels. Remove any such board and replace after sealing off the source of moisture. Check flashing over windows, gutters and spouts to see that they carry off rain water as intended. If they do not, repair them before repainting.

Check window putty, removing hardened and cracked pieces. Touch up exposed wood with priming paint and, when dry, replace putty. Examine for holes and cracks near window and door trim. Fill these openings with caulking compound, using a caulking gun.

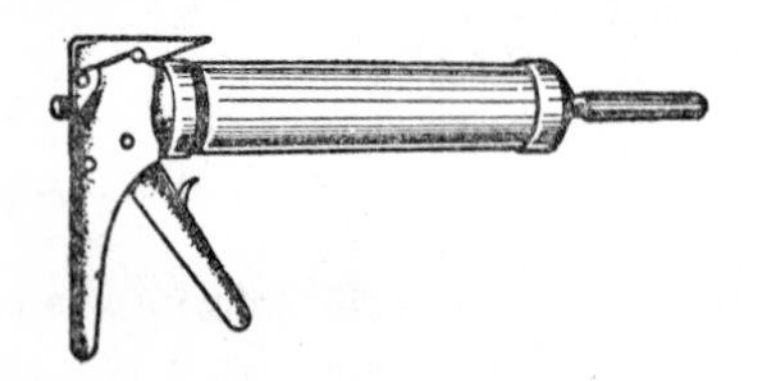

Fig. 8. A caulking gun.

Removal of Old Paint

For speed use a gasoline blowtorch, being careful not to burn the wood. Or use one of the exterior paste or liquid types of removers. This method is much safer than the blowtorch, but somewhat slower and costlier. With either method, scrape off loosened paint with a stiff-bladed, broad knife. Rub stubborn spots smooth with sandpaper.

You can also employ an electric paint-remover. It heats the paint until soft and ready to be scraped. This method takes more time than either of the others, but, although it takes a

Fig. 9. A blow torch. It is very useful for removing paint, but handle it carefully.

short time to get the feel of it, it is safer than using a blowtorch.

Wire-Brushing

If the paint is only slightly imperfect, rub it with a wire brush. This removes loose paint and smooths over the edges of remaining paint.

Repainting

Sound paint can be refinished with one or two coats. Houses painted every one or two years need only one coat. Longer intervals between painting demand two coats for a satisfactory job. The first coat should be a good-quality, manufactured exterior undercoater. For the second and final coat employ a reliable exterior paint.

Surfaces from which the paint has been removed need three new coats. When the surface is clean and smooth, apply a coat of exterior primer. Follow this with a coat of good, manufactured exterior undercoater, and finish with a coat of high grade exterior paint.

Masonry

Brick, cement, or stucco surfaces should be repainted with oil-base paint only cement binder paints do not adhere to oil base surfaces. The roughness of masonry ensures adhesion. Painting masonry wears out brushes fast. Use only old or inexpensive ones.

Wood Shingles

Painted. Dust off loose paint, check for moisture conditions, and paint. Apply two coats, an exterior undercoater and a good exterior paint.

Creosote-Stained. To renew the stain, purchase a creosote stain of the desired color and apply. This thin liquid spatters and flies on the breeze. Use it before applying finish paint on the rest of the building, then wipe off any that has spattered on other surfaces.

To paint creosote-stained shingles, use a good grade of exterior aluminum paint for the first coat. This seals the stain and provides a solid base for the finish coat of a reliable exterior paint.

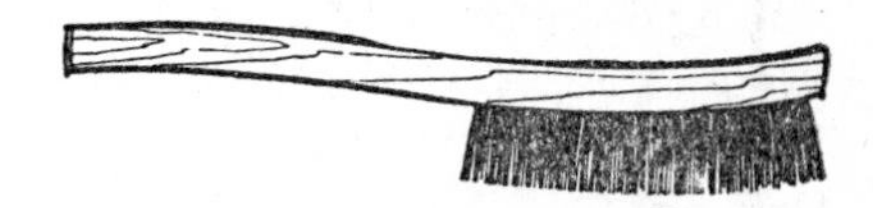

Fig. 10. A wirebrush. It is used chiefly for scraping off loose exterior paint.

Metal

Iron. Wire-brush all loose or rusty spots; dust off loose scale and rust. Touch up bare spots with a rust-inhibiting primer. Paint over all with an exterior metal paint, either an enamel or a regular exterior metal paint.

Galvanized Iron. Wire-brush any rusty spots and loose paint off the metal. Touch up bare spots with a good rust-inhibiting primer. Paint over all with one coat of a good grade of exterior enamel or implement paint.

Copper and Bronze. Wipe with a turpentine rag to remove dirt or grease. Coat with one coat of a good grade of spar varnish.

SPECIAL PROJECTS

Patching Areas in Interior and Exterior Painted Surfaces

Most damage to painted surfaces involves the material on which the paint lies. It is this material which should be repaired first. Even moisture damage causing blisters on paint should be eliminated before the surface is touched up. After the surface damage has been taken care of, you can safely proceed with the painting of the area. Treat the repaired surface as you would any new paint job. Prime, undercoat, and finish coat. On interior work you can frequently save waiting overnight for the priming to dry by priming with shellac; use a two-pound cut. Mix the final touch-up color and try it out on a sample stick or in some inconspicuous part of the room. Let it dry for an hour or so to check its dry color. If necessary, adjust the color and, when right, apply it to the patch.

Radiators and Heating Pipes

The heat makes most paints unsuitable for coating heating equipment. Very few oils or resins will stand the constant expansion and contraction of the metal and very few colors will remain stable. There are two solutions to the problem. If you are painting equipment in the li ing area of a home, it is best to use the cheapest oil paint available. There is so little oil or resin in it that it will remain stable. Lithopone is reasonably stable at the temperatures found on household heating equipment, so that the combination of inexpensive vehicle and pigment makes a paint which will serve satisfactorily. The other and obvious solution is to buy one of the specially made heat-resistant paints. These are the best but are also usually considerably more expensive. In the use of either paint, be very careful of any tinting colors you use. The most stable are the earth colors, raw sienna and raw umber. Burnt sienna and burnt umber and black are almost as reliable.

Stove Pipes

The old fashioned stove-pipe enamel—so well known to our parents—is still available. It is essentially a low-temperature baking enamel. Most brands should be applied when the pipe is cool or just warm, after cleaning of course. They dry when the heat is applied and, incidentally, smell in the process.

Metal Shower Stalls

The painting of shower stalls with any of the air-drying paints available to the homeowner should never be considered more than a cleaning-up operation. None of the normal paints or enamels will stand the alternate wetting and drying, heating and cooling, and the alkalis of the soaps without showing deterioration within several months. For best results, thoroughly clean the metal surface. This means scrubbing it down to the bare metal unless the present paint is unusually sound. Prime the clean and dry metal surface with one of the zinc type of primers, preferably one made for use in water. Lightly sand in order to smooth the surface, and apply two coats of high-grade enamel. Allow the enamel to dry thoroughly between coats, and sand before flowing on the last coat. The smoother the finish, the longer it will take to accumulate imbedded dirt.

The touching up of chipped places is best done with one of the touch-up enamels made for refrigerators, after you have cleaned and sandpapered the area (see below).

Baked Enamel and Porcelain Finishes

Chips or scaled patches on appliances with baked enamel and porcelain finishes should be cleaned with ammonia water or washing soda to remove any trace of grease. Thoroughly rinse and dry the area. Then touch up with one of the porcelain enamels made for the purpose. These are very thick in consistency. For a smooth job you will do well to put a little of the enamel in the cap of the bottle or can and thin it for the first and second coat. In this way you can apply it so that the level of the chipped area is brought up to that of the surrounding surface. Do this work with a soft artist's brush to get the proper flow of the enamel.

Fig. 11. Painting metal. You must prime the metal first.

Painting Glass

In spite of the experiences you may have had in scraping the paint off windows after painting the sash, paint does not stick well to glass. The glass should be absolutely clean. You can make it so by washing with ammonia water, with one of the white abrasive cleaners, or with one of the non-residue solvent type of cleaners. Many of the glass polishes sold for household use leave a residue which will prevent the paint from sticking. When clean and dry, you should apply an enamel. If it is one of the darkly pigmented types—brown, red or black—it will cover solidly in two coats. Most of the more lightly colored enamels will look streaky with less than three coats. The glass surface is so smooth that if you try to apply the enamel too heavily, it will run and sag.

Recently a "frost" type of paint has appeared on the market. Upon a clean glass surface they will simulate the effect of etched glass. They are entirely satisfactory for the purpose. Follow the manufacturers directions for application.

Whitewash

There are special circumstances when you want only a temporary paint on glass, such as in greenhouses or chicken coops. This is generally done with white wash. It is applied to the inside of the glass and is expected to chip off in spots. And it is readily removable by washing with a hose.

Tools, Toys, and Sporting Equipment

Tools. The metal surfaces of tools are frequently painted to prevent rusting and for purposes of identification. The procedure is the same as for other metal—clean, prime, and paint. The implement paints, or semi-enamels, which is what they really are, will give a good solid finish in one coat on top of the primer and will last very well. Wooden surfaces should also be cleaned, sanded, and primed, and they can be finished with the same type of paint. Or the wood can be thoroughly cleaned, sanded, and varnished. This method is actually better, as you will be able to see any defects that develop in the wood through the varnish.

Toys. The only unusual problem involved in the painting of toys is the possibility of the paint's being eaten. Children frequently put toys in their mouths and the paint disappears. Consequently you should be very careful in the selection of the pigment used in the paint. Some of the bright greens are made with arsenic, white lead is frequently the white pigment. Either of these is fatal if consumed in large enough quantities. None of the ordinary vehicles contains anything harmful.

Probably the implement paints will make the brightest and most durable finishes. Simply prepare the surface by cleaning and priming, and finish with a good, well flowed coat of the implement paint. Use a soft brush and flow on the paint; it will dry to a glossy, smooth, washable surface.

Sporting Equipment. For the most part, the wood surfaces of sporting equipment are varnished. This is done not only for the decorative effect but also to make possible the early detection of splits or other defects. Finishing or refinishing should always be done from the bare wood. Clean, sand, and apply varnish. The synthetic, exterior types of varnishes are generally best because they both dry hard and resist the action of water, either salt or fresh. Decorative colors can be applied by using implement paint or enamel.

The usual treatment for gun stocks is to finish them with boiled linseed oil. The rule is: One coat a day for a week and then one coat a week for a month.

Fibre Rugs and Canvas

Fibre rugs are usually stained rather than painted. Any oil stain of a color that pleases you will do. It is very advisable to take the rug out of doors and spread it on paper. You have to apply the stain generously, and if this is done on the floor in the house, it would probably also stain the floor. Simply brush on the stain with a large brush. If you apply it generously enough to get an even coat, you will cover about one hundred square feet with a gallon of stain. Of course, this will vary somewhat depending upon the thickness of the rug.

Canvas can be painted. There are specially made paints for the purpose. Their main characteristic is that they remain flexible after drying. Heavier canvases absorb more paint than the thinner types such as duck. Brush on the paint generously. If you do not, the paint probably will not cover and will show brush marks. Ordinary oil paints can cause canvas to rot; this, added to their tendency to stiffen the cloth, makes it unwise to use them.

Interior Metals

Iron, wrought iron, and steel are generally coated with Coach Black. This is simply a black pigment ground in Japan varnish. It covers very well in one coat and can be left dull, the way it dries naturally, or can be varnished with one of the interior varnishes—which type is not important—to give it a high gloss. Before painting, the metal surface should be thoroughly cleaned by rubbing with steel wool and turpentine or alcohol. If there is rust present, this should be wire-brushed off first.

Copper and brass are usually simply cleaned or cleaned and polished, and then are coated with one coat of two-pound-cut shellac. Shellac that is used on metal is frequently called lacquer.

CHAPTER 6

BRUSHLESS PAINTING

SPRAY PAINTING

Modern mechanical developments inevitably led to the invention of the spray gun, a device which speeds up the application of paints, enamels, varnishes, stains, and other materials. The spray gun works with air under pressure directing a stream of paint through a spray head. The spray head breaks up the stream into small particles. It also aims the particles toward the surface to be painted.

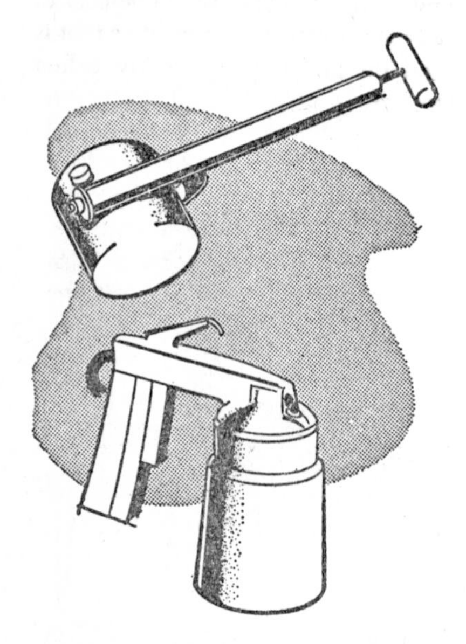

Fig. 1. Household types of spray guns are available at almost all paint and hardware stores.

It also makes possible the application of fast-drying lacquer and synthetic gums. Unfortunately, its speed is not entirely a blessing for it has introduced the hazards of fumes and inflammable vapors. For this reason its use on a large scale is generally limited to factories where hoods and ventilating systems can be installed. Fumes are the mass of particles of the pigment which do not stay on the sprayed surface. They float in air and, if poisonous, like white lead, can be harmful to the operator. The vapors are the volatile thinners. All thinner vapors, with the exception of water, are highly inflammable in concentration and must be directed away from the work area.

Spray Guns

Spray guns are available in several models. They vary from the simple hand-pump type used for white-washing cellars to complicated automatic types used in assembly-line production work.

Household Type. Small motor- or magnet-driven types are manufactured for household use. They are good if their use is limited to occasional pieces of furniture and hobby work. They will not lay in a large area with evenness or the speed of a professional model. However, the cost is

Fig. 2. The more professional types of spray guns have a compressor, which pumps air into the storage tank. You will be wise to get one with some sort of pressure control.

only about one twentieth that of a complete professional outfit. You must show care in cleaning the apparatus if you expect favorable results. Follow the directions for maintenance, and note carefully recommendations for the types of paints to use. These machines do not build up the pressure nor the volume of air necessary to handle the heavier paints, especially the new synthetics. These machines are good, within limits.

Compressor type. All professional machines are basically composed of two parts—gun and compressor. The compressor is generally electrically-driven and pumps air into a storage tank. The more expensive types have automatic controls which cut out the pump when the pressure falls below or rises above set limits. The less expensive ones generally have a safety blow-by valve. When pressure in the tank exceeds the setting, air is released until the danger is passed.

In the interest of safety, or to avoid the cost of a burned-out pump motor, have one or both of these controls on your compressor.

The air under pressure is led through a regulator which drops the pressure from 100 or more pounds to the working pressure of between 20 to 70 pounds. The amount of working pressure depends upon the type of paint and the type of gun you are using.

Heavier paints, like the synthetics, require heavier pressures to spray effectively.

When buying a compressor, an important factor to consider is "cubic feet of air per minute." No compressor having a capacity of less than four to five cubic feet should be considered. Better yet, contemplate getting one which delivers eight, ten, or twelve cubic feet per minute. Too much air will seldom spoil work, but to run out of air in the middle of a big panel can be more frustrating than losing a big fish. Better to buy a big compressor and a small gun than the reverse.

Guns. The principal differences in guns lie in the spray heads and the

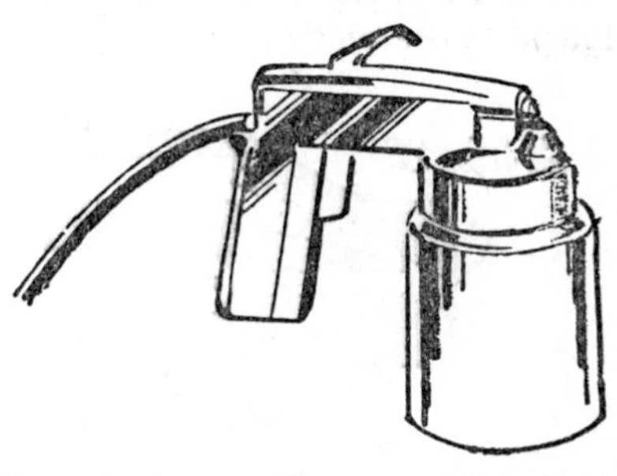

Fig. 3. In this type of spray gun the paint is drawn from the attachable cup into the nozzle by suction.

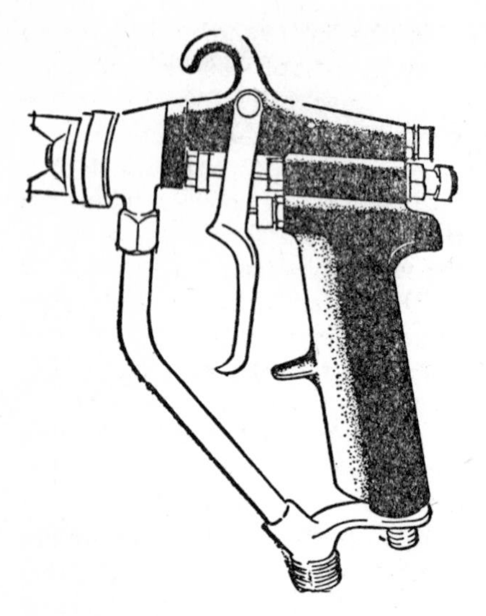

Fig. 4. The spray gun that works by pressure may have a cup that is attached directly to the gun or a tank that is connected to the gun by a hose. The pressure type of gun is recommended for use with synthetic paints.

method of supplying the paint flow to the spray head. Paint is either directed to the spray head by suction or pressure. Almost all small types of guns have cups attachable to the gun. By suction they draw the paint up and into the nozzle. However, a pressure-cup type is recommended if you intend to use synthetic paints. Large commercial types have paint tanks of two- to five-gallon capacity which stand on the floor. Air under pressure is fed to the tank, thus forcing paint up through a rubber hose to the gun.

Spray Heads. The spray heads are either internal- or external-mix types. Of the two the internal-mix type is less popular. It mixes air and paint inside the spray head. The vaporized paint and air are blown out through a slot. Some slots are made to handle a certain kind or consistency of paint or finish. If you change the paint material for which the slot was designed you may lose the spray pattern.

The external-mix spray head with its multiple jets thoroughly atomizes the paint. Also, it fans out the paint spray into a wide and evenly distributed pattern. This spray pattern is very important in obtaining even, wide coats of paint. Each sweep of the gun, held 6 to 10 inches from the surface, should deposit an even band of paint 6 to 12 inches wide. The thickness of paint should not be heavier in the center. It should not thin or feather out until it reaches the last inch of each end of the pattern. With this good pattern one need only overlap an inch on each stroke of the gun to get a perfect job.

Size. If you intend to use several paint materials, get a gun with a removable head and several nozzles. These come in a variety of sizes, from A to G. They are made in sizes to accommodate different kinds of paint materials. Nozzles E, FF, FX, and F are the most commonly used sizes. The larger nozzles, A to D, are used for extremely heavy paints.

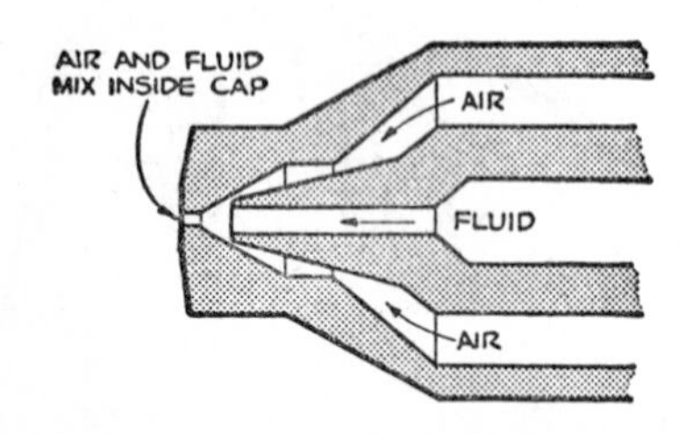

Fig. 5. An internal-mix spray head. The mixture of paint and air is blown out through a slot. A variety of slots is available.

Before you buy expensive equipment, investigate the market thoroughly. Manufacturers will cooperate in supplying you with complete information.

Paints. The best paints and finishes for spraying are those made especially for this purpose. Many painters who are dismayed by brush marks in their work, think spraying is the answer to the problem. Unfortunately this is not necessarily so. Ordinary paints or enamels when sprayed have a tendency to run or sag, since they are not fast-drying. In addition, the average gun will not spray very successfully when held in a vertical position. You must turn each piece on its side to do the top. If you consider the annoyance and danger of fumes and vapors, the extra handling of each piece, and the preparation and clean up, you will find that sometimes you have not saved so much after all. However, if you use recommended materials, especially on production work, you will save time and get a better job.

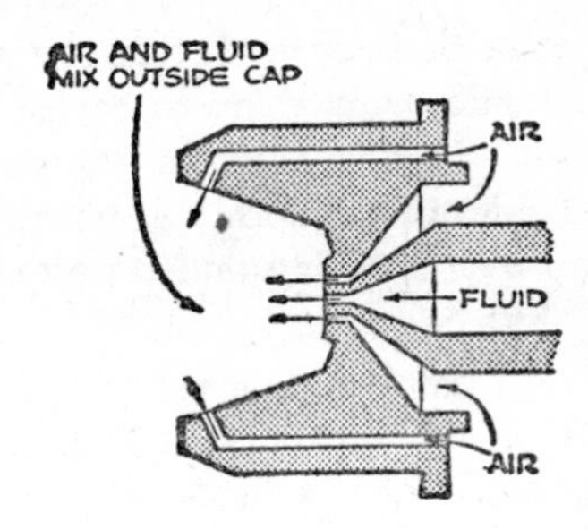

Fig. 6. An external-mix spray head. This type is the more popular. It gives a good spray pattern for the general run of painting jobs.

Spraying

Load the cup with properly thinned material. Test the air pressure and clear the nozzle by pulling the trigger part way in. Practice on a piece of old board to check the adjustment and operation of the gun. There is no set rule for the pressure, because it varies with the nozzle, paint, and surface to be covered.

Hold the gun perpendicular to the surface to be sprayed and 6 to 10 inches away from it. Move the gun beyond the edge of the surface to be painted. Now you are ready for the first stroke. Pull the trigger all the way back. As the spray begins, move steadily across the surface to be sprayed, always holding the gun perpendicular to it and taking care to maintain the distance of 6 to 10 inches. No exact directions can be given for the speed of the stroke. This will vary with the material used. Use a free arm motion, and release the trigger before the end of the stroke; this is known as feather-cutting. Stop an inch or so short of outside corners.

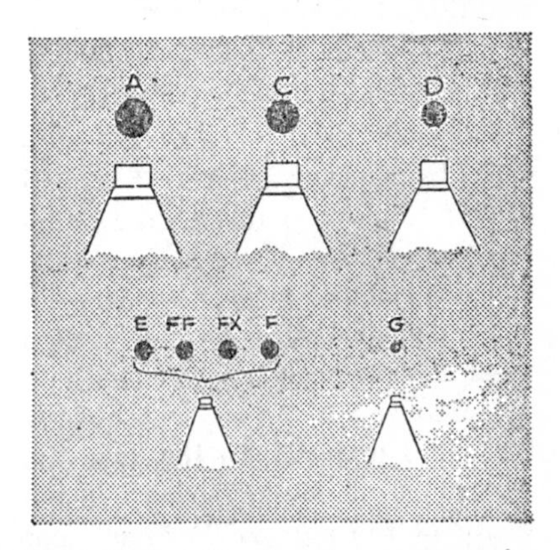

Fig. 7. Comparative sizes of spray-gun nozzles. Different nozzles are used with different paint materials.

To paint these corners, turn the gun on its side or turn cap to horizontal position. In this way you will cover both sides of the corner at once and avoid over-spraying and consequent sagging.

If the paint sags or runs, you are spraying too slowly. If it looks dull and does not cover properly, you are moving too fast. A little experience will guide you. The trick is to put on the thickest coat which does not sag or run.

Troubles. The fan pattern of the spray may be heavy on one side. This is probably caused by dried material in the vents that clog up one side of the air passage. Thinner should be used to dissolve the dried material. Sometimes the material can be reamed out, but this should always be done with something soft like a straw or matchstick so as to avoid damaging the openings. It may also be necessary to remove the air nozzle and clean it, but first check to see that it is tight. Some defects in spray patterns are merely the result of a loose nozzle.

Incorrect pressure may be indicated by a spray pattern that is more or less divided in the middle or by one that is either heavy in the middle or has a salt-and-pepper appearance. You may also get a divided pattern when the pressure is correct because you are trying to get too wide a spray with thin material. In this case the answer is, of course, to reduce the width of the spray. "Blushing" and blooming," excessive offspray and fogging of adjacent areas are also the result of faulty control of air pressure.

Defects. Chief defects that may occur in the gun itself are spitting, air leakage, and paint leakage. Spitting is the interruption of an even flow of mixed paint and air by alternate discharges of the paint and the air. To locate the causes of the interruption, check the following: 1. The packing around the needle valve has dried out. Place two drops of oil on the packing; in extreme cases, replace the packing. 2. The material nozzle is loose or its seat is dirty. Clean with thinner and re-install tightly. 3. Nuts on the siphon cup or material hose are loose. Tighten or replace the nuts. 4. Water and lubricating oil have accumulated in the gun. Remove the oil and water. This possibility should be checked frequently; water can accumulate in the gun by condensation.

Air leakage may result from improper seating of the air valve or from wear or damage in some part of the air-valve assembly. You may be able to correct the condition by tightening, by cleaning, or by lubricating. If there is some damage or excessive wear, the affected parts must be replaced.

Paint leakage usually indicates something wrong with the fluid needle. Check to see if it is damaged or dirty or improperly seated. If none of these is the cause, check the packing nuts to see if they are too tight.

There are other troubles you may run into, like orange peeling, splattering, streaking, and fogging. These are described in the literature obtainable from manufacturers. No gun

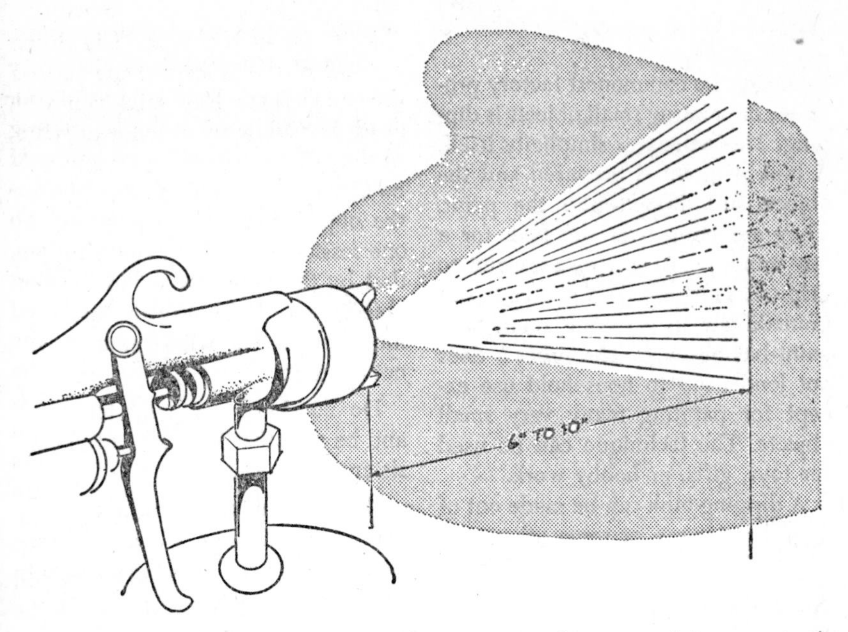

Fig. 8. Where to hold the gun to get a good spray pattern. Correct use of the gun not only does a better job but a much quicker one, too.

manufacturer wants you to blame his equipment for the trouble.

When spraying indoors, have the room ventilated but without drafts. When spraying outdoors, you must choose a time when there is no wind at all unless you aren't going to be bothered by flying spray.

Masking. It is impossible to spray to a sharp line the way you can paint to one with a brush. In order to achieve this you must cover the areas not to be painted with paper. And to make this paper stay in place, a tape with an adhesive back is used. Simple masking is usually done with wrapping paper or other heavy papers. Cut pieces of wrapping paper to almost cover the area to be masked out, leaving a thin strip of space at the edges to be covered by the outer half of the tape. Lay the paper in place. Stick the tape partly on the surface and partly on the paper. Spray paint the remainder. When the paint is dry, remove tape and paper.

Stencils (see Chapter 10, page 150) can also be used for masking. But unless made with an adhesive back, the spray paint tends to blow or creep under their edges, producing a sloppy job.

Liquids which can be painted on and later stripped off like a sheet of gelatine are available. They are particularly good for working with glass.

Protection. It is always advisable to cover the head, especially the hair, when spraying. A simple respirator mask is often advisable too.

DIPPING

One of the commonest factory processes of painting small objects is dipping. The process is simplicity itself. A tank of paint is prepared and the objects are dipped into the paint. They are hung over the tank for a few minutes to allow excess paint to drip off. They are then generally put immediately in a drying room or a paint-baking oven. The process does not lend itself to household use except for painting many very small objects. The technique can be used for toys, gifts, or hobby work.

A dipping tank can be made out of an old paint can or some other container that is the proper size for the objects you have in mind. The closer the size of the tank is to the size of the objects, the less paint you will need, but allow some room to spare so that you can work freely and will be able to put in enough paint for all the objects you are going to dip in one session. Otherwise, you may find that by the time you get to the last object, you have already used so much paint that what remains will not cover it.

Do not have the paint too thick and be sure that it is of an even consistency throughout.

Objects can be dipped most conveniently by means of a simple wire hook. They need be immersed only

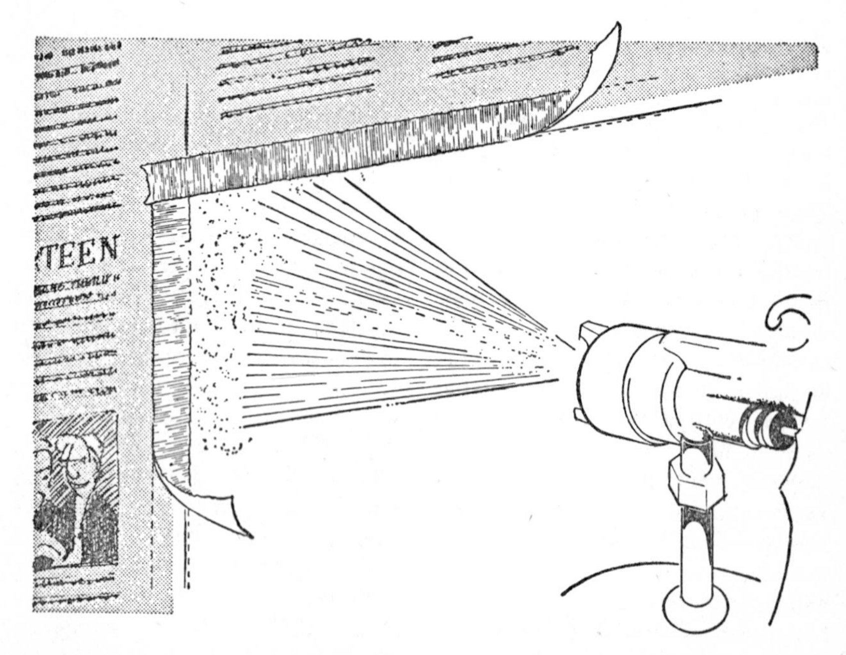

Fig. 9. Masking tape or an adhesive tape and wrapping paper provide the simplest way to mask areas that are not to be sprayed.

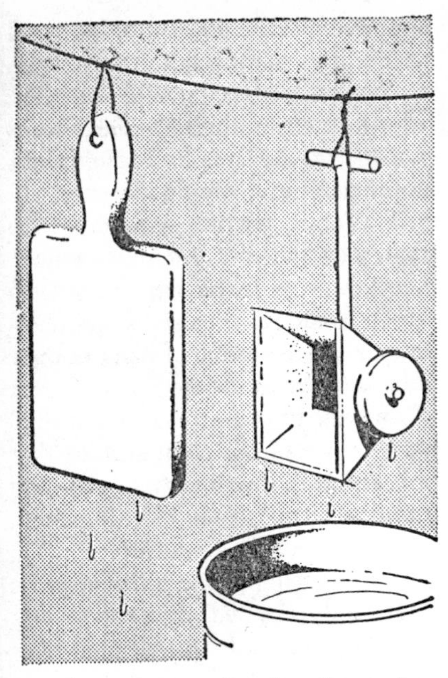

Fig. 10. A simple tank and a place to hang objects are all you need to "go into production" painting small things around the home.

long enough to be sure that the paint has reached every part of the surface. They do not need to be swizzled around. A practical method of work for the home is to make a wire hook for each object and a shallow trough with an open end that feeds back into the tank. Thus, when the object has been dipped, it may be hung over the trough to allow the excess paint to drip off. When the paint has ceased dripping, the objects may be left hanging or they may be placed on wax paper to dry. If placed on other materials, the wet paint or enamel will make them stick. Drying may be hastened by placing the objects near the furnace if it is not too hot or by directing a gently turning fan at them.

Dipping can also be used for larger objects, such as fence posts and pickets, by building a trough of sufficient size and filling it with paint. This is usually too expensive a method for painting, but it is often used for staining shingles and for soaking wood in preservatives.

PAINT ROLLERS

Household paint rollers are available for the application of wall paints. They are generally about 2 to 2½ inches in diameter and about 10 to 12 inches long. The outside of the roller is covered with a rough material. You roll this tool back and forth in a trough or pan of paint to cover the roller. Then you roll the tool over the wall or ceiling. The paint comes off the roller on to the surface.

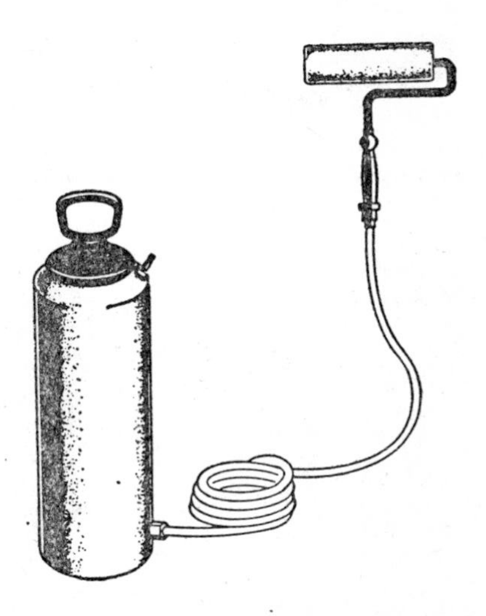

Fig. 11. A pressure-fed paint roller. Air is pumped into the tank, and the roller is thus kept loaded as you work.

A new variation is the pressure-feed roller. A tank standing on the floor is filled with paint. The pump on the side of the tank is used to build up pressure in the tank. A hose from the tank carries the paint to the roller, where it oozes through the porous surface of the roller These rollers apply paint in a stippled texture.

Fig. 12. The use of a mechanical roller is simple and quick, but remember, it won't get into corners.

The chief trouble with rollers is that they will not get into corners. Corners have to be painted with a brush. Some rollers also have a tendency to leave a ridge of paint at their edges. However, while rollers do not allow you the control over the final appearance of the paint surface that a brush does, it will not take you long to acquire the knack of using them and they will do a fast job.

The covering of the roller must be thoroughly cleaned after use or else replaced. They can be cleaned with the same materials used to clean brushes. The simplest method is to remove the excess paint from the trough or pan, if you are using one, put some turpentine or benzine in it, and clean the roller in this. After the roller is clean, the same turpentine or benzine can be used to clean up the pan.

CHAPTER 7

FLOOR FINISHES

KINDS OF FLOORS

About a dozen woods are regularly used for interior flooring in homes. There are two principal types, hardwood and softwood.

Those in the first category include mahogany, oak, chestnut, cherry, walnut, maple, beech, and birch. These are also identified as "broad-leaved type, porous group." The complexity of the fibre structure is the distinguishing characteristic of these woods. The hardwoods wear more uniformly than softwoods, are less likely to sliver, take a better finish, and are generally better looking.

Softwoods. In this group are southern pine, fir, poplar, and cedar. Somewhat less expensive than hardwoods, they are entirely satisfactory for flooring in the less-frequented rooms of a home, such as bedrooms, closets, and can be used instead of plywood for floors to be covered with composition flooring.

Hardwoods. Most often used in flooring for homes are oak and maple, with beech and birch ranking next in quantity. Each piece of wood usually bears the trade name of the association under whose rules it was graded.

The softwoods regularly manufactured into flooring are southern pine,

Fig. 1. Both hard and softwoods are regularly manufactured in vertical (a) and flat-grain (b) stock. Vertical grain is cut at about right angles to the annual rings of growth, while flat-grain is cut approximately parallel.

Douglas fir, western hemlock, western larch, western red cedar, redwood, and southern cypress. As in the hardwoods, each piece of softwood flooring is usually stamped to show the trade mark of the association under whose rules it was graded, the grade name, and the name or mill identification number of the manufacturer.

Grains. Both hardwoods and softwoods are regularly manufactured in flat-grain and vertical-grain stock.

Flat-grain lumber is simply sawn plank after plank from one side of the log to the other. Other terms for flat-grain are slash-grain, "bastard" grain, plain-sawed, and tangential cut.

Vertical-grain lumber is that in which the wide surfaces have been sawn in a plane approximately at right angles to the annual rings of growth. It is also known as edge-grain, rift-grain, comb-grain, and quarter-sawn.

The vertical-grain is generally considered to have better wearing qualities in both hard and softwoods and has a more pleasing, uniform figure.

Whether it be hardwood or softwood, interior or exterior, the home-owner's problem is to apply a finish that will stand the ravages of time and active living. No one type of finish is better in every respect than any other. The secret of good floors lies in thorough understanding of the nature and limitations of the particular kind of finish chosen. No less important are care and maintenance after the job is done.

Composition Floors. Among the various materials included under the heading of "composition" flooring are linoleum, asphalt tile, cork, rubber tile, and mastics. Cement floors for basements, garages, and porches also come under the heading of flooring and are treated below.

Exterior. Open or semi-open porches of cement or wood flooring and car ports made of either material are covered under exterior floors.

Where the owner's chief requirement is a long-lasting finish, varnish and shellac are likely to prove most satisfactory. The durability of coatings can be improved and preserved by keeping them properly waxed. Fresh wax every four to six months is a general maintenance procedure. The time interval will naturally vary according to the amount of wear on the floor.

DESCRIPTION OF FINISHING MATERIALS

The following list of finishes is intended only to identify the various types and their customary use, with some of their advantages and disadvantages. The details of preparation and application are given below.

Varnish. Although tending to show scratches, this finish has a durable, glossy appearance which is highly resistant to spots and stains. The application is simple; use a 3- or 4-inch brush and flow on a good even coat. Some skill is needed, however, to patch worn spots without leaving lines of demarcation between old and new varnish. Varnish will give satisfactory results if properly waxed and otherwise maintained. It is available in quick 4-hour or regular 24-hour drying types.

Shellac. Its quick-drying qualities and ease of application make this a widely-used floor finish. It has only moderate resistance to water and other types of stains, and will spot if liquid is allowed to dry on it. Among other qualities, it has a high gloss, is transparent, and does not darken with age as quickly as varnish does. As in the case of varnish, durability of the finish is increased by waxing and care.

Floor Sealer. For floors subject to heavy traffic, floor sealer produces excellent results on oak, maple, beech, birch, and edge-grain pine and fir floors. It is a finish which shows wear less than varnish or shellac, but soils more easily. The process requires application of wood filler, sealer, and wax.

Lacquer. This finish has about the same durability as varnish. It provides a glossy finish and worn spots may be retouched with good results. Lines of demarcation are not visible because the new lacquer dissolves the old application rather than forming an additional layer. It is extremely difficult to apply, however, because of its quick-drying properties. It has less depth of finish than varnish and is somewhat more expensive.

Wax. Important in finishing and maintaining wood, composition, and cement flooring is wax. Not only does it give a shine, but it also forms a protective film that prevents dirt from penetrating the pores of wooden floors. When it becomes dirty, it can be cleaned easily and new applications of wax made. It comes in paste or liquid form requiring rubbing to polish. Self-polishing types are also available.

Paint. This finish is more suitable than any other coating for exterior floors of both wood and cement. Though painting interior wood floors is sometimes done, it is not recommended because paint wears more rapidly than other finishes. Also, it hides the natural beauty of woods. Varnish and shellac do not. Basement floors are satisfactorily painted, thus helping to preserve the material and keep the dust down.

Stains. If you want to change the natural color of the wood, then colored oil stains are an answer. They are used to give a darker color to a natural wood. Popular types are oil, penetrating oil, and water stains.

PREPARATION OF FLOORS

Preliminary to floor finishing or refinishing, surfaces should be checked for loose boards, slivers, unfilled cracks, loose joints, stains, and other defects. The flooring should then be scraped or sanded. Stains and burns should be sanded out. In brief, the surface should be smooth, free from marks or gaps in the wood, and ready for the succeeding steps of finishing.

Previously finished floors may be mopped or scrubbed with warm water and a mild soap. Wash worn spots with a detergent soap and water. Some discolorations can be removed with a mild bleach. (see page 104). Your floor must be free of all traces of oil, grease, and wax or the finishing materials will not adhere properly. It must also be perfectly dry.

Sanding

You'll need a sanding machine. They can be rented by the day from

Fig. 2. Wash worn spots with detergent soap and water. Mild bleach will remove discoloration.

Fig. 3. For finishing or refinishing floors, you'll need a sander. They can be rented complete with instructions.

most builder's supply houses or paint stores, complete with instructions. You'll also need a small edger for scraping near the baseboards and inside closets.

Surface dirt should be swept up before using the sander. On softwood floors move the sander with the grain at all times. Start with a coarse sandpaper, then use a paper of medium coarseness. Finish up with a paper of fine grade in the last scraping operation. Carefully sweep up the dust each time; if possible, use a vacuum cleaner. Hardwood floors are sanded the same way except that the rough scraping is done either across the grain or at an angle of 45 degrees to the direction of the grain. (Finish sanding is always done with the grain.)

The floor should not be walked on after the last scraping until the stain, filler, or first coat of finish has been applied and has dried thoroughly. For such walking as is unavoidable, wear heavy socks over–or without–shoes. It is important that at least the first coat of the finish, no matter which method is used, be applied the same day as the final buffing in order to prevent moisture in the air from raising the grain of the newly sanded floor.

Fig. 4. Fill cracks in flooring before finishing. You can use wood paste or wood putty.

Special Repairs

Cracks. Cracks in wood floors should be filled before sanding, finishing, or refinishing. Slivers or wedges of wood can be cut to fill large cracks. Glue them in firmly and fill the recesses remaining with wood paste or wood putty. Finally, sand or plane smooth the repairs you have made, unless, of course, you are planning to sand the entire floor.

Smaller cracks can be filled with the wood paste or wood putty alone; color it to match the floor.

Use slivers and paste or putty of approximately the same color as the surrounding wood, if possible. The sliver should preferably be of the same kind of wood as the floor, but you can stain it if you can't make a match otherwise. The wood paste and putty are usually available in a variety of colors, but if you can't get what you want, match the shade by mixing a little color into the material.

Replacing Damaged Floor Sections. Patching badly battered sections of flooring becomes necessary when other repair techniques fail. It means lifting up old flooring and inserting new sections of wood.

Boards which have been warped or worn are replaced by cutting through their width approximately 2 inches on either side of the damaged area with a compass saw or floor saw, taking care not to cut into the subfloor. Then split the board down the center of the damaged area with a chisel and pull out the two pieces. Next, measure a new piece of flooring, saw it to length, and cut off the bottom edge of the groove. Set the new piece of board in place and nail it into the subfloor. Tap the nails slightly below the surface with a nail set, fill the hollow with wood filler, and sand smooth.

If your flooring is not tongue-and-groove (single flooring), the problem of replacing floor sections is somewhat simplified.

Drill a hole right through the floor on either side of the worn board large enough for you to insert the point of a keyhole saw. Cut the plank so that it is flush with the joists at either end. Nail some 2" x 3" wooden cleats to the sides of the joists to support the new plank. Measure and cut the new piece of flooring and nail it to the cleats. With a nail set, countersink the nails, fill with wood filler, and sand smooth.

Repairing Creaky Floors. Some creaking floors are caused by the omission of subflooring. Others have inadequate joist support or are improperly nailed.

For floor boards that have lifted slightly from the joists or the subflooring, better at first try tapping them down. Lay a piece of old burlap or carpeting over the bulge. Place a block of wood over this, and tap with a wooden mallet or the flat back of a hatchet, taking care to hit the wood block and not the floor. If this doesn't bring results, try driving 10d nails

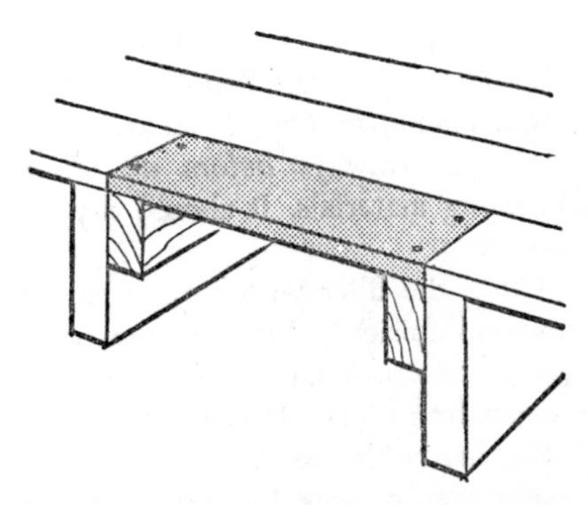

Fig. 5. To repair damaged sections of single wood flooring, cut sections flush with joists. Nail cleats to joist for support of new sections.

around the loose areas in the boards. Sink the nails just below the surface, fill with wood filler, and sand smooth.

Another method of stopping creaking floors is possible if you can get at the joists. Tap a slim wedge under the joist near the offending area of flooring. Do not overdo this or you will raise the floor boards at the wedged point and create the worse problem of an uneven floor. In the event that you can't drive in a wedge, nail a wooden cleat to a joist so that it supports the flooring at that point where the creaking occurs.

APPLYING FINISHES

Wood Filler

The purpose of wood filler is to fill the surface pores in large-pored woods. It prevents the top coating of finish from sinking into the pores by making the surface flush and flat. It is generally used with the hardwoods and generally not used with the softwoods.

For a natural or light-colored floor, use colorless wood filler; of course, colored wood fillers are used for a dark-stained floor. You apply the wood filler *after stain,* if you are using stain, but always *before all other* finishing materials. It should dry 24 hours.

Thin the filler with turpentine or mineral spirits to the consistency of thick cream. Using a short bristle brush, brush it freely across the grain and then with the grain, rubbing it well into the pores. Don't try to cover too large an area at one time. When the surface appears dull, indicating that the volatile portion has evaporated, wipe off the excess with burlap or a wad of excelsior or use a floor-buffing machine. The wiping operation is important and is done first across the grain and then lightly along the grain.

Varnish

In using varnishes, select the type made especially for floors. All-purpose varnishes will not dry hard enough. Instructions for the application of varnish vary from product to product. In any case, follow the directions of the manufacturer. As a rule, three coats are required when varnish is used on bare wood. Two coats where a wood filler has been used and one where a coat of shellac has been applied is usually enough. Make very sure that each previous coat is thoroughly dry before applying a new coat. The application and flow of varnish are best at 70 degrees;

Fig. 6. Select a varnish made especially for floors. As a rule, three coats are needed when varnish is used on bare wood.

below 60 degrees it will not flow to an even surface. After the last coat has dried, apply wax and polish. See page 105 for refinishing.

Shellac

This finishing material is often used as an undercoating for varnish. As stated before, it has the advantage of drying more quickly than varnish. As an undercoat for varnish it makes a good bond between raw wood and the varnish. A proper type of shellac is also satisfactory as a final interior coater, and it is somewhat cheaper than most standard varnishes.

Application. The shellac should always be fresh – it spoils when left around. Shellac that has stood long in metal containers may have salts of iron that discolor oak and other woods containing tannin. It should be applied with a wide brush and the strokes should be long even ones. Take care to join the laps smoothly. The first coat on bare wood requires 2 to 4 hours to dry. It should then be rubbed lightly with steel wool or sandpaper, after which the floor should be swept clean. A second coat should be allowed to dry 2 or 3 hours, and then gone over with steel wool and swept again before the third and last coat is laid on. Three coats are generally required for hardwood floors; for softwood floors two coats will usually be satisfactory. After applying the last coat of shellac, don't use your floor until the next morning if possible. If you must use the room, then wait at least three hours. As in other finishes, an application of wax should be made to maintain the appearance and preserve the finish. Wait at least 8 hours after the last coat has been put on before applying the wax. Avoid using water-emulsion waxes manufactured for linoleums and composition floors, as the water may cause the shellac to bloom, that is, become milky in appearance. See page 105 for refinishing.

Fig. 7. Most shellacs need thinning before use. Use only 190 proof denatured alcohol. See chart for reducing shellac.

Thinning. Some shellacs need thinning to conform with a consistency needed for a particular job. The correct thinner for reducing shellac is 190 proof denatured alcohol. Never use anti-freeze alcohol or methanol, as they usually contain water.

QUANTITIES FOR REDUCING SHELLAC

Shellac	*Amount of Alcohol*
5-lb cut to 3 lb.	3½ pints to 1 gal shellac
5-lb cut to 2 lb	1 gal to 1 gal shellac
5-lb cut to 1 lb	2⅔ gals to 1 gal shellac
4-lb cut to 3 lb	1 qt to 1 gal shellac
4-lb cut to 2 lb	¾ gal to 1 gal shellac
4-lb cut to 1 lb	2⅛ gals to 1 gal shellac

Recently, colored shellacs, known as French lacquers, have become available to the consumer. Looking like enamel, they have all the sealing and surface qualities of regular shellac. They come in white and black, and can be tinted by mixing in dry colors dissolved in denatured alcohol. They are extremely difficult to apply. They must be put on with great skill and under ideal conditions or they won't flow to a smooth finish. They are not recommended for use by the amateur.

Floor Sealer

This finish is good for floors getting heavy traffic. The process requires the application of wood filler, sealer, and wax. For the application of filler, see above in this chapter.

The floor sealer is essentially a thinned varnish, a spar varnish with more volatile and correspondingly less nonvolatile matter in it. Its application requires no special skill. Apply the sealer with a paint brush, a lamb's wool applicator, a mop, or a squeegee. Apply as much sealer as the floor will absorb. Depending on the type of grain, some boards will absorb more sealer than others. After the first coat has been applied, spread out the surplus sealer with an applicator or cloth to areas which will absorb it, and then wipe off any excess before it becomes tacky. Before the first coat dries, burnish the surface with steel wool. Allow it to dry overnight. Apply the second coat in the same way, but do not use more sealer than the floor will absorb. Repeat the burnishing operation with a power-driven steel-wool burnishing machine and allow the floor to dry overnight. Lastly, apply wax.

Lacquer

The difficulty for the beginner in applying lacquer is a factor limiting its use. It dries so quickly that it takes quite some experience to apply it well. It is not recommended for the amateur. If it is used, particular attention should be given to the instructions of the manufacturer. It has about the same finishing properties as varnish.

Wax

Almost all finishing operations require wax to intensify the beauty of the floor and to preserve the finish. Two types are paste or liquid wax. Water-emulsion waxes, commonly called non-rubbing or "self-polishing" waxes, are widely used on cement, linoleum, rubber tile, cork, asphalt tile, mastic, and other floorings. Follow the directions of the manufacturer for applying a particular product.

Wax on varnished floors tends to make them slippery unless it is kept thin. To insure having a non-slippery surface, allow the wax to dry from 30 minutes to one hour before polishing. Be careful in using water-emulsion or self-polishing waxes, since the water base frequently results in the raising of the grain of the wood, which in turn results in a rough surface. Apply a good-quality paste wax over the final shellac, varnish, or floor sealer finish, and polish, either by hand or with a buffing machine.

Application. To apply paste wax, put a thin coat on the floor, using a cloth applicator or machine. With cloth, fold the cheesecloth into a thick pad and place the wax between the folds; pressure on the pad forces wax to the rubbing surface and assures an even coating. Let the wax set for about 15 to 30 minutes, then polish the surface with a polishing machine or by rubbing with soft cloths on a weighted floor-brush.

Holding a Brush. You can easily make a floor polishing brush by attaching an old broom handle to a piece of plank about eight inches wide and 12 inches long. Use a strap hinge so that the handle can swing up and down as you push the polisher back and forth. Cover the bottom with five or six thicknesses of burlap or other strong cloth and wire or secure a couple of bricks onto the top side of the plank. This added weight will speed up the polishing.

Cement Floors

Painting concrete with either oil or concrete paints is not entirely satisfactory as both are surface treatments which show wear at a fairly early date. The most thorough coloring of concrete is achieved when the concrete is mixed by the addition of alkali-resistant colors. Most manufacturers of these colors recommend that the dry colors be mixed in water and this mixture added to the concrete mix. Of course, the mix must be thoroughly stirred to disperse the color evenly throughout.

In addition, there are on the market chemical stains for the treatment of concrete. The surface of the concrete must be etched by mopping on a coat of muriatic acid, usually a 5% solution. When this is dry, the chemical for staining is mixed in the directed amount of water and brushed on the concrete. The chemical reacts with the alkali in the concrete to form a color. There is penetration and permanence with this method. There are

Fig. 8. After the floor-finishing operation, waxing is important for preserving your finish and maintaining the appearance.

also variations such as blending of the various colors available or intensifying them. For interior use, chemically stained concrete can be waxed and polished. It will take several coats of wax to bring up a tile-like gloss. The moisture and alkali in concrete usually breakdown a varnish film, so the use of this material is not recommended except in the very driest parts of the country.

Painting. Although paint is not as good as the methods given above for permanently coloring concrete, cement floors are often painted and will prove quite satisfactory. The paint will also help hold down the dust.

It is generally not advisable to paint a cement floor until it is at least one year old. The reason is that new cement breaks down ordinary paints. If you must paint sooner, you can neutralize the salts in the cement by applying a solution of 2 pounds of zinc sulphate in 1 gallon of water. When it is completely dry, you are ready to paint.

Readying the Floor

The general procedure for painting previously unpainted cement floors is to clean, to repair, if necessary, and to neutralize, if necessary, and then paint. To clean, wet the surface with clean water and then apply a solution of 2 to 2½ ounces of washing soda to a gallon of hot water. Sprinkle a good scouring powder uniformly over this. Then brush the surface and rinse with clear water. Do not use an ordinary soap because it will form a scum of lime soap, which will prevent paint from sticking to the surface.

After cleaning, you can remove loose paint with a stiff wire brush. Repair cracks by scraping out loose particles and then filling with a prepared cement crack-filler.

The two kinds of paints most used on concrete floors are varnish-base deck paint and rubber-base paint. The varnish-base paint is best used on floors not subject to dampness. The rubber-base paint is used where dampness is prevalent, especially for basement floors.

Varnish-Base Paints. Apply these when the humidity is low. To make the first or priming coat, add to each gallon of the paint one quart of spar varnish and ½ pint of turpentine. Brush it out well and allow it to dry thoroughly. The second coat does not need to be thinned. Two coats are usually enough.

Rubber-Base Paints. Rubber-base paints do not adhere well to a smooth surface. If the concrete has been troweled to a smooth hard surface, it should be etched with a solution of 1 pint to 1 quart of muriatic acid to each gallon of water. The etching roughens the surface. After etching, wash the floor with water and let it dry thoroughly. Wear rubbers on your shoes and rubber gloves on your hands. This acid will harm leather and clothing. For the first coat, thin each gallon of paint with 1 quart of mineral spirits or the thinner recommended by the manufacturer. The second and third coats can be applied unreduced. Two coats are frequently used, but three coats are recommended. This type of paint should *not* be used over other types of floor paint.

Wax. A thin film – preferably a liquid floor wax of the organic solvent type – will protect any of these finishes. Cement floors can also be waxed without painting. However, while the wax makes the floor somewhat more water-repellent, it tends to darken it, too.

Refinishing. To refinish a cement floor, if it is in good condition and there is no wax on it, cleaning is all you have to do. Wash or mop with plain water—slightly soapy water may be used on very dirty floors—and rinse with clean water. If wax is present, you will have to remove it. This can be done by applying turpentine or petroleum spirits and scouring with steel wool while still wet. Then clean, if still necessary, and paint.

If the old paint is peeling, it should be removed. One method of doing this is to soak the surface for about 30 minutes with a solution of 2 pounds of caustic soda (household lye) dissolved in 1 gallon of hot water. Another method is to cover the floor with a thin layer of sawdust that has been soaked in the lye solution, allowing it to remain overnight. In either case, the old paint can afterwards be removed with a wide steel scraper and the surface rinsed thoroughly with clean water. *Caution:* Be sure to protect yourself with rubber gloves and goggles. If some of the solution spills on your skin, flush the spot immediately with water and brush it over with vinegar to prevent a burn.

After wax and paint have been removed as necessary, make whatever repairs are required. Touch up the new patches of cement with zinc sulphate solution to offset the alkalinity of the material. Then, with a clean, dry floor, put on one or two new coats of paint. Large areas that have been worn or repaired should be primed before you put the new coats on.

Painting Exterior Wood Floors

Although paint is not generally suitable for indoor floors, it is better than any other coating for exterior wood floors. It is more durable than varnish or sealer and usually affords greater protection against weathering.

Painting wet wood is not recommended at all, of course. It is also very unwise to paint damp wood. Make certain that wood floors are free of moisture before painting. Wood floors in contact with the earth are usually damp. Adequate provisions for dampproofing them should be made. This means separating the wood from the earth by metal, cement, or air.

You must also consider the weather. Choose a day when the humidity is low and the temperature is pleasant. Paint dries very slowly at low temperatures, so do not paint when the level is expected to fall below 40 degrees.

Preparation. Do this by cleaning dust and dirt and smoothing rough or uneven spots. Fill all nail holes, open joints, and cracks with putty after the surface has been primed. One of the softwoods is generally used for exterior flooring; if so, filler will not be needed. If a large-pored hardwood has been used, you should make use of filler.

Painting. The painting procedures are the same as described for varnish-base paints under *Cement Floors,* page 102.

Repainting. If the paint has worn away but is generally in good condition, showing no blisters or flaking, spot-prime the worn areas and apply one coat of paint over the entire floor. For severe paint failures, such as blistering, flaking, alligatoring, and cracking, strip the old coating from the wood surface, using paint and varnish removers. Determine whether construction defects are responsible for paint failures and correct, if necessary. Prepare and paint the surface in the same way as for new surfaces.

Oil Finish

Floor oil finishes are used for surfaces which are subjected to heavy traffic and frequent scrubbing. Oil finishes are easily applied and dry quickly, permitting the use of the floor in a short time. They are obtainable in a variety of colors, brown, dark, and natural tones being generally preferred. Do not use mineral floor oils; they will permanently darken the wood.

After preparing the floor as for other finishes, apply one coat of oil. Mop the oil on the floor and rub it in along the grain, using a stiff strong brush. Remove excess with a clean dry cloth or mop and allow 24 hours for the oil to penetrate and dry. Apply wood filler on open-grain woods. Apply sealer and wax for finer finish. See below for refinishing.

TOUCHING UP A GOOD FLOOR

Restoring a floor in fair condition is simple. Hardwood floors with some finish will stand a good washing with one of the detergent washing powders and water. Apply with a mop and scrub the stubborn spots with number 2/0 steel wool. Rinse with clean water and mop up excess water. If you do the washing carefully, using a minimum amount of water, and do not leave it on the surface, the amount of absorption will not harm the wood.

Discoloration

Check the areas of greatest travel for wear and discoloration. The discoloration can generally be removed with one or two applications of an oxalic acid bleach. Place ½ pound of oxalic acid crystals in a quart of warm water and mix thoroughly. Spread some of the solution over the discolored areas. Wear rubber gloves or make a small mop by tying a rag to the end of a stick. The oxalic acid is very poisonous. When the bleach has dried you will find a frost-like layer on the wood. Remove this with a moist rag. If the area has been bleached enough, it is ready for touch-up staining. If not, apply the bleach again.

Purchase a small quantity of penetrating oil stain similar to the color of the floor and touch up the bleached area. Blend out the edges with a dry brush to eliminate the dark line of the stain. Apply one coat of shellac or varnish to the stained area. When dry, shellac or varnish the whole floor. Always work towards the door through which you are going to leave the room. This treatment of washing, bleaching, touching up, and finishing will work equally well on an unstained, finished floor. Simply omit the staining operation.

Crack Fillers

If the joints of the flooring are open as a result of shrinkage, you can fill them successfully by the use of one of the prepared crack fillers. Select the color which most closely matches the color of the finished floor. After the first coat of shellac or varnish, push this paste into the open cracks with your broad knife. Wipe off the excess with a turpentine rag before it has a chance to dry too hard.

Scraping

If the floor is softwood, the finish poor, or the boards warped, it is best to scrape. Do this as described above, page 95.

Proceed with the finishing by staining, by staining and filling, by filling alone, or by simply shellacking on the raw wood. For repainting cement floors see page 103.

REFINISHING OLD FLOORS

Where floors have become badly discolored and worn by neglect or improper maintenance, the most practical procedure, and often the only one that will restore a fine finish, is to have the old finish removed and the floor reconditioned by power sanding. Where the floors have been reasonably well maintained but the finish has become dingy with age, refinishing without power sanding may be practicable. The method of removal of the old finish depends upon the kind of finish that was used originally.

Floors Originally Finished with Varnish. Old, discolored varnish is usually removed most easily by power sanding; if desired, this can be done with liquid varnish remover. Alkaline solutions in water and removers sold in powder form to be dissolved in water should not be used. The directions for using liquid remover should be followed carefully. Since some of the old, discolored varnish remains imbedded in the wood, complete restoration of the natural wood should not be expected. Traffic channels where the old varnish has long been worn through and dirt has been ground into the wood should be cleaned by sanding.

Floors Originally Finished with Shellac. Old shellac and wax finishes that have merely become soiled by dirt in the wax coating may be cleaned by going over the floor with steel wool saturated with clean turpentine. Any white spots in the shellac caused by contact with water may be taken out by rubbing lightly with a soft cloth moistened with denatured alcohol. But the alcohol must be used with care to avoid cutting the shellac coating. On floors where the dirt is ground into the shellac itself or white spots penetrate through the coating, more drastic treatment is necessary. First, wash the floor with a neutral or mildly alkaline soap solution followed by clear water, using as little water as possible in each operation. Then scour the floor with No. 3 steel wool and denatured alcohol. If the floor boards are level and are not warped or cupped, the scouring can be done to advantage with a floor-polishing machine fitted with a wire brush to which a pad of the No. 3 steel wool is attached. After the scouring, the floor should be rinsed with a minimum amount of clean water, mopped up to prevent blooming, and allowed to dry thoroughly before refinishing with shellac or other finish.

Floors Originally Finished with Oil. Clean the surface with water and detergent cleaner and apply a new coating of oil. Make necessary repairs and smooth rough spots if the floor is in poor condition. To remove oil, wet about 10 square feet of floor with a mop and warm water and sprinkle the area liberally with a mixture of one part soap powder and three parts trisodium phosphate. Scrub the floor with a stiff brush, using only as much water as needed to form an emulsion and float the oil to the surface. As the oil is loosened and comes to the top, remove it with a squeegee and mop. Rinse the area with clean water and mop dry. Treat the other sections in the same way. When the entire floor has been cleaned, let the surface dry 24 hours, then sand with a machine and finish as desired.

FLOOR MAINTENANCE

To reduce the need for frequent refinishing of floors, you must be familiar with the principles of floor cleaning and maintenance. You should clean floors with wet or damp cloths or mops only often enough to meet sanitary requirements, because repeated wetting and drying softens varnish coatings, thus causing more rapid wear. Strong alkaline soap also softens wood and raises the grain, causing splintering.

Wood Floors. Dust unwaxed varnished and shellacked wood floors with a soft brush or dry mop. Rub the floor with an oiled mop or a cloth slightly moistened with turpentine, floor oil, kerosene, or furniture polish. In general, avoid using water, but if surfaces are badly soiled, wipe them with a mop or cloth dampened with warm, slightly soapy water, and then with a cloth moistened with clear water. Wipe the surface dry at once and polish it with an oiled mop or cloth. Apply wax to worn surfaces.

Oil and Painted Floors. Use a soft brush to sweep them and then rub them with an oiled mop or cloth. Occasionally, they may be washed with slightly soapy water and rinsed with a wet cloth or mop, then wiped dry and polished with an oiled cloth or mop. Floors may usually be reoiled or repainted without sanding.

Waxed Floors. Clean these with a soft brush or mop. Do not use oil, since the oil softens wax. To remove a dirt-and-wax film which darkens the surface, use a cloth dampened with warm soapy water. Although gasoline and turpentine are more satisfactory than water, these liquids are inflammable and care must be taken to avoid having open flames in the room.

Water dulls and whitens many waxes. If water-cleaning has already whitened a waxed floor, restore luster and color by rubbing with a woolen cloth or a weighted brush, applying a little wax if needed.

Daily sweeping with an untreated dust mop is one point of good maintenance. If you should spill water on the floor, wipe it up promptly with a dry cloth.

Finishing While Painting. As mentioned elsewhere in this book, the dust created by sanding is so fine that it penetrates the dust bag of the machine and settles on all of the exposed surfaces in the room. If the floors are to be finished and the room is to be painted at the same time, it is best to complete the floors, except for the final coat of finish, before doing any painting.

After applying the first coat of finish and allowing it to dry, cover the floor. When you have completed the painting, remove the paper, remove any paint spots on the floor with a turpentine-soaked rag, and proceed with the finishing.

Fig. 9. Materials used in floor finishing often contain highly inflammable substances. Don't smoke or work near an open flame while using them.

PRECAUTION: Gasoline, turpentine, volatile mineral spirits, acetone, and many other volatile organic solvents are highly inflammable. Care should be taken when using these solvents or preparations containing them. Have good ventilation and avoid open flames and smoking in the rooms or other spaces where they are used. Pilot lights should be turned off. Oily and greasy rags should be kept in closed metal containers or spread like washed clothes to dry. Animal and vegetable oils are very likely to cause spontaneous combustion.

CHAPTER 8

WALLPAPER

Wallpaper is one of the simplest and most attractive ways to decorate a room. By looking at one of the sample books available in any paint supply store, you will be able to plan the color harmony and the decorative effect of the finished room. Almost without exception, the manufacturers of wallpaper have staffs of color consultants for the development of the colors and designs found in their papers. Many of the designs are reproductions of those developed during famous periods of decoration. These designs maintain their popularity on the basis of good taste and experience. Modern artists often contribute to the development of new examples of wallpaper designs to go with modern interior decorating.

Wallpaper has a sound historical background as a form of decoration. The Chinese were the first to use it—more than two thousand years ago. Traders with the East brought back rolls of it. Soon after it was manufactured in Europe. Early in the history of our own country, its manufacture became one of our industries. In many museums you will find examples of actual Colonial papers. By carefully removing them from the walls of old houses it was possible to restore them on reconstructed rooms in the museums.

Economy of Wallpaper

You will find that using paper may even be economical in the decoration of your rooms. A wallpaper which costs seventy-five cents a roll amounts to little more than two cents a square foot. You cannot buy paint to do an adequate job as cheaply. Of course, this doesn't include the cost of tools used on the job. But if the price of the tools is divided over several rooms, the cost is still low. In addition, the labor involved is considerably less in comparison with a good paint job. The ceiling and the woodwork can be completed, the paper hung, and the room is ready for use.

Types of Wallpaper

Wallpaper is available in a wide variety of types, many more than there is room to describe here. But we can list the broad classifications and some of their characteristics. The simplest wallpapers are merely a good grade of uncoated paper stock upon which a water-color paint has been applied. If a decorative design is wanted, this is printed on top of the water-color paint. The obvious disadvantage of this type of paper is its sensitivity to water. However, it is the least expensive of all.

Manufacturers have also developed washable papers. These are made with casein water paints. As you know from the discussion on paints, casein glue becomes insoluble in water when it dries. Emulsion binders and even oil paints are used, too. The latter have required the development of very special types as most oil paints would become too hard and would crack. These papers are water proof and reasonably washable. To further improve the washability of the wall covering, some manufacturers use a light grade of cloth instead of paper. The added strength of the fabric makes washing a safer procedure.

Embossed Paper. Paper stocks are also embossed. This type of paper is not enjoying the popularity it once had, but as texture becomes more and more important in our modern decoration of large flat walls, it may return to general favor. The colors and designs are usually of the water-color type, though some of these papers are advertised as being washable.

Border Papers. Border papers are available in almost all the types and are made in the same ways. They are simply narrow and intended to be used as a border.

Metallic Papers. Metallic papers are very popular. There are two types: one is coated with a metallic pigment such as aluminum; the other is coated with a metallic foil. The first type presents no unusual problems to the paperhanger. The second, however, has probably made aspirin addicts of many would-be decorators. When the paper backing is pasted, it expands a bit while the metallic foil facing does not. This causes the wallpaper to curl in from the edges, making it difficult to hang properly. In addition, when the back curls over the paste frequently soils the fragile metallic face. It is possible to minimize the problem by using one of the adhesives with a low moisture content, but it is better for the amateur to avoid the problems raised by this type of paper.

Wood Papers. Real wood papers are available to the home decorator. The Japanese have supplied the market with a wall covering made of wood sliced so thin that it can be handled like paper. Needless to say, it is fragile, but when applied and waxed it makes an attractive wallcovering. An American manufacturer has solved the problem of using real wood by mounting thin slices on fabric backing. This is strong and satisfactory but it requires special techniques for hanging. If you choose this type, the manufacturer will be glad to supply you with all the necessary information. The method was developed with the assistance of master paperhangers and works very well.

"Scenic" Paper. For impressive decoration jobs there are the "scenics." These are the royalty of papers. They are sold in sets and by the strip. Frequently they are hand-painted or hand-blocked and almost always make attractive wall coverings. If you plan hanging this type it is suggested that you get experience with paperhanging first. Actually, they are no harder to hang than ordinary papers but the higher cost should make one think twice before trying the job without previous experience.

Ready-Pasted Papers. Finally, the latest development in the field of wallpapers is the ready-pasted type. The manufacturer applies a paste to the backside of the paper and lets it dry before rolling. Full instructions for the wetting and hanging of these papers are included in each package. Follow instructions carefully and your job will turn out satisfactorily. The greatest danger is in blistering, but thorough preparation of the surface and careful smoothing will eliminate this.

MEASUREMENTS AND TOOLS

Measuring Quantities of Wallpaper

The standard of measurement for wallpaper is 36 square feet. No matter how wide or long the paper, the standard American roll is 36 square feet. You have to reduce your measurements of a room to this figure to determine the number of rolls to buy. This number of square feet is also known as a "single roll," though wallpaper rarely comes in single rolls. Generally, it is packaged in double or triple rolls.

Wallpapers are made in various widths, the narrowest being 18 inches and the widest, 48. The most frequently used widths are 18 and 30 inches. A convenient length for the narrower papers is the double roll. An 18-inch paper would then be 48 feet in length. In the average room this would provide six strips for hanging, each 8 feet long. The wider 30-inch paper is usually sold in the triple roll. It is approximately 43 feet long, providing five strips for the average room. The horizontal measure in a room provided by either of these two sizes of rolls is about 12 feet. You will cover the same area of wall surface with either.

Measuring Strips of Wallpaper. If all ceilings were of equal heights, the problem of packaging wallpaper would be easy.

Though the paper is bought in rolls, it must be hung in strips of the appropriate length. Measure from the baseboard to the ceiling or picture moulding; this will give you the approximate length of each strip. For straight patterns or lining paper, three to six inches additional length at the top and bottom is enough allowance for waste. But for drop patterns you may have to allow as much as an extra two feet or more depending on the pattern size. (The difference between these two types of paper design will be explained later in the chapter, page 115.) By dividing the proper length of each strip into the known length of the roll of paper, you will be able to determine the number of strips in each double or triple roll. When you have determined the number necessary to cover the walls, you can easily figure the number of rolls to buy.

How Much Paper Should You Buy? The easiest way to estimate wallpaper needs is to make a small sketch of the floor plan of the room. Measure the length of each wall and mark it on the sketch. Divide this by the width of the paper and you will know the number of the strips. Subtract the area of any large openings, such as archways, but include doors and windows. The pieces which would cover these areas will come in handy at the tops and bottoms of the windows, over doors, and for other small spaces. When you know the length of each strip and the number of strips, then you know the number of rolls to buy. It is wise to buy several more rolls than you need to allow for errors in cutting or pasting. Any good paint store will be willing to take back clean and uncut full rolls of paper. It is standard trade practice. So order extra rolls.

The trade practice in estimating quantities of wallpaper is to take the wall area and add 10 to 20 per cent to allow for waste in cutting. But this method requires knowledge of the type of paper used and of the physical characteristics of the room. However, you can use it as a quick check on your own estimate.

Tools

You should have the tools listed below to do a good paperhanging job. If you use the ready-pasted wallpaper or have your paper trimmed at the store, you can eliminate the special table and straight edges. But there are disadvantages to these methods, as indicated in the descriptions. Sets of these tools are available from the larger mail-order houses as well as from your local paint store.

1. Table, Top: 3 (white pine) boards 6′ x 12″ x ⅜″; Legs: two folding trestles or other adequate support
2. Straightedge, 6 ft long, true, can have brass edge
3. Paperhanger's knife
4. Scissors, preferably 12″ blades
5. Paste brush, 7″ or 8″, similar to calcimine brush

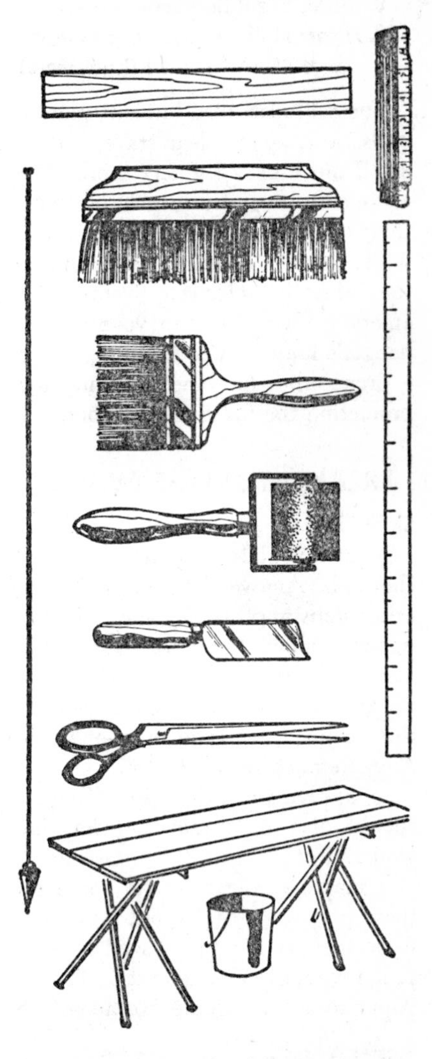

Fig. 1. A complete set of tools for paperhanging can be ordered from the larger mail-order houses or from your local paint store.

6. Seam roller, either 1″ or 1½″ will do
7. Smoother, make sure it has plenty of bristle
8. Plumb bob, line, and blue chalk
9. Rule, 2′ folding type
10. Tear stick, short straightedge, 2½′ x 3″ x ⅜″ (make it yourself)

You will also need ladders, planks, pails, a sponge, clean rags, and a small piece of #0 emery cloth. The sponge and rags are used to clean up the paste which you get on the woodwork. One of the pails is for paste and the other for cleaning water. The emery cloth is to keep your paperhanger's knife sharp. Newspapers or a dropcloth will come in handy for protecting the finish on the floor.

PREPARATION OF WALLS

Light Fixtures

All switch plates or lighting fixtures should be removed before taking any other steps in preparing the walls for paper. Remove the correct fuses and cut the wires if necessary; they can always be easily reconnected by using the simple twist type of connector. Any other fixtures which will interfere with applying a full strip of paper should also be removed from the walls. After you gain some experience you may be able to avoid some of these preparatory jobs, but it is wise to do them until you are well able to judge where to do the cutting in the paper to accommodate obstacles.

Plaster Walls

New plaster walls should be tested for free alkali. Apply the testing procedures outlined in Chapter 3, page 47. If necessary, neutralize with the suggested zinc-sulphate solution. In addition, make sure necessary patching is done to eliminate any cracks or checks in the surface. The next step is to size the plaster so that the paste will adhere properly to the surface. Size is made of glue. Actually, it is simply a thin mixture of glue. You can make your own, but this is not recommended as glues vary greatly in strength. Considering the small cost involved, it is better to buy one of the standard brands and follow the directions on the package. Apply this size generously to the plaster surface and let it dry. Avoid any holidays, that is, untouched spots, by working from a window towards the darker part of the room. You can then constantly check the surface just covered by its wet shine.

Wallboard

Wallboard presents no difficulties. Joints have to be filled and covered with tape and all nail holes have to be filled. See page 47.

Hard Wallboard. After the preliminaries described in the paragraph above, apply a coat of size as directed for plaster. If the manufacturer of the wallboard recommends some particular size, you will do well to follow his advice.

Soft Wallboard. After taking care of the joints and nail holes, apply one coat of glue size.

Painted Walls

Previously painted walls should be cleaned by washing if necessary. If the paint is one of the glossy types, either real enamel or one of the enamel-like paints, you should use washing soda or a similar strong solvent to cut the hard surface of the paint. The glue size will usually crawl on a smooth shiny surface. Steel wool is also useful in cutting through this hard surface. Now cut out all plaster cracks and patch them as instructed in Chapter 3, page 33. Small checks or dents can generally be spackled out smooth. Follow the instructions for this found on page 34.

You are now ready to apply the size. Add about four ounces of household vinegar to each gallon of size and the possibility of crawling will be lessened—the vinegar will aid the size to penetrate the paint. If the manufacturer of the size you have bought recommends the addition of something else, or states that it is not necessary to add anything, follow his instructions. Once again, spread the size generously and make sure that every part of the wall has received its fair share.

Plywood

Plywood can be successfully papered if you follow the instructions issued by its manufacturers. They suggest covering the surface with a paper felting material before hanging the wallpaper. This is recommended because the paste used for wallpaper would raise the grain so much that it would show through. The felting is hung with a special adhesive and should only be done after all the joints have been previously filled and taped over.

Papered Walls

Previously papered walls can be successfully repapered either over the old paper or—better—after removal of the existing paper. It is considered reasonably safe practice to place up to three layers of paper on a sound wall. More than this will almost certainly pull the under layers loose and your work will be wasted.

In papering over old paper, make sure that there are no loose patches. If you find any, scrape them off and sandpaper down the edges until they are smooth with the surrounding wall. Carefully check all the joints, scrape any loose ones and sandpaper all of them. If the paper is one of the shiny-surface varieties or has been coated with shellac or one of the preparations for making it washable, you will have to wash it so much that you may as well remove it. The paste will not stick to any of these materials and they must be removed. While you are doing that much work, you might as well add a little more and remove the paper entirely.

Removing Paper

This can be done in one of several ways. You can soak the paper enough so that the water will penetrate and loosen the paste underneath. Then the paper can be stripped off in large sheets or gently scraped with a broad knife. Simply remember to be very gentle with the broad knife as every dent you make in the wall will have to be patched out later. Apply the water with a large brush such as a calcimine or old wall brush. Do not hesitate to put on five or six coats.

Keep testing as you go along. When the paper is loose enough, it will come off readily. If the paper seems unusually stubborn, add about one cupful of paste to each gallon of water. This will slow up the evaporation and aid the penetration.

The second method is to use one of the chemicals made for removing wallpaper. They are quite effective, though they are an added expense. Follow the directions on the label and apply until the paste softens enough to strip off the paper.

Fig. 2. In straight patterns, the matching design will be found on opposite edges of the strip and on the same level.

The third and easiest method is to use one of the steam machines made for the purpose. These are steam-generating boilers with a pan-like device for concentrating the steam on a small area of the paper. Between the heat and the moisture of the steam, the paper will rapidly yield and can be stripped off by hand if it hasn't already fallen off. These machines are by far the most satisfactory method for removal of the old paper. They are also the most expensive from the standpoint of the amateur. Once the paper is off, the usual patching operations follow. Cracks are cut out and patched, checks and dents spackled, and the walls sized.

PREPARING THE PAPER

Lining Paper

Before proceeding to the actual hanging of wallpaper, it would be well to consider the use of lining paper. This is a plain uncoated type of paper applied to the walls to provide a better surface upon which to hang the wallpaper. It is inexpensive, costing less than the cheapest wallpaper, and is simple to hang. If you are going to run into any troubles with adhesion, they will show up in the lining paper job and can be remedied. Follow the instructions for a butt-jointed job as described later in this chapter.

Types of Wallpaper Patterns

Before describing methods of cutting wallpaper into strips before pasting it for hanging, let us consider the two chief types of paper patterns.

Straight Patterns. In this type of pattern, if you find part of a design, such as a flower, at the left side of the paper, you will find the other half on the right-hand side directly opposite. This is the easiest type of wallpaper to cut into strips and hang as each strip is exactly the same as the one next to it.

Drop Patterns. When the matching part of the design is at a different level on each side of the paper, it is known as a drop pattern. This type gives greater freedom in decoration and reduces the effect of repetition at the same level around the room. The repetition is not eliminated but it is lessened by the wider spacing between the repeats. Also, the pattern becomes saw-toothed rather than horizontal. This type of pattern slightly complicates the hanging of the paper, but not greatly. If you cut your strips continuously from one roll of paper, there will be considerable waste. But if you use two rolls and cut all the odd-numbered strips from roll one and all the even-numbered strips from the second roll, the waste will be minimized. Further instructions for the cutting of this type of pattern will be found in the next section.

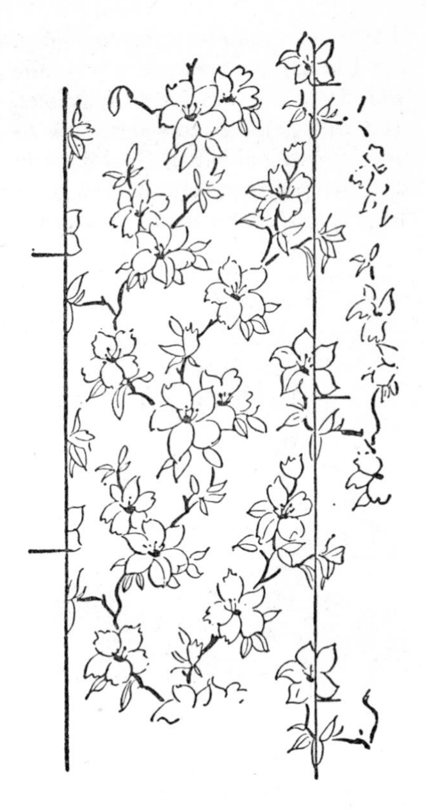

Fig. 3. A drop pattern allows for greater freedom of design. In hanging, simply cut alternate strips long enough to allow for the drop pattern.

Cutting, Pasting, and Trimming

Cutting. Measuring from baseboard to picture moulding or ceiling will give you the actual dimension for placing patterns, but this is too exact for paperhanging. It is customary to allow at least three inches at the top of each strip and the same amount at the bottom. If you are hanging lining paper, simply unroll a strip to the actual measurement and add six inches. Lay the strip on the table. Placing the tear stick in position, grasp the roll in the right hand. Lifting up and away from the tear stick, tear the paper. Match the two torn ends and use the piece you have just torn off to measure out another one. Repeat the tearing operation. When you have torn the correct number of strips, you are ready for pasting.

If the paper is a decorated one, you will have to decide what part of the design you prefer at the top edge. Hold an unrolled end at the top of the wall and study the design for effect. You will generally get ample assistance from members of the family in this, so prepare yourself for some lengthy discussion before a decision

Fig. 4. For cutting lining paper or wallpaper, into strips, use a tear stick.

is reached. If the paper is of the drop-pattern type, you had better hold up two strips, properly matched, so that all the possibilities can be explored.

When all assembled have reached a decision, mark the first roll about three inches above the picture moulding or the ceiling line, this will be your guide for cutting all the strips. Lay the first roll on the table and measure out the first strip, including the extra three inches at the top and bottom. Place the tear stick at the measured length and tear off the first strip. Place the roll at the other end of the table and unroll enough to match the pattern on the first strip at its top end. Unroll the roll to the tear stick, place the tear stick on the second strip and tear to the same length as the first strip. Continue the operation until you have enough to go around the room.

Drop Patterns. Using this pattern, you will have to be more careful in the matching of the design so that your strips are all long enough. By planning your work and knowing how many strips you are going to need to go around the room, you will be able to do the cutting of the drop-pattern strips with the same ease. Place a roll of the paper on the table and measure out the length of strip number one, not forgetting the necessary extra top and bottom for trimming. Simply continue to tear strips to this length until you have a number equal to half of the total required strips. Then carefully match the design on the second strip to that on the first, unroll to the proper length, and tear Again, continue until you have torn the remaining half of the total number of strips. You are now ready for the pasting operation.

Pasting. For best results in hanging the paper, use a prepared paste. Homemade mixtures may prove to be satisfactory, but don't chance using them. Only winter wheat should be used in the mixture and it is quite difficult for the average grocer to know whether his flour is of the winter variety or not. The paste is such a small part of the cost of the job that it hardly pays to save on this material. Simply follow the directions on the label.

Turn the paper over on the table, placing the pile at the back of the table. Pull the top sheet to the front and let the edge extend about one-quarter of an inch over the front. Spread the paste evenly, but generously, over the paper for the full length on the table. Then pick up the end of the pasted strip and fold it nearly to the other end of the table (this is the long fold). Gently smooth the pasted sides together and carefully match the outside edges. Pull the strip back across the table so that the overhanging end is now on the table. Then paste the remaining dry back of the paper. Fold this in towards the center (this is the short fold), lapping over the already pasted section about one or two inches. Again carefully match the sides of the paper. Fold this pasted strip once more and set it aside to let the paste soak into the paper. Draw the next strip to the front of the table and repeat the pasting operations as for the first strip. Set this one aside and finish all the pasting. The folds will keep the paste wet while you are doing the hanging. If the paper is a drop pattern, make two piles of the pasted strips so that you can alternate them in hanging.

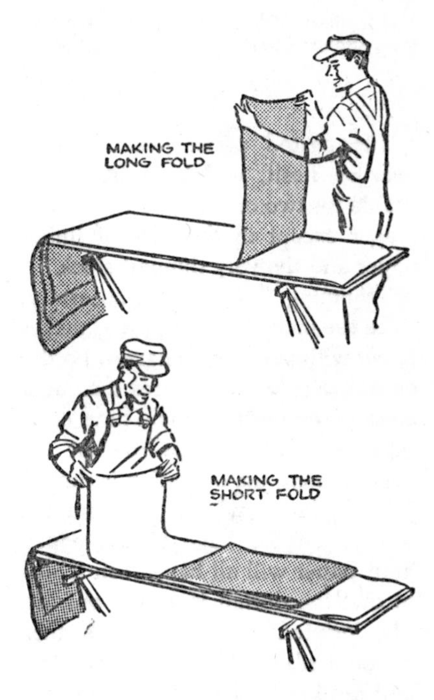

Fig. 6. Pick up the end of the pasted strip and fold nearly to the other end of the table.

Fig. 5. When pasting, lay the paper on the table and apply paste generously over the length.

Fig. 7. Trimming the selvage gives you a perfectly straight edge to make clean butt joints.

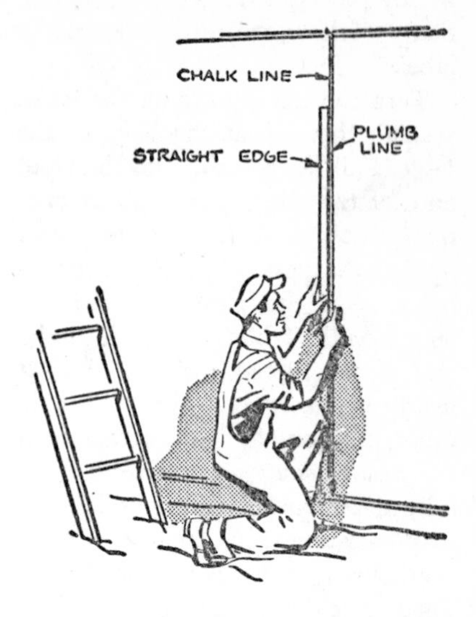

Fig. 8. Hanging the pasted paper should always proceed from a plumb line for accuracy.

The pasted paper, when folded over on itself, will keep fresh and usable for two or three hours or even longer except in the case of lining paper and the very thinnest stock.

Trimming. Trimming is necessary, since the manufacturer always makes paper with a selvage, a narrow border on either side that insures a straight edge to the design. If you have carefully folded the strips so that the edges match, the operation is simple. The marks to which you trim are printed on the edge of the paper. Your paper will all have been folded so that the design is on the outside. The printed trim marks are then plainly visible. Fold the paper end for end until it is slightly less than the length of the straightedge. Lay the straightedge on the paper so that only the selvage to be cut projects beyond it. Hold the straightedge down with one hand and cut off the selvage by running your paperhanger's knife along the side of the straightedge. Spin the paper around so that the other selvage is now on the working side of the table and repeat the cutting operation. This strip is now ready for hanging. Repeat with the other strips and you can proceed with the hanging.

It is possible to buy store-trimmed paper. Some stores have one of the patented trimming tables and will gladly do the trimming for you. Remember, though you cannot return trimmed paper which you have not used. However, if you are certain of the quantity of paper to be used, this trimmed paper will reduce the number of operations in putting up your wallpaper. The ready-pasted types of papers are trimmed by the manufacturer.

HANGING THE PAPER

Hanging paper should always proceed from a plumb line so that the design will be straight up and down. Chalk your plumb line and hang it at a distance of about 17½ inches or a little less from a window or door trim. A string with an ordinary weight will serve as a plumb. When the bob has stopped swinging, gently draw back the string and let it go. You will find a neat chalk line on the wall. This is the correct distance for the regular 18-inch papers. If the paper is wider, snap the line at a distance of at least one-half inch less than the width of the paper. It is generally best to strike the line on the right-hand side of the door or window and proceed with the hanging in that direction.

The First Strip. Lift this and hold it so that the short folded-in end can readily be placed at the top of the wall. Mount the ladder and gently strip apart the folded-in end. Place this at the top of the wall so that the extra three inches extends above the picture molding or against the ceiling and so that the left-hand edge is on the chalk line. Gently press several feet of the strip of paper in place,

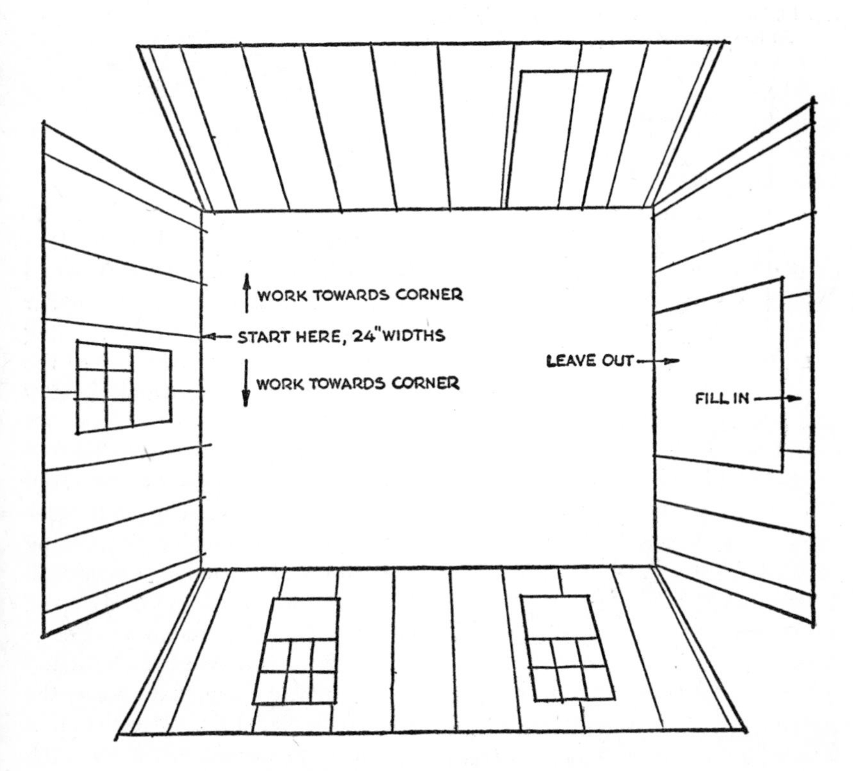

Fig. 9. The sequence of paperhanging is outlined above.

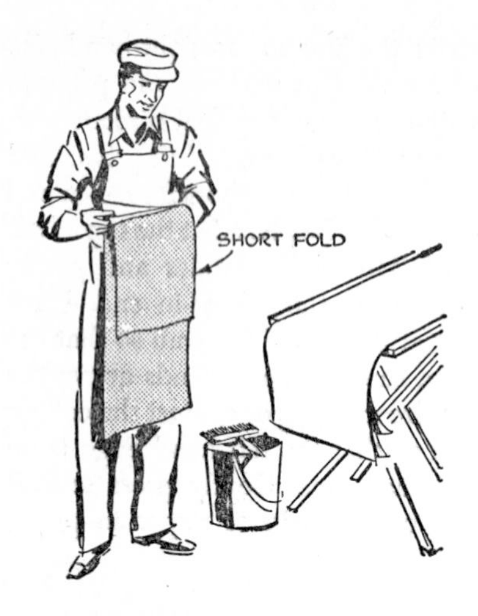

Fig. 10. The short folded-in end can easily be set into place at the top of the wall.

Fig. 12. When the left-hand edge is in place, smooth the rest of the paper to the wall.

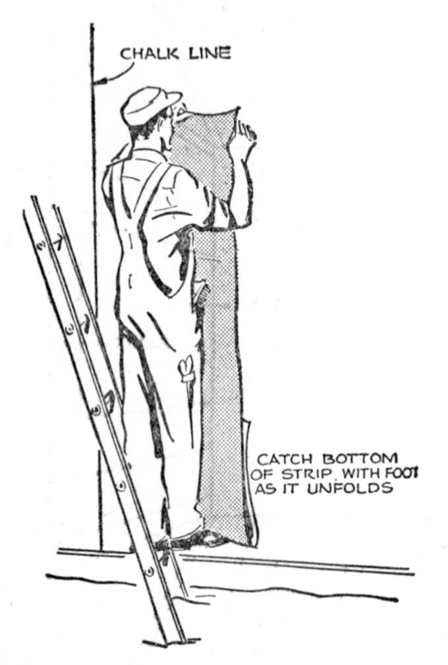

Fig. 11. Gently press the first few feet of paper in place, being careful to have the left-hand edge on the chalk line.

being careful always to have the left-hand edge on the chalk line. You can support the rest of the strip with your foot while you are pasting. Using your smoother, brush the rest of the opened strip in place without forcing or stretching it. Now, come down off the ladder and reach behind the loosely hanging part of the strip. Carefully separate the fold in the bottom section of the strip by grasping the end and gently pulling downward. When the paper is completely open, continue pressing the left-hand edge to the chalk line. When the left-hand edge is in place, smooth the rest of the strip to the wall. Do not stretch or pull the paper in any of these steps or the right-hand edge will not hang

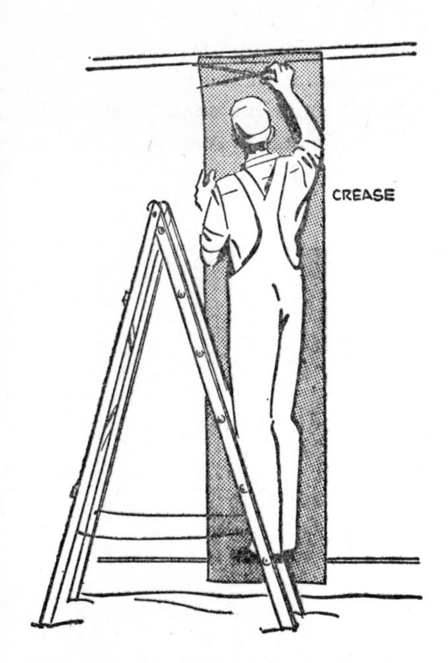

Fig. 13. To trim top and bottom, run the point of a scissors against the paper along the joint of the picture moulding or the ceiling.

straight. If it is necessary to adjust the paper, pull a goodly length loose from the wall and smooth it into correct position. The wet paste will withstand several of these removals and replacings though it is not recommended that it be done often. If the paste should show signs of drying, place the strip back on the table and repaste.

The top and bottom must now be trimmed. Remount the ladder and run the point of your scissors against the paper along the joint of the picture moulding or the ceiling. This will mark the surface of the paper. Now pull the paper loose from the wall for a distance of about one foot. Using your scissors, cut along the line and smooth the paper back in place. Do the same at the bottom of the strip. The first strip is now hung

The Second Strip. Hang the second to the right of the first, and so on around the room. You have your choice of hanging by the butt method or the lap method. The butt method makes the most workmanlike job. It takes a little more effort than the lap but is worth it. However, if you use the lap method you eliminate the trimming of the right-hand selvage of each strip of paper.

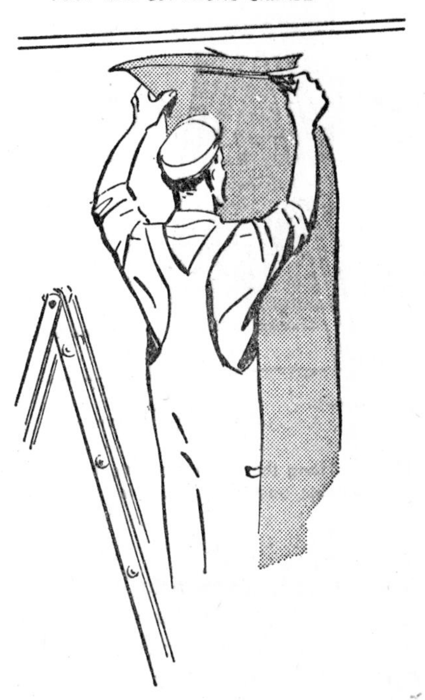

Fig. 14. You can neatly fold the section to be cut by pulling the paper away from the wall about one foot.

Lap and Butt Joints

Lap Method. In using the lap method, mount the ladder with the second strip over your arm and loosen the pasted top. Press the paper in place with the design matching and the trimmed edge overlapping the previously hung strip to the selvage trimming mark. This should leave you with the extra three or four inches at the top. Continue down the wall as for the first strip and smooth into place. Roll the seam gently with the seam roller to prevent the paper from curling. If you press too hard, you may both shine up the paper and also squeeze some of the paste from underneath onto the surface, where it will be difficult to remove. Mark the top of the paper and cut with your scissors to the proper length. Press back into place and repeat the operation on the bottom. Continue strip after strip around the room.

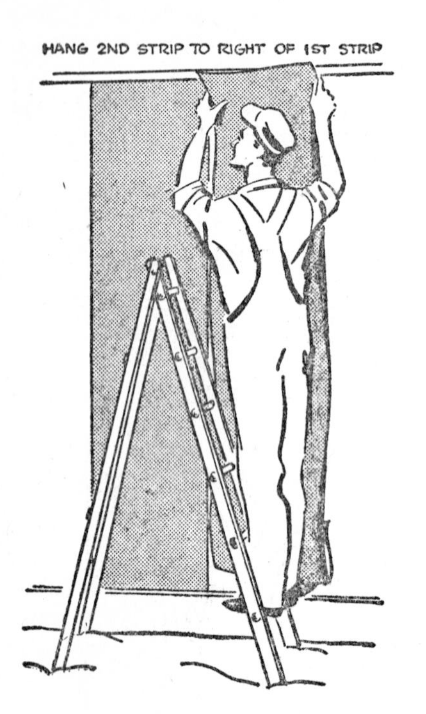

Fig. 15. Hang the second strip to the right of the first, and so on around the room.

Fig. 16. For lap joints the trimmed edges overlap the previously hung strip and then it is trimmed.

Butt Method. Butt joints simply mean that both sides of the seam lie flat on the wall. The paper must be trimmed on both sides as described earlier. The first strip is hung as instructed above and then you are ready for the joining of the second. Holding the second strip over your arm, mount the ladder, loosen the top pasted section, and place it next to the right-hand edge of the first strip. Match the pattern and make sure the excess extends up above the picture molding or the ceiling joint. Join the right-hand edge of the paper on the wall and the left-hand edge of the new piece by gently pressing the new one in place. Again do not stretech or pull the paper into place or the right-hand edge won't lie true. Once again, pull the paper loose from the wall, if necessary, and reapply. Continue down the wall by loosening the folded paper and placing it against the right-hand edge of the previously hung paper. Mark the top with your scissors, cut, and replace. When you have done the same on the bottom of the strip, gently run your seam roller down the joint and flatten the seam.

Cutting Around Obstacles

It would be a strange room in which there were no openings. Special procedures are necessary for hanging around doors, windows, and the like. Experienced paperhangers can come to an opening and measure their way around it, coming back to fill in after. This is not recommended for the amateur. It is for him better to hang a strip which partly covers the opening and cut as necessary. If possible, get someone to help you when you do this operation.

Drape a strip over your arm and mount the ladder. Loosen the top part and butt or lap the joint, always allowing for the excess at the top and always matching the pattern. Let your

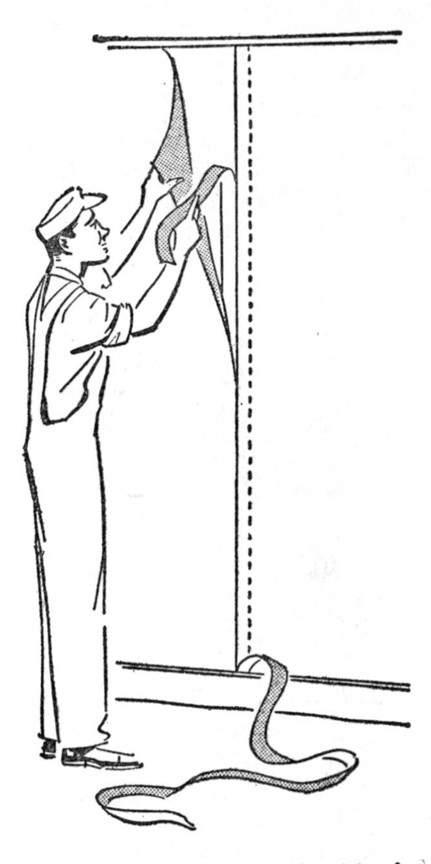

Fig. 17. It is possible to make butt joints by hanging the muslin with the selvage and then stripping off after the fabric is hung.

helper hold the rest of the strip of paper while you find the place to cut across the strip by outlining it with your scissors. Cut and press the upper section of the paper in place. Now continue the joint by loosening the bottom section of the strip and placing it against the previously hung strip. If the opening is a window, you can rule in across the bottom of the trim and cut to fit. Smooth the bottom section into place. Now you can trim off the excess down the side of the window trim. Use your paperhanger's knife. Simply run the knife down in the corner of the trim and wall. There are knife rollers for this purpose and they are the best tool to use. But if you are careful and do not pull the paper, you can do a satisfactory job with a knife. You can help prevent rough cuts by placing a thin ruler or straightedge on the wall next to the trim and pressing on it while you do the cutting. If the opening is wider than the next strip, simply cut the strip to a length slightly in excess of the distance from picture molding to top of trim.

Fig. 18. You'll probably have to cut around some obstacles. If it is a window, rule in across the bottom of the trim and cut to fit.

You may find it wise to strike a new plumb line when you have located the place for the first seam to the right of the opening, because the short distance from the picture molding or ceiling to the top of the opening would not give you a true line to the baseboard. Take the right-hand edge of the strip that will partly cover the opening on the right and hang it to the line and you can proceed safely along the wall.

Fitting for Wide Openings

Wide openings, such as archways, can be pieced out on the top with parts of full length strips cut for the purpose. Simply make sure you match the pattern on each succeeding strip and you will have no trouble. When you have determined where the first full length strip will start at the top of the wall, strike a plumb line and hang the strip to this line on its right-hand edge. Continue along the wall until you come to the corner.

Papering Corners

Seams should never end in a corner of the room. It is customary to have the paper go around the corner for at least two to four inches. It is best to assume that the corner is not square. Butt the joint on the left and smooth the paper around the corner. To make sure that the seams on the new wall will all be plumb, you should strike a chalk line at the right-hand edge of the paper hung around the corner. You can place your straightedge on the wall and carefully cut the edge of the paper to a true line. The matching may suffer slightly in this operation, but that is not as bad as having the whole wall out of square. You will barely notice the small mismatch in the corner. Continue butting the seams along the new wall and you will have a neat job.

Removing Excess Paste

The small amount of paste which inevitably gets on the trim and moldings should be removed with the sponge as you go along. Dip the sponge in the pail of clean water, wring it out, and gently wipe the surfaces on which the paste has accumulated. If the paste has not dried, it will come off readily and will not shine the painted surface in the process.

SPECIAL PROBLEMS

Papering Over Wallpaper

Hanging paper over a previously papered surface requires only that the old and new seams do not coincide. Strike the plumb line for the first strip so that the new seam does not fall on the present one. Continue around the room, being careful not to locate the corner seams on top of those already there. Doing this avoids a double pull

Fig. 19. Just hang small sections with full-width sheets of wallpaper.

in the shrinkage, which might open up the under seam and make a difficult job of repasting.

Border Designs

Borders come in two types: narrow borders and cutout borders.

Narrow Borders. The narrow borders are printed parallel to one another on an 18-inch-wide paper. They must be cut to width after being torn to appropriate lengths—usually about eight feet. Paste the back side of the paper, fold the pasted side in, and cut into proper widths with the straightedge and the paperhanger's knife.

The hanging is simply a matter of placing the border where you want it. The corners are generally mitered, that is, cut at angle of 45 degrees, if the border is hung in a panel.

Cutout Borders. Cutout borders are perforated on the bottom edge of the design and are printed parallel on an 18-inch-wide roll. They are cut to width the same as the narrow borders. Then they are pasted. Finally, when the paste has softened the paper, the border can be separated along the perforations by gently pulling on the side. The hanging is the same as for the narrow borders. The corners are mitered.

Papering Panels

Panels to be hung with wallpaper should be carefully measured and their centers located. Strike a plumb line down the center of the panel and hang the paper either way from this line to the outside molding of the panel. The top and bottom should be trimmed exactly as you would if hanging the full length of the wall.

Papering Ceilings

Ceilings can be hung with wallpaper, though this can be troublesome for the amateur. The problem of supporting the paper until enough of it is fastened up to continue the smoothing operation is usually the stumbling block. Probably the best way is to fold the pasted paper into a short enough length to carry over one arm while with your free hand you smooth the short length which hangs free. You will have to work to a line previously marked on the ceiling to make sure the seam is straight. It is usual to start near a window wall and work away from it.

Horizontal Wallpapering

Paper can also be hung horizontally. Some interior decorators have used the striped papers to good effect in this manner. Mark on the wall a line that is parallel to the ceiling or picture molding and lower by the width of the paper. Hang to this line. Striking a line parallel to the floor is not as good as striking one parallel to the ceiling. It is generally better to have any irregularity at the base line rather than near the ceiling where it would be more obvious.

Two Patterns in One Room

Do not be afraid to use one paper on one wall and another on an adjoining wall. It is popular to have a patterned paper flanked by a plain paper. Use your knowledge of color harmonies to determine the proper choices (see Chapter 9, page 129). This is a good device to indicate the divisions of a room. For instance, the dining end of a living-dining room or the sitting end of a large bedroom can have contrasting paper designs. Use your imagination freely.

Fabric Wall Coverings

In addition to wallpapers, there are fabrics which can serve as wall coverings. It was a custom years back to cover walls to be painted with muslin, either plain or specially prepared. The muslin was hung like wallpaper and provided a pleasant texture to the paint. It also hid the inevitable cracks which appear in plaster walls. The unbleached muslin is available in any width up to 108 inches, but the narrower widths, up to 36 inches, are recommended as they are easier to handle. The prepared canvas, as the prepared types are called, generally comes in a 48-inch width and has a filling which makes it easy to paste and handle. Butt the joints as you would for a paperhanging job.

Matching Shades

Your principal problem in paperhanging will be the shading of the paper's color. The manufacturers try to match each run of the papers as faithfully as possible, but you may find that the shade of several rolls will vary slightly. You can either return the paper to the store or use the two different shades on different walls. Make the usual joint in one of the less conspicuous corners, and you will scarcely notice the variation in the shading. But the next time you buy paper, look at the mill run numbers on the edge of the paper and make sure they are all the same. Then you can be sure the paper was all made with exactly the same color.

PATCHING AND REPAIRING

Blisters. Blisters, a common failure in paperhanging, can be repaired in one of two ways. The simplest is to cut the blister with two lines at right angles to one another. Gently fold back the paper and apply just enough paste to the backside of the paper to wet it. With a large, bunched, clean rag, gently push the paper back into place and hold it there for five or ten minutes until the paste has set. Do not let the paste have a chance to soak into the backside of the paper before pushing it back on the wall as it will swell and create an overlap. The second method is to put a little paste into a hypodermic needle, insert the tip into the blister, and squeeze in some paste. Better to squeeze in too little than too much—too much and the blister will never lie flat again.

Seams. Seams and joints which have opened should be repasted with a very small brush and gently held in place until the paste has set. Be careful to avoid excess paste as you may smear the wallpaper in wiping it off.

Bruises. Bruises not only damage wallpaper but also the plaster underneath require the repair of the plaster first. Remove the damaged paper to a point just beyond the bruise. Clean out the loose plaster and patch. When this plaster is dry, apply a little glue size, just as you would for a new wall. While this is drying, rough-tear a piece of the same wallpaper as is on the wall to a size slightly larger than the patch. Carefully apply paste to the back of this piece and stick the paper patch in place. The feather edge of the rough-torn paper will almost blend into the rest of the paper if you have been careful of the amount of paste.

Stains. Grease stains can rarely be completely removed from most wallpapers. But they can be so reduced that they will be hardly noticeable. Make a paste of carbon tetrachloride and Fullers earth. Get the Fullers earth at a large paint supply store or a drugstore; carbon tetrachloride is the common dry-cleaning fluid. Apply this paste to the stained area and, when dry, dust it off. Apply a second and even a third coat to remove stubborn spots.

Absorbent types of wallpaper cleaners are available and will clean loose airborne dirt from wallpaper. But if not kneaded and rolled over the surface of the paper properly, they will streak it. Very fresh bread used to be the standard paper cleaner and is almost as effective as the rubber-like absorbent cleaners common today.

The dark streaks generally found over exposed radiators are caused by the circulation of warm air which carries dust with it. This dust becomes so well imbedded in the wallpaper that it will not yield to the absorbent type of cleaners. You can remove part of it and reduce the amount of dirt, but you are unlikely to get it all off. Water streaks can rarely be removed. Generally it is better to try to repaper the soiled strips. If the existing paper is in good condition, you can usually paper right over it. If it is loose, remove all of the strip and rehang.

BONNIE

CHAPTER 9

COLOR HARMONY, MIXING AND MATCHING

Color is the art in painting. It is the most difficult part of painting to the inexperienced. It requires more careful concentration than any of the other skills that painting develops. You can paint competently after limited experience. But the selection of colors, the matching of colors, or the determination of color schemes requires experience and knowledge of the factors involved. This chapter will give you the necessary fundamental knowledge to work successfully with color. But each pigment does reflect light of a definite wavelength. When seen by the retina of the eye and interpreted by the brain, a particular lightwave causes the sensation of a particular color. Without light no color could be seen. Because of these circumstances, the light source is as important as the pigment used. Problems of color used on the exterior of a house are simplified by the fact that the light source is not variable. Interior painting, on the other hand, involves variations among sunlight, incandescent light, and fluorescent light, as well as the color effects of lamp shades, which must be borne in mind when planning a color scheme.

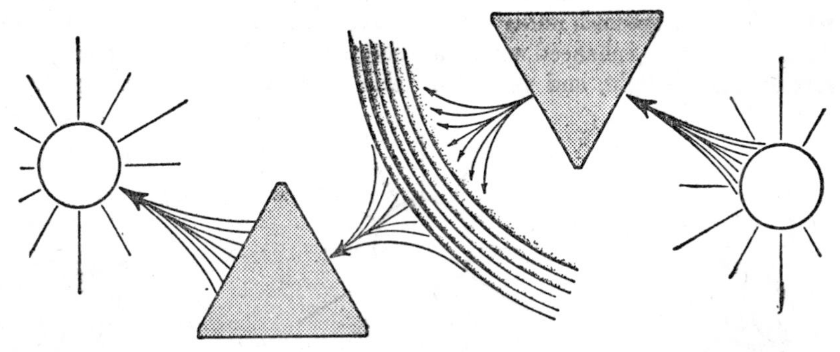

Fig. 1. Clear sunlight contains all the colors, which may be demonstrated by passing it through a prism. The result is a rainbow of hues.

Color and Light

If you understand what color is, many of the problems simplify themselves. To begin with, pigments in paint do not in themselves have any

Effects of Light on Skin and Color

The color surfaces of your home furnishings, flat wall colors, and even skin color take on a startling variety of shadings depending on the type of lighting in your home.

There are six, perhaps more, types of illuminants to consider in choosing color harmony. These are natural daylight, incandescent filament lamps, and at least four basic kinds of fluorescent lamps with more types being developed all the time.

With each manufacturer of fluorescent lighting developing a different type of light, the problem of the interior and home decorator is to predict and design with adequate assurance a color scheme which will respond harmoniously to the varying reflections.

To illustrate this, if your skin type is normal, daylight fluorescent light will reflect pale. The same skin will reflect a sallow greenish under white fluorescent light, enhanced under a soft fluorescent light, and yellowish under incandescent light. Similarly, for tanned, dark-skinned persons, or those wearing light or heavy make-up, all the color reflections will vary vary according to the different types of lights.

You should observe, when purchasing fluorescent or incandescent lighting, what effects will result in the colors and textures used in your interior decorating.

The light source that is taken as a standard is clear sunlight. Science tells us that it contains all colors, the sum of which is white light. When we place vermilion pigment in this light and look at it we see a red color. If we now place an ochre pigment in it, we see a tan yellow. As far as our present purposes are concerned, these pigments vary only in that they reflect different wavelengths of light. They are not, however, as precise as we might wish; along with the dominant wave, they reflect others that are shorter or longer. This lack of precision and differences among light

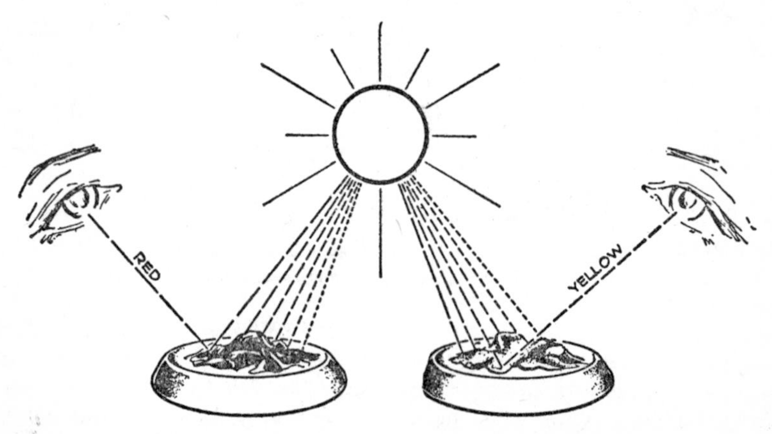

Fig. 2. Different pigments reflect different wavelengths of light.

sources cause the apparent changes of color in paint pigments under varying conditions. An incandescent light, even if of the daylight type, gives off a light considerably yellower than sunlight and consequently tends to yellow all colors. This light does not

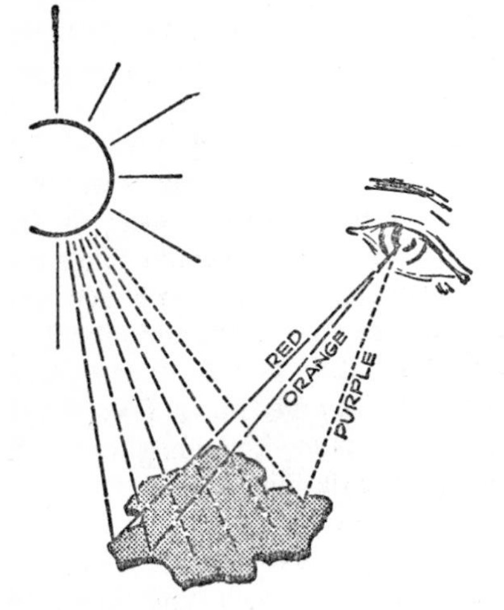

Fig. 3. Pigments do not reflect just one wavelength of light, but subsidiary wavelengths as well. This is one cause of apparent color changes.

seriously affect a yellow pigment like ochre, but it does turn the bright vermilion from a clear red to a slightly orange-red. If these changes in color under varying light conditions are anticipated, many disappointments can be avoided.

Psychology of Color

It seems hardly necessary to describe in detail the purposes of using color as everyone accepts it and would surely notice its absence. However, so much can be done to improve the use of color through the intelligent application of the principles of

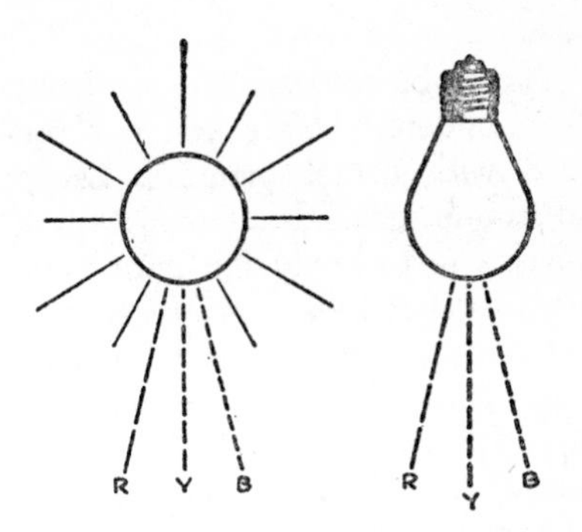

Fig. 4. Even a "daylight" incandescent light is considerably yellower than sunlight.

color psychology that the time spent in studying these principles will be well rewarded. It has been established statistically that normal persons respond similarly to various colors of pure hue. Occasionally an individual may have an aversion for one or another color, but the rest of his reactions will follow the statistical pattern. With few exceptions people find clear red an exciting color, yellow a cheerful color, purple a subdued color, blue a calming color, green a refreshing color, brown a neutral color, and white to be clean and black either depressing or dramatic. Gray is variable in its effect. You may not find these descriptions exactly to your taste, but it is probably the descriptions themselves rather than the actual effect of the colors to which you take exception. And variations in shades and intensities will produce some variation in the normal reactions. But if you use your colors with these normal effects in mind, the impression upon the occupants of the room is reasonably predictable, and you can decorate accordingly.

Tints

The problem of colors in mass must be considered before you can proceed with actual painting. Except under unusual circumstances it would be unwise to apply the pure colors often used by artists because they are much too intense for use on the large areas of walls and ceilings. Generally a pure color is reduced in intensity by adding some of it to a white pigment. This makes what is called a *tint.* (Do not, generally, mix white to a pure color to get a tint.) Tints are most commonly used for color in mass. There are so many possibilities in tinting white paints – by varying the amount of pure-color pigment or by adding two or more pigments – that you may become bewildered. When you realize that the normally perceptive human eye can distinguish about 400,000 tints, shades, and hues, you can see how easy it is to become confused. But once again, by ignoring the apparent complexity and following simple rules, you can achieve painted colors that are entirely satisfying.

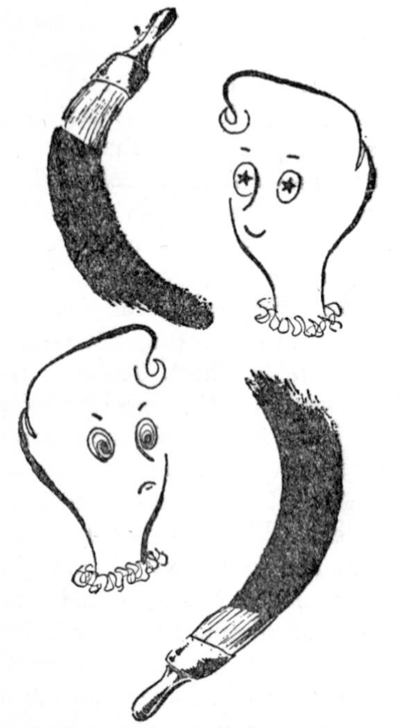

Fig. 5. Emotional reactions to various colors follow a definite pattern.

It is possible to buy a variety of tinted paints at almost any paint store. In order to satisfy the tastes of the greatest number of people efficiently and economically, the manufacturers make these tints bright and relatively few in number. For many uses these tints must be toned down. If you have to do this yourself, you might as well do all your tinting. Furthermore, you will probably want to match some specific color or work out a color harmony, and you will find that the ready-made colors are frequently not close enough to what you want to make their purchase worthwhile. Most often the carpets or rugs, the draperies, the upholstery or some important piece of art or furniture will affect your choice of color more than anything else. However, no matter what particular hues you choose, you must select colors in "correct" harmony for satisfactory results.

In order to select colors wisely, it is well to understand some of the simple rules of color harmonies, of which the simplest is based on the relations of analogous colors. These and all other color relations are most easily understood by studying the construction of a color wheel.

COLOR WHEEL

The color wheel is based upon the fact that with three hues—red, yellow, and blue—you can mix any other color you wish. These three colors are called the *primaries*. Admittedly there is much discussion by chemists and physicists about the composition of colors, but a simple experiment in mixing, using either oil or water colors, will satisfy you that this rule will work to your satisfaction. Try this experiment, if you have not already done so, both to satisfy your curiosity and to get a sense of mixing colors. Yellow and red when mixed in equal amounts will give you a good orange; yellow and blue will give you green; and blue and red will give you purple. These three mixed colors are called the *secondaries*.

Intermediate colors between the primaries and secondaries should be mixed next to complete a twelve-color wheel. With this simple device you can learn a great deal about combining colors harmoniously.

Color harmony means simply the congruity of hue, intensity, value, and contrast. You must choose colors so that they look right together, and they will look right if you follow the rules for color harmony. Some people have acquired through experience what is called "color sense." When this color sense is analysed it is found to be an

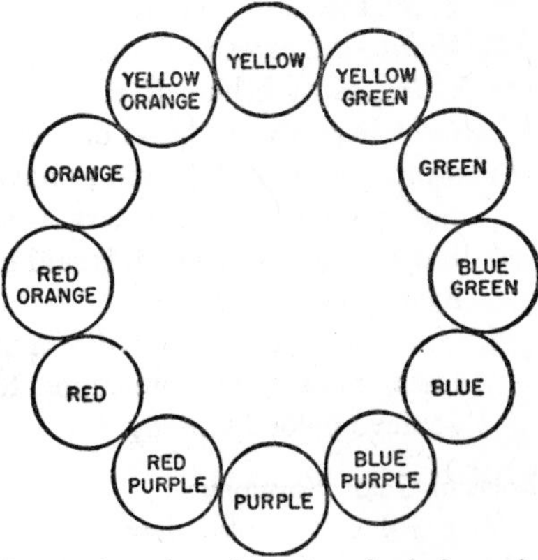

Fig. 6. A twelve-color color wheel shows the primaries, the secondaries, and the first range of intermediates.

unconscious recognition of the rules of color harmony. In order to under-

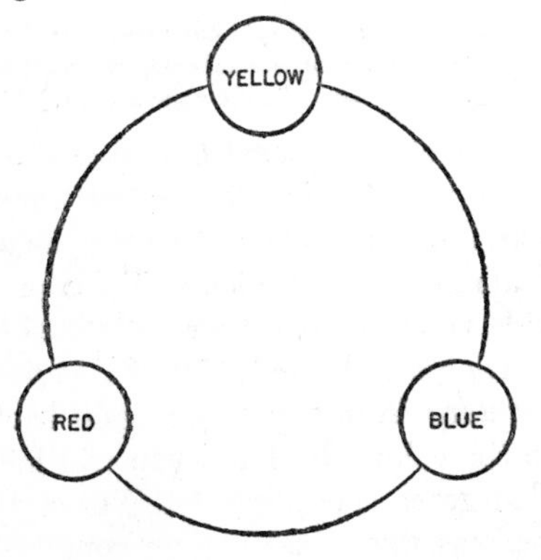

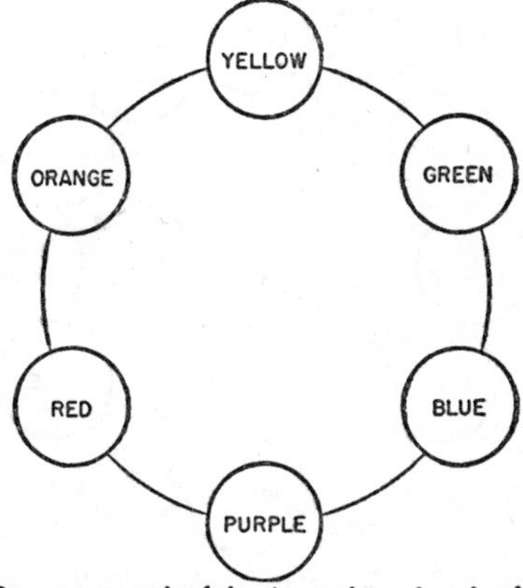

Fig. 7. The first two steps in making a color wheel. Step one, at the left, shows the primaries in place. Step two, at the right, shows the secondaries added.

stand one another in the following discussion, let us agree upon a meaning for the four principal terms used in the discussion of color harmony.

1. *Hue:* a particular color, that which distinguishes the color from any other color.
2. *Intensity:* the purity of a color or hue. The closer it is to the primary, the more intense it is.
3. *Value:* indicates the lightness or darkness of a hue. If it is very light from the addition of much white pigment, it is said to have high value; if it is very dark from the addition of black, it is said to have a low value.
4. *Contrast:* the use of different hues, values, or intensities to achieve color harmony.

Rules of Color Harmony

The rules of color harmony to which we have referred can be reduced to two, with subsidiary variations. The simplest rule is that of *Analogous Harmony.* If you look at the 12-color wheel and block out with a sheet of white paper all but any three adjacent hues, you will find that the combination of any two or three is pleasant. Experiment will prove that the value of any of these colors can be changed at will with results that may be even more pleasing. Keeping the value of one of the three at its original intensity and changing the values of the other two will introduce you to the decorator's favorite trick of having an accent color in your scheme. You now have the first basic

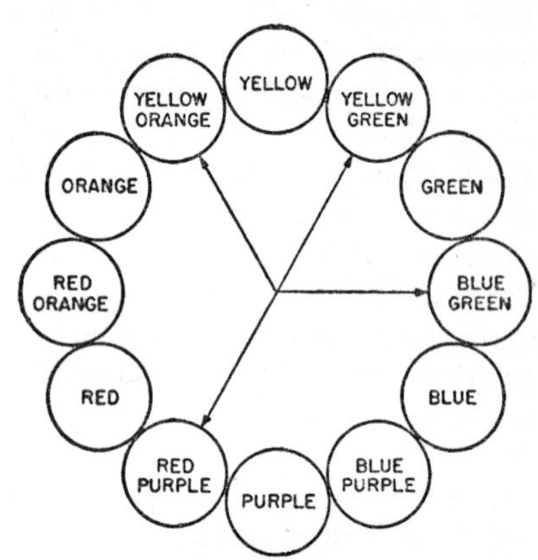

Fig. 9. A variation of split complementary harmony. If you use such a scheme, you must be careful with the values.

rule: *Colors adjacent to one another on the color wheel are in harmony.* Variations are achieved by the use of different values, which will also provide you with variations in intensity.

The second rule is that of *Complementary Harmony.* Once again back to the color wheel and you will find that green is opposite red. For some persons, this makes a happy combination. Just think of Christmas decorations. Eastertime decorations illus-

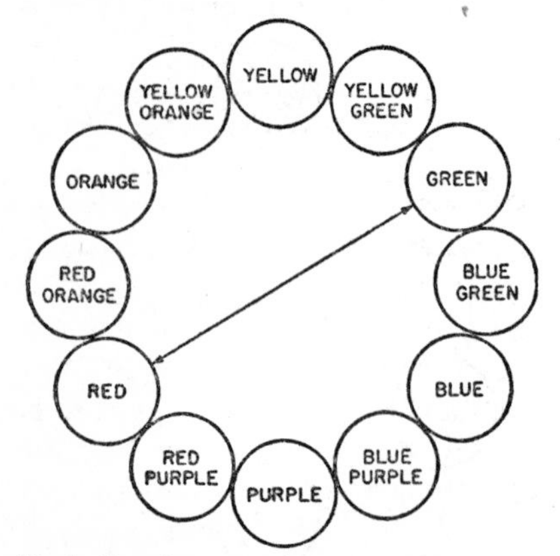

Fig. 8. Complementary harmony: Colors opposite to one another are in harmony.

trate equally well the congruity of yellow and purple. And while we do not have any holiday decorations to illustrate blue and orange, the same holds true for them. However, only under the most extreme circumstances would you be likely to paint a room half red and half green, using the intensities of the color wheel. But it would not be at all unusual to place red mahogany furniture in a gray-green room or to put a green carpet on the floor of this gray-green room and bright red-and-green chintz curtains at the windows.

You now have the second basic rule: *Colors opposite to one another on the color wheel are in harmony.* You can vary the values or intensities of complementary hues. In addition, you can apply the rules of analogous harmony to complementary harmony; you can use either or both of the adjacent hues of one of the original colors to form a harmony known as *Split Complementary.* Again, it is wise to vary the values for interest.

When you have developed facility in basic harmony, try more subtle ones based upon variations of complementary harmonies. There are *double complements.* For instance, yellow-orange with blue-purple might be one pair and yellow-green with red-purple the other. In such combinations, extreme care must be exercised in the choice of intensities. A third possibility is *Triad Harmony.* This is not a true complement, but if great caution is used in handling the intensities, the results can be very pleasing. Triad harmony is simply the selection of any three hues that are equally spaced around the color wheel, like red, yellow, and blue. Frankly it is not recommended that you try these last two variations until you have developed a great facility in the use of color. When used in subdued values, success can be achieved

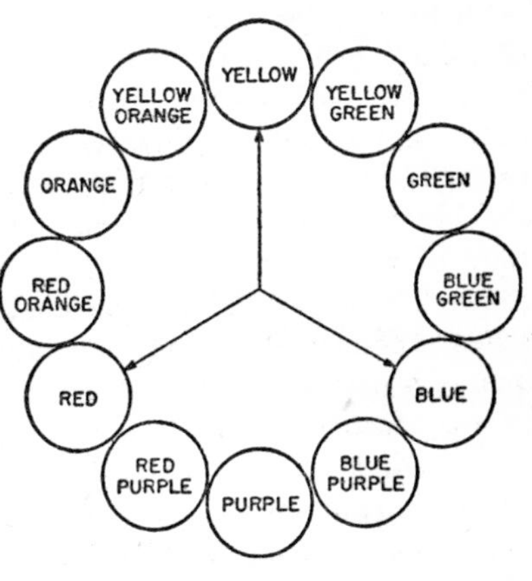

Fig. 11. Triad harmony. The colors are equally spaced around the color wheel. This scheme is difficult to handle successfully.

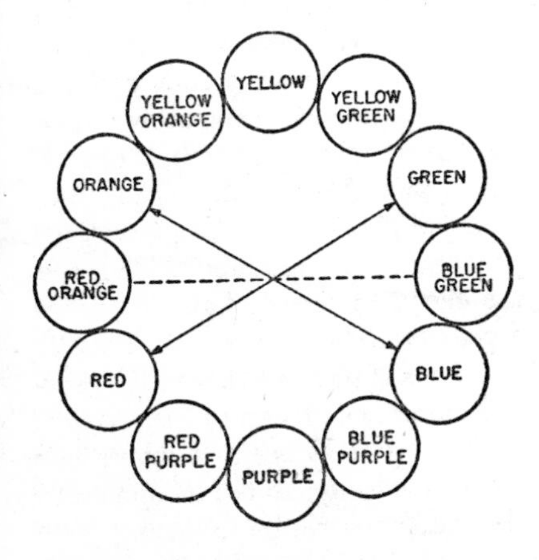

Fig. 10. Double complementary harmony: a subtle scheme calling for caution and imagination in the variation of the intensities.

with them. But prepare sample boards of generous size and study the visual effects under different light conditions before you proceed with painting a whole room. You need have no hesitation, however, in using these harmonies for such hand-painted decoration of furniture as Pennsylvania Dutch or "peasant" art motifs.

Sources of Color Schemes

There are color schemes all around us. All we have to do is open our eyes. Nature provides an inexhaustible variety – in the greens and browns and yellows of a landscape, in the greens and blues of a seascape, in the mottling of a leaf or the veining of a stone. There are the chance color schemes of a street and the deliberate ones of a painting, an advertisement, or a room. Some of these are good, some bad, some are suitable for our use, others are unsuitable. By merely being aware of the color all around us we can develop a sense of harmony and discover many unusual effects.

The simplest way to choose a color scheme for a room is to visit a museum where "period" rooms have been arranged or a furniture or department store with sample room displays, and adapt a scheme you see and like as directly as the circumstances warrant.

Another simple method that nevertheless gives you full opportunity to use your taste and imagination is to buy a packet of papers in various colors and shades and "play around with them" until you develop what you want. You will have to test out the final results carefully because the texture of the paper and size of the actual surfaces you are going to cover can play tricks with your color effects. Just the same, while this method is not nearly so thorough as getting the feel of pigments and learning to mix colors, as described below, it is more economical, less troublesome, and will teach you a lot.

Pigments

The next thing to learn is the pigments used to make particular colors. If all painting were done with five simple pigments – yellow, red, and blue in combination with white and black – our problems would apparently be simplified. Actually they would not be, as the only primary colors available are much too expensive to use and are frequently too unstable for house paint. Consequently we use a wide variety of pigments that are more feasible from the standpoints of permanence, clarity, and economy. It would be ridiculous to use an expensive yellow and red plus black to make cocoa brown when we have inexpensive burnt umber, which provides the same result. And this applies to all the colors except the primaries. Nature's abundance and the chemist's science have produced a great variety of pigments–literally hundreds of hues, more than the average painter can begin to use.

If you wish to begin to investigate colors modestly, it is recommended that you acquire the following ones; they can be obtained in cans of 1/16 or ⅛ gallon–or 4-oz. tubes will do.

1. Vermilion (English or American)
2. Medium chrome yellow
3. Ultramarine blue
4. Medium chrome green
5. Raw sienna
6. Raw umber
7. Burnt umber
8. Venetian red
9. Lamp black

These nine colors will give you the colors necessary to make your color wheel. They are the most used by painters.

These colors may be purchased either "in water" or "ground-in-oil" for further details on this, see page 143). It is recommended that the oil variety be purchased as this is the form most commonly used. If the

TABLE OF COLORS AND COLOR CHARACTERISTICS

Color	Characteristics
Reds:	
1. English vermilion	Bright, clear, slightly orange-red
2. Turkey red	Bright, clear, slightly less intense
3. Permanent red	Bright, clear, fire-engine red
4. Venetian red	Brick red, dull
5. Indian red	Bluer than Venetian, dull
6. Rose pink	Purplish red, bright
Yellows:	
1. Chrome yellow medium	Clear, egg-yolk hue
2. Chrome yellow orange	Clear, orange-yellow
3. Chrome yellow light	Clear, greenish, light
4. Ochre (French or domestic)	Dull, tan, wheat
5. Golden ochre	Brighter and lighter than Ochre
Blues:	
1. Ultramarine blue	Clear, dark, purplish
2. Cobalt blue	Clear, light, sky-blue
3. Prussian blue	Clear, dark, greenish
Greens:	
1. Chrome green medium	Clear, dark, bluish
2. Chrome green dark	Clear, darker, bluish
3. Chrome green light	Clear, yellowish
4. Mitis green medium	Clear, light, bright, yellowish
Browns:	
1. Burnt umber	Medium, clear, chocolate-brown
2. Raw sienna	Light, tan, brown
3. Vandyke brown	Dark reddish brown
4. Burnt sienna	Very reddish brown
5. Raw umber	Very grayish brown
Purple:	
1. Madder lake	Bright, dark, reddish
Black:	
1. Lamp black	Clear, sometimes greenish
2. Drop or ivory black	Clear, occasionally brownish

cans or tubes are kept well covered or stoppered, there will be little loss of material. A simple trick is to add about two tablespoons of turpentine to a can before closing it. This will prevent the formation of a skin on the surface of the paint.

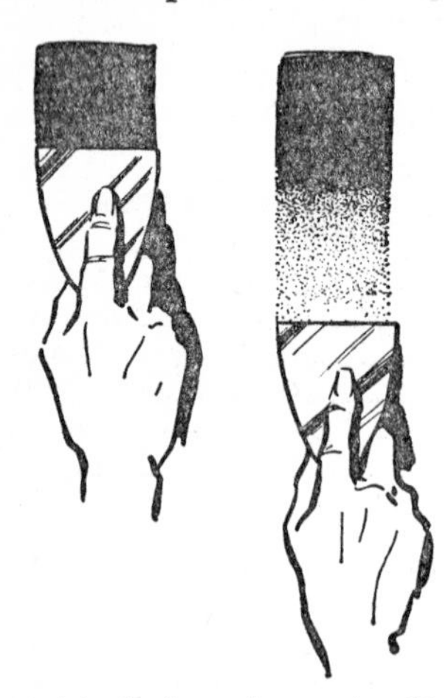

Fig. 12. Put a dab of color at the top of a white card and draw it down with your broad knife so that you get the full range of values.

The thorough painter really familiarizes himself with at least twenty or twenty-five of the color pigments. He gets to know them in their exact hues, their tinting strengths, their ease of mixing, their permanence, and their compatibility with other pigments. Much of this information can be given to you, but it would apply only to the product of one manufacturer. While you are mastering the mixing of colors, it is recommended that you always buy colors made by the same company so that you will not have the added difficulties of the variations in differently manufactured pigments. And needless to say, it is wise to select one of the better companies; then you can count on the consistency of the material. See previous page for lists recommending hues and their color characteristics.

MIXING

The simplest way to begin studying colors is to put a dab of pigment about as big as a lima bean near the top of a piece of white paper and draw the color down with a broad knife. The intensity should be greatest at the top of the paper and thin out to nothing at the bottom. The laboratories of the paint and pigment manufacturers use this method under

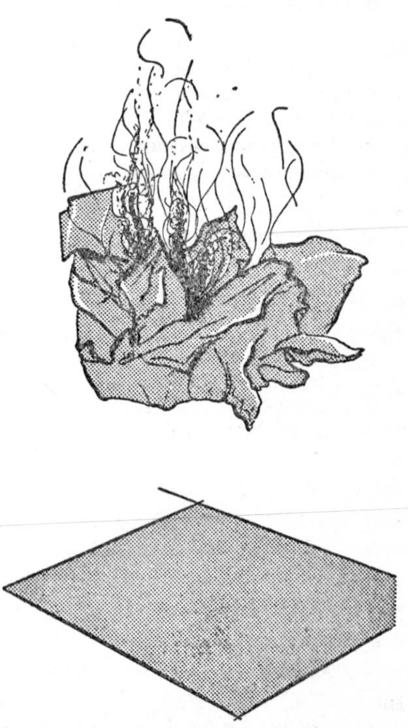

Fig. 13. Spread out cleaning rags after use to avoid spontaneous combustion.

Fig. 14. Make yourself some sample cards. They are useful for studying colors and indispensable for deciding on a color scheme.

controlled conditions to establish the tinting strength of a pigment. You can use it to study the hue with variations in value. However, you would do well if you also mixed the various pigments with different white pigments in order to familiarize yourself with subtle changes in hue and value.

Study Cards. You can cut up some smooth Bristol cardboard into pieces about 2 x 6 inches. Give these pieces a coat of good white paint. When the cards are dry, mix your study colors and apply them to all but one inch of one end of the cards. This will give you a handy size of card, of which you can hold several at one time for comparison. In addition, the white will give you an immediate check on the value of your color.

These cards can be used to study and compare values of different colors, as explained above, or each one can be covered with the same shade throughout, except for the white space at one end, and the collection used to work out a color scheme. Always let the paint dry completely before starting to work with it, as colors almost invariably are lighter when dry than when still wet. And make a practice of recording on the back of the card the ingredients and quantities that went into the color; in this way you will be able to repeat any effects you wish and will have a control for mixing larger amounts of paint when you have decided on the colors you want.

The mixing is best done on a piece of glass because glass can be so easily cleaned with a rag. And spread that rag out when you finish cleaning up; otherwise it might catch fire.

Procedure. It is recommended that matching be approached in this manner, using small quantities of paint. It will save you much time and frustration, not to mention the gallons of paint involved. Once you have determined the exact pigments to use, larger quantities should hold no terrors for you. Simply increase the amount of ingredients in proportion to the quantity of paint desired. If you are not sure of the amounts, try less than you think necessary and add a little bit more at a time until you reach the right point. At each stage, paint a sample on a piece of material similar to the surface you are going to cover and let it dry before you add any more pigment to the paint.

Fig. 15. Boxing insures a good distribution of pigment.

Study your results under different light sources so that when the lights go on your blues don't turn green and your beautiful, soft gray doesn't turn tan. No hard and fast rules can be given about this problem as there are so many possible variations. The home-owner who does his own painting has an advantage here, because he can anticipate what kind of lighting will be used and test his colors accordingly, while the professional painter must rely on his judgment. If you must rely on judgment, one method is to compromise and make the color in daylight slightly bluer than you actually want it to be; fluorescent light will not yellow the color as much but enough for you to consider it when mixing the color.

All painters, amateur and professional, have the problem of apparent color strength in the bareness of a room that is being painted. Light streams in the uncurtained windows and makes the color on the wall look so much brighter than it did on the sample that you can hardly be blamed for wanting to tone it down. Don't! You were right the first time. Your studied color sample, prepared in the proper color harmony and with the fabrics to be used, should be your guide.

MATCHING

Once you have familiarized yourself with colors, harmonies, and pigments, you are ready to begin the delicate job of matching a color. Approach it respectfully; it has been one of the greatest sources of friction between painter and owner, husband and wife, journeyman and apprentice since man began rubbing colored clays on the walls of his cave. Always try to do the actual mixing or matching at a window with a northern exposure so that the light will be constant. Avoid a window with reflections from a large tree, wall, or other colored surface, as this is certain to cause off-color matching. You cannot be too careful in this matter; very slight variations in the light can seriously affect balances in your colors. For instance, a light with too much green in it will make blues look grayish, reds brownish, and yellows grassy. What may have been a good color balance or harmony loses all of the characteristics you were striving for.

Simple Matching. With luck, you'll be matching a paint sample made with only a single colored pigment added to white. One of your study cards (made as suggested before) will rapidly determine exactly which pigment to use to mix the batch of paint. Add a little of the correct pigment to the white paint until you reach the right value. A simple trick if the color is light is to thin the pigment with an equal volume of turpentine before adding to the paint. This will reduce the amount of stirring you have to do to make a thorough mix. When the batch matches the sample, pour it back and forth from one pot to another five or six times; this is known as boxing the paint and it insures good distribution of the pigment.

Then carefully clean out one pot by brushing and then wiping it. Place a piece of cheesecloth or, better, a piece of thin muslin over the top, tie a piece of string around the outside to hold the muslin firm, and strain the paint into the pot. This may seem like an unnecessary step but you will see it is well worthwhile when you note the absence of streaking on the painted wall.

Matching Mixtures. You will rarely have the fortune to have to match a simple color. Practically all tinted

Fig. 16. Straining will help to prevent streaking.

paints are made with two or more colored pigments in addition to the white. Here you will have an opportunity to make generous use of your color cards and your good judgment. You must learn to see the component parts in a color. Do not fear the process. You may have seen your dentist do the same when he matches two or three porcelain teeth to your teeth to determine which colors to put into a batch of porcelain to make an invisible filling. He has seen hints of the hues in his sample teeth and has added appropriate amounts of each hue to make the match. A dye-mixer in a cloth-processing plant will frequently get out skeins of yarns dyed in single pigments and pick out different ones, the sum of which equals the sample to be duplicated.

You will not find it too difficult if you approach the problem in the same way. Determine the basic hue—is it yellow, is it bluish red, or is it a greenish blue? Now, which are the tinting pigments that most nearly approximate these hues? If the sample is a greenish blue and your pigment is too greenish, better select a blue and make it greenish by the addition of a little yellow. Now what yellow to use? Is it a dull greenish blue or a clear one? If a clear one, a bright yellow such as medium chrome yellow is indicated, or if a dull greenish blue, ochre will probably do it. If you find it is still too bright, a touch of Venetian red, the complement of your green, may contribute the faint brown grayness that is missing. When you have determined the pigments to be used on a small sample or palette, proceed as before, stirring well, and boxing and straining thoroughly.

Fading

Lucky is the painter who has to match another oil-paint sample. His only serious problem is the fading that probably took place since the sample was originally painted. There is no such thing as a truly permanent color in paint. Many misunderstandings can be cleared up if this is understood. Once it has been established whether the original color or the faded color is preferred, you can proceed with the color matching. Sometimes you can pretty well revive the color temporarily by wetting the sample with water. This partially eliminates the effect of the chalking in the paint, but it cannot restore the actual fading of the color pigment due to the action of the ultraviolet light from the sun.

Frequently the faded color is the preferred one, in which case your ingenuity is extended. You must visualize the original color and the pigments used to make it. Then make a small sample as close to the original as you can, and afterwards add modifying pigments to simulate the fading. These modifying pigments should contain some white, as all faded colors are somewhat lighter than the original. Raw umber is one of the most helpful of these modifying pigments as it provides the grayness that almost always accompanies fading. Only in rare instances is it possible to exactly duplicate the hue of a faded paint without resorting to the use of a glaze. (See Chapter 10, page 155.)

Matching the Effect. Often the word "match" is used lightly. It is impossible to duplicate the translucency or the transparency of the original object. Many home-owners do not recognize one obvious limitation of a mass of paint—its opacity. This is one of the major characteristics of paint and means its quality of obscuring the surface it covers. That immediately precludes any possibility of transparency, and translucency can only be approximated by applying a glaze. So you will have to determine the major color and the modifying pigments, and strive for the color effect rather than an exact match. No precise instructions can be given for the variety of ceramics, flowers, metals, glass, shells, even fur, which you may want to match. However, a simple procedure to determine the basic color is to make a peephole in a piece of white cardboard and view the sample through it. Hold the peephole so that you cannot see the form of the object and so that it appears hazy. Then the real color will become more apparent. This is similar to the artist's trick of bending over and looking at a landscape through his legs. The landscape's being upside down makes it essentially unrecognizable and he can study the colors without preconceptions. It is also one of the principles used in camouflage in wartime. Make the form unusual by painting in distorting patterns. No doubt you will evolve some tricks of your own as you gain experience and confidence.

Water Colors

Water-color samples will most frequently come in question in the form of wallpaper. Even the majority of the papers marked "washable" are made with water color containing an insoluble binder. These papers present an interesting problem in color matching as the pigments used are generally different from painter's colors and the finish of the paper is generally duller than most paints. Also, the use of aniline dyes gives the wallpaper manufacturer greater latitude in color. This makes for difficulty if you have to match one of the intense colors. Frequently it can only be solved by the use of pure-color pigment. This means compounding your own paint. It is not impossible to do this, in fact it was the custom fifty or seventy-five years ago. But it is difficult. The problems of getting the mix smooth and with the proper flowing quality are beyond the equipment available to the average painter.

Fig. 17. A peephole makes the real color of an object more apparent.

One possibility, however, is to use "colors ground in Japan" (see page 146 for more on this). Thin the color, brush it on, and, to protect the surface, apply a coat of flat varnish.

Often the background color of the paper is the one selected for matching in paint. This is relatively easy as the color is generally neutral and with a dull finish. If the wallpaper is vigorously figured in other colors, you will do well to cut or tear out a piece containing only the color you must match. Colors in close proximity have a very definite effect upon one another and they lose some of their individuality. You must avoid matching the apparent color, and this can best be done by isolating the actual color. Either remove or cover the others.

Glossy Finishes; Fabrics

The use of a gloss or semi-gloss paint or enamel on the woodwork of a papered room is common practice.

Fig. 18. A "window" makes color matching easier.

And it is a good one because the finish is more readily washable than is the case with flat paints. However, this in turn raises the problem of matching a gloss paint to a dull paper. All glosses dry somewhat darker, so that if you mix the paint lighter and let a sample dry beforehand, you can make a creditable match.

Matching a fabric is a more difficult process due to the effect of its texture The type of yarn, the twist, the pattern of the weave, piece- or yarn-dying, and finish all affect the color. The attempt to match a fabric sample usually results in "getting the feel of the color," rather than in reproducing the exact color. Determine the basic pigment to use and tint a sample of the white paint to almost the same value. This may require two pigments, but no more than that should be necessary. Hold your sample so that no gloss is reflected from the paint surface and then place the fabric close to it. Examine to see what is missing in the color. Here, a helpful variation on the use of the peephole mentioned earlier is to cut a hole about 4 x 4 inches in a piece of stiff white paper and then to place the hole so that it reveals some of the paint and some of the fabric at the same time. This will eliminate the influence of other colors and help to focus your attention.

The simplest fabrics to match are probably the chintzes, and the most difficult the velvets. Printed linens have the same matte surface as paint and consequently present no unusual problems. Any fabric with a heavy texture or pile requires a compromise. Even if you apparently match the color exactly, it will not look the same on the wall. Resort to matching for effect and the results will be more pleasing.

Printed Samples; Flowers

Quite often you will want to match a color from a magazine, book, or other printed matter. You should know that this color is rarely a pure or mixed pigment. If you look at the printed surface with a reading glass, you will find that it is composed of red, yellow, blue, and black dots. The size and frequency of the dots of the various colors determine the final color. For instance, large red and yellow dots make an orange color. The same method is used for all the other colors, shades, and tints. In addition to this basic "four-color process," there arc many variations in the number of colors used and the methods of obtaining color effects.

Matching to these printed samples becomes somewhat simpler when you recognize that all the colors are tints achieved by visual mixtures of primary colors. You will not be able to make an exact match because of the texture and probable gloss of the paper, among other things. But by using the peephole technique, you should be able to come close enough to satisfy yourself.

Flowers, either fresh or dried, present one of the most frustrating experiences in color matching. No paint yet made can duplicate the effect of the texture on the surface of a petal. It is the petal's texture and translucency that create the subtlety of the flower's color. This is easily demonstrated by passing a cold iron over the petal and flattening it out onto a piece of white paper. The color loses that quality which distinguishes it as a flower color; it becomes quite easy to match but it is not what it was. The best method for matching a flower color is to use the hole in the paper technique, varying the size of the hole to fit the flower. It is not easy, since flowers are rarely obliging enough to have flat petals. But care and perseverance will reward you with a reasonable facsimile of the original color. Dried flowers are considerably easier to match since they are faded, of matte finish, and generally more opaque than fresh ones. Simply determine the major hue, tint to it, and add modifying pigments to finish the match.

Source of Pigments

These color pigments we have been studying are interesting in themselves. They are either natural or are made chemically. Ochre, sienna, and raw umber are natural clays or deposits that are simply cleaned and are then ready for use. To make burnt sienna and burnt umber, the raw pigment is merely burned or calcined and the chemical change induced by the heat modifies the original color. With the exception of Vandyke brown, all the other colors are made chemically. The processes in many cases are complicated and require a good grounding in chemistry to understand. Vandyke brown is the decomposed vegetation you can find in low spots in the damp parts of the woods.

Forms of Pigments. For the use of painters these pigments are available in many forms: ground-in-oil, water or poster color, ground-in-Japan.

Pigments ground in oil start as a dry powder and are mixed with raw linseed oil, after which they are ground between steel rollers. This grinding process forces the oil into every irregularity on the surface of each particle of pigment, thus thoroughly wetting it. The process also breaks down the larger particles so that the finished material has a uniform fineness. If the process is hastened, the color can be "burned." The frictional heat developed by the compression as the paste passes between the rollers becomes high enough to cause chemical changes in the pigment or oil which result in loss of intensity of hue. The final pigments are packed in tubes for the use of artists and in cans and barrels for the use of the painting industry.

Water or poster colors are simply ground in appropriate water-soluble adhesives, generally one of the glues. They come in cakes, tubes, or jars.

Colors ground-in-Japan are made in the same way as ground-in-oil colors except that a quick-drying matte-finish varnish is substituted for the oil. In general these colors are the finest obtainable. They are widely used in the furniture industry and were once used for coach and auto painting. They still are used for tinting lacquers, though pigments made for lacquer-spraying are available.

CHAPTER 10

DECORATIVE PAINTING

STRIPING

One of the simplest ways to heighten the eye-appeal of a room or piece of furniture is to stripe it tastefully. Stripes set off innumerable objects, from lampshades to steamship funnels. In clothes they shorten, lengthen, slenderize, or draw attention to the figure. With paint you

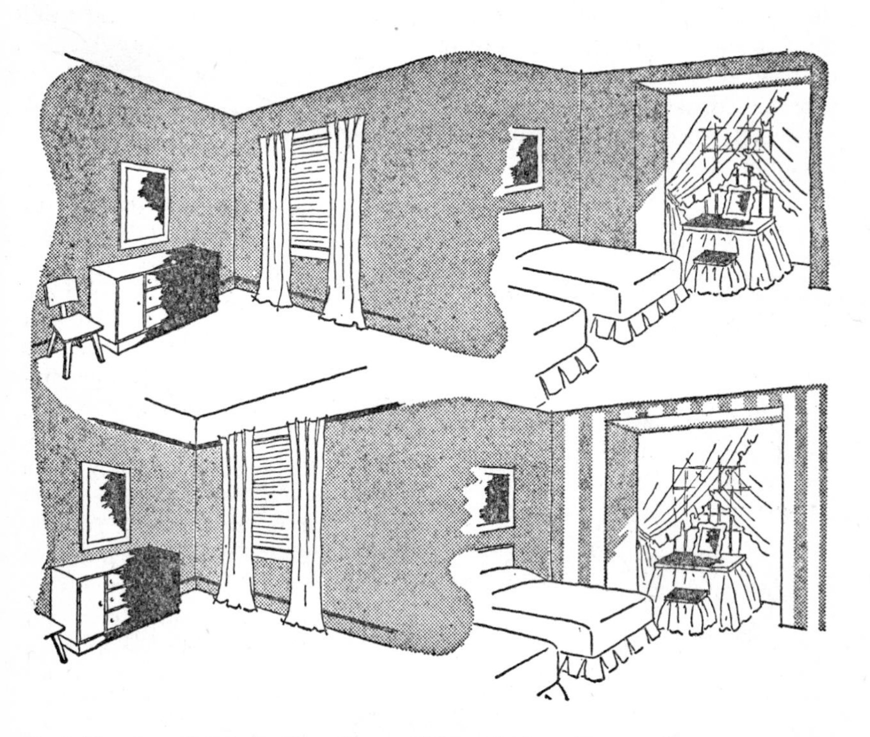

Fig. 1. There is no limit to the decorative possibilities of stripes either to enhance a room or to conceal its faults. See the difference that the addition of vertical stripes and horizontal lines has made in the "bare" room at the top of the illustration.

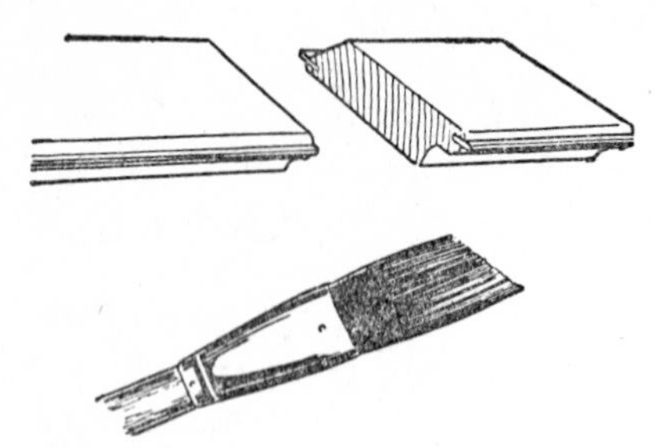

Fig. 2. An angular striper and a straight edge. They are used for painting stripes on flat surfaces.

may, correspondingly, point up the best features of an interior or play down the worst.

Observe how often stripes carry out the decorative schemes of modern theaters and restaurants. Notice panels banded by color, main doors emphasized, dimensions seemingly expanded by stripes straight or wavy, broad or slender. You can modify

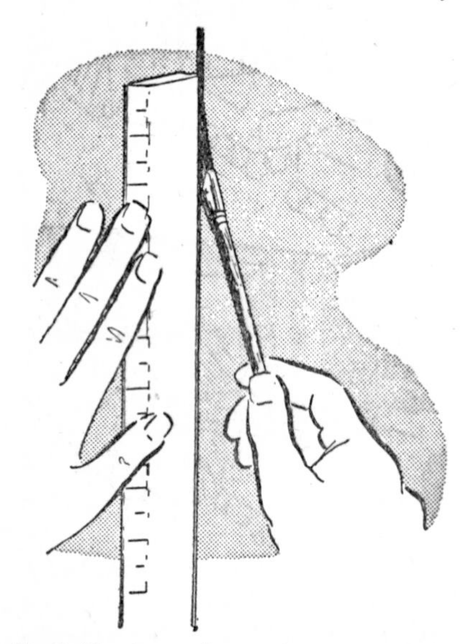

Fig. 3. How to use the angular striper with the straight edge.

these techniques to instill fresh sparkle and character into your home. Let the material on color harmony in Chapter 9, page 133 of this book guide your choice of colors.

Paint and Glaze

Either paint or glaze will serve. Paint gives a solid opaque color. It can be bright, dull, light, or dark but it is always solid. Translucent glaze (see below) lends a more subtle effect. If you are decorating in one of the period styles, the use of a glaze stripe is almost a must.

Fig. 4. A sign painter's quill, often used for striping.

Paint used for striping must be slightly thinner than for regular wall or wood work. Add a little turpentine and test it. For proper coverage employ a well-loaded brush or a long, soft-haired brush.

Glazes for striping generally come a little heavier than wall glazes (discussed later in this chapter). You can thicken a glaze by adding a little dry zinc. Adding oil pigment tends to make the glaze dry with a gloss but this is rarely desirable. To attain a real gloss, use an enamel.

Brush and Straight Edge

One easy way to apply stripes to a flat surface is to use a special brush, called an angular striper, and a straight edge. Angular stripers come in sizes from ¼ to 1 inch. The straight edge should have a beveled side and be used as in Figure 3. A 3-foot straight edge is the handiest length. You can make your own so easily it is hardly worth buying one. Select a in various widths. After using, rinse these brushes in two or three changes of turpentine or benzine. Then dip them in a mixture of half castor oil and half turpentine. Squeeze them clean between your fingers. Shape the quills and wrap them in wax paper. They will last years if cared for.

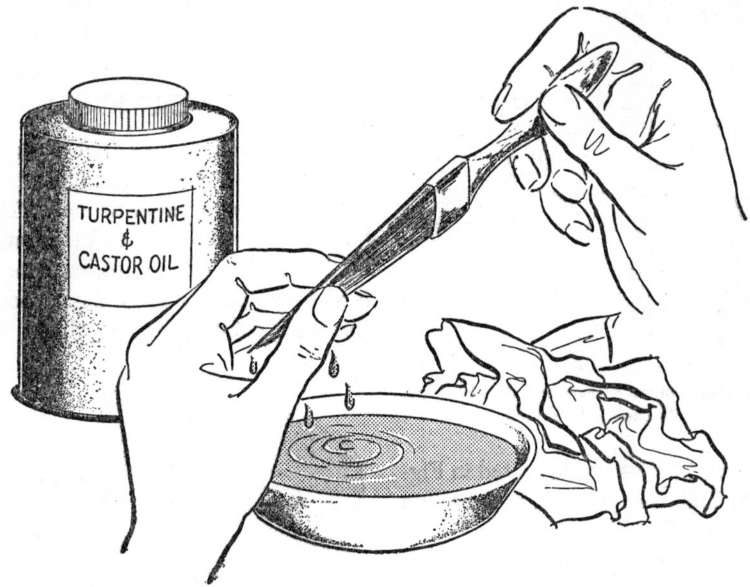

Fig. 5. Sword stripers and painter's quills will last for years if properly cleaned and shaped before storing.

clear-grained piece of wood that will not warp (Philippine mahogany is very good) that is about 2 inches wide, ¼ to ⅜ inch thick, and 3 feet long. Plane a bevel like that on a ruler, on two sides. (This keeps the edge off the surface to be painted.) Sandpaper the straight edge smooth and give it two coats of shellac or boiled linseed oil.

Some painters use sign painters' quills for striping. These cost less than other kinds of brushes and come

Application of Stripes

Mark out the corners or the extremities of the stripes you want with chalk or charcoal. A moist rag will remove these markings after the paint or glaze has dried. Using these points as guides, place the straight edge so that the bevel faces the surface to be striped. This prevents the paint from running under the straight edge and making a sloppy line. Hold the brush as shown in Figure 3. To make broad lines, use a flat liner. Hold it against

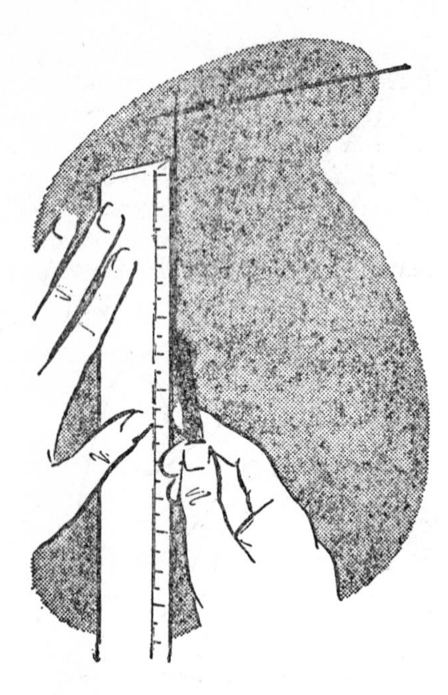

Fig. 6. Mark out the corners and sides of stripes with chalk or charcoal.

the straight edge as illustrated in Figure 7. This way you can make a line as wide as 1½ inches.

Apply heavier paint or enamel with a camel-hair sword striper. Load the brush carefully, as shown in Figure 8, and use your fourth and fifth fingers to follow the straight edge; this brush holds so much paint that it would otherwise drip down the bevel and leave a messy line. When you have mastered this technique you can use it even for picking out parts of a moulding in stripes.

Other Methods

Another, and perhaps simpler, method of striping is to apply masking tape or other adhesive tape on either side of the lines you have marked. Paint in the space between the tape. When the paint is dry, remove the tape.

You may also use a mechanical roller striper. This requires that the paint be of exactly the right consistency. If the paint is a little too heavy, it won't flow on to the roller. If it is too thin, it will trace an uneven line.

STENCILING

To apply many repetitive designs, use a stencil. A stencil is simply a hole cut in a piece of paper or metal. The hole outlines the area to be painted in. The best paper to use for stencils is a heavy stock made for the purpose. But any oak-tag paper which has

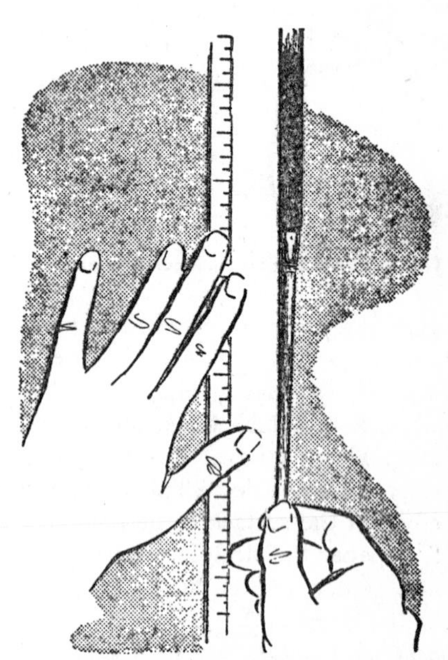

Fig. 7. How to use a flat liner to make broad lines.

been coated with boiled linseed oil on both sides and hung to dry will do.

One-Color Stencil

For simple, single-color stencils, lay out the design on a piece of paper.

Fig. 8. Load the sword striper carefully, it holds a great deal of paint. The lid of the can will make a convenient paint holder.

Determine where to put the ties least conspicuously. The ties are uncut strips of the stencil paper which hold in place portions that would otherwise be entirely cut around and fall out of position. For instance, if a

Fig. 9. Using masking tape is the simplest way to get straight edges.

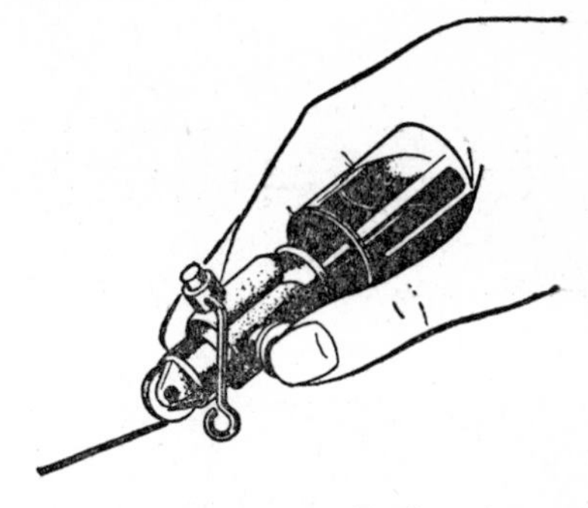

Fig. 10. A roller striper is handy and a great time-saver, but the paint must be of exactly the right consistency.

square or circle of stencil paper is to remain in the middle of the design, it will require strips in at least two, preferably four, places to hold it in position.

Fig. 11. A stencil is simply a hole cut in a piece of paper or metal.

Crayon or otherwise color in the sections to be cut out. Place this drawing over a piece of the stencil paper, and tack both to a cutting board, bread board, drawing board, or piece of plywood. With a sharp knife cut

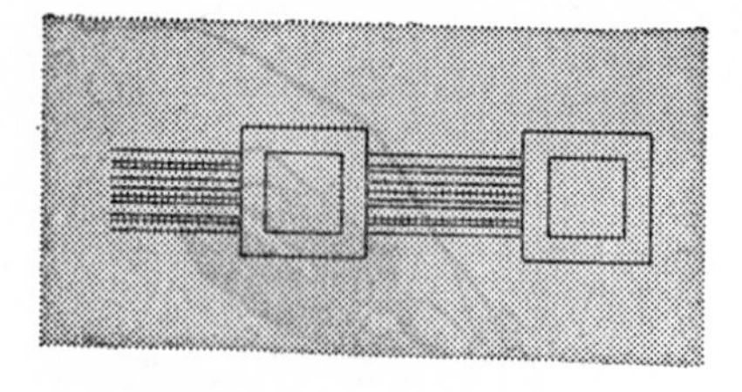

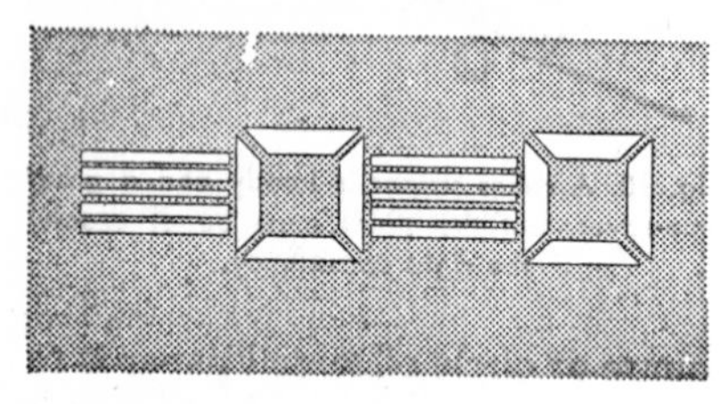

Fig. 12. Steps in the making of a single-color stencil. Above, the design laid out on the paper. Below, the design cut out, showing the position of the ties.

through both pieces of paper. When all the colored-in sections have been cut out, locate the keys. The keys are small cut-out parts of the design, arranged so that you can place the stencil correctly for the next decoration. With keys you can make a series of the design, equally spaced. Measure the length of the space in which you intend to put the stenciled design to make sure it will fit evenly.

Two-Color Stencil

A two-color stencil simply requires a little more work on the drawing board. Make your design in two

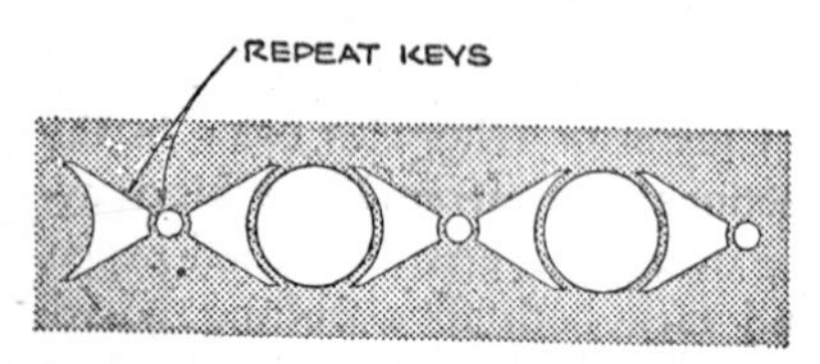

Fig. 13. Keys are used to position the stencil correctly for the continuation of the design.

strong colors on a sheet of white paper. Lay a piece of tracing paper over this and hold it in place with a piece of cellophane, adhesive tape or tacks

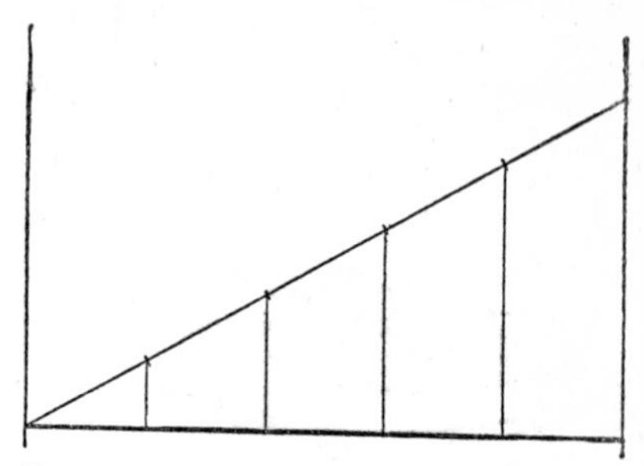

Fig. 14. Measure the space on which you are going to apply the design and divide it equally. Make your stencil to fit these divisions, so that it will fit evenly throughout. The illustration shows how, by dividing a horizontal line into equal spaces and drawing verticals at the divisions, you can in turn divide a diagonal line evenly.

at each corner. Trace the first color you are going to apply. Locate and mark in the ties. Lay a second sheet of tracing paper on top of the first. Remove the cellophane tape or tacks from one corner at a time and attach the second sheet. This way you will not move the under-sheet of tracing paper.

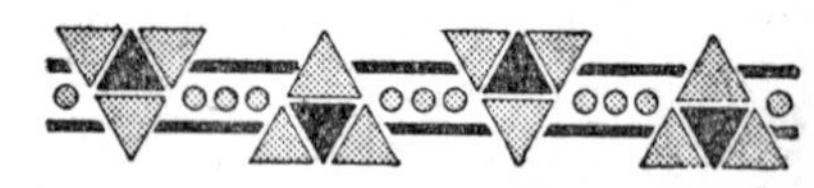

Fig. 15. Many different effects are possible with the use of two-color stencils.

Trace the outline of the second color. Then locate the ties on the second color design. Mark in keys so that you can locate the second stencil over the first. These keys are small cut-outs of part of the first color design, but they should be so located that you will not stipple through them with

Fig. 16. Preparing to trace the second color of a two-color stencil. To fix the second sheet in position without moving the first, lift the tape at one corner at a time.

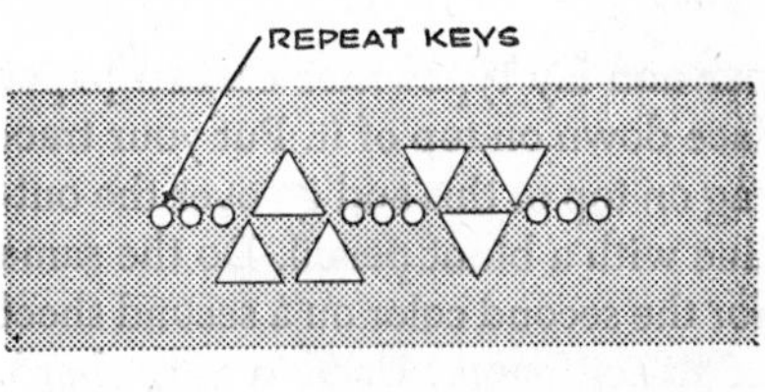

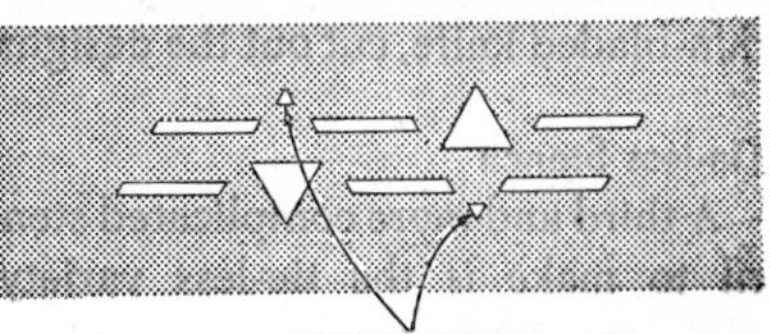

Fig. 17. Keys in a two-color stencil. Above, keys used to control the continuation of the design. Below, keys used to control the position of the second color.

the second color. Try to locate them diagonally opposite one another so that they will help keep your work square and even for a professional job. Remove both sheets of tracing paper and place the repeat keys on the first color tracing. Do this by moving the tracing the proper distance to the left or right. Mark the keys. Next tack down a sheet of prepared stencil pa-

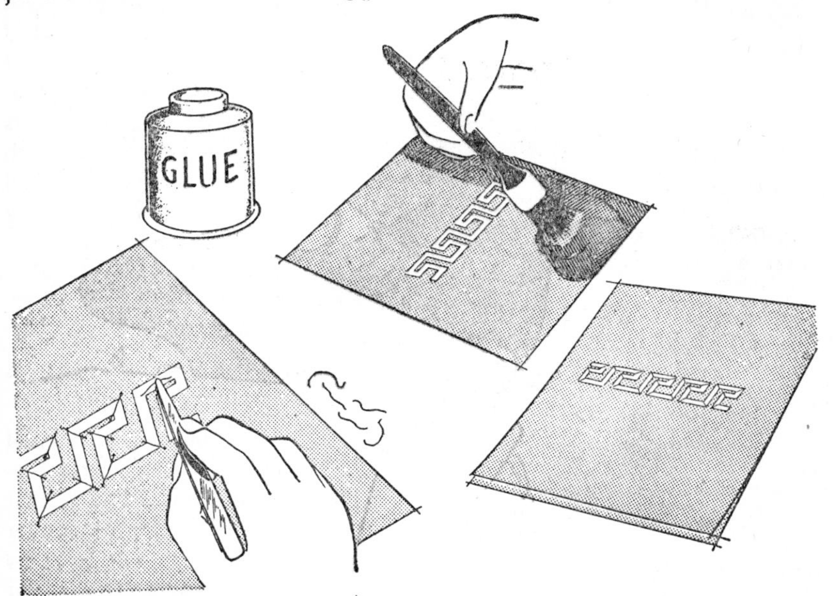

Fig. 18. Steps in the preparation of a tie-less stencil. Left, putting in the thread ties. Top, gluing the bottom side of the top sheet. Right, the two sheets correctly positioned.

per and lay typewriter carbon paper face down on top of it. Put your tracing on top of this and go over the outline with a blunt pencil. Do the same for the second color on a second sheet of stencil paper. Using a very sharp, thin-bladed knife, cut out the designs.

Fig. 19. How to bind a sash tool to make it into a stencil brush.

Tie-less Stencil

A third and more complicated stencil to make is the tie-less variety. Make two tracings of the original design on *very* heavy tracing paper. Place the two exactly over one another on your drawing board. Cut out the design through both pieces of paper. Set the top piece aside.

Cut pieces of horse hair or silk thread to lengths to serve as ties. Dip the ends in glue and place them on the bottom sheet. When you have put enough of these thin ties in place, paste or glue the bottom side of the top sheet. Carefully lay this in place on the bottom sheet and cover all with weights until dry.

Painting Stencils

Use ordinary paint, a little thick. Dab some on a palette of metal, glass, or wood. Dip the stencil brush into the paint vertically. Rub in a circular motion to load the brush. Holding the correctly located stencil with one

Fig. 20. Use of the repeat keys to locate the stencil for repetition of the design.

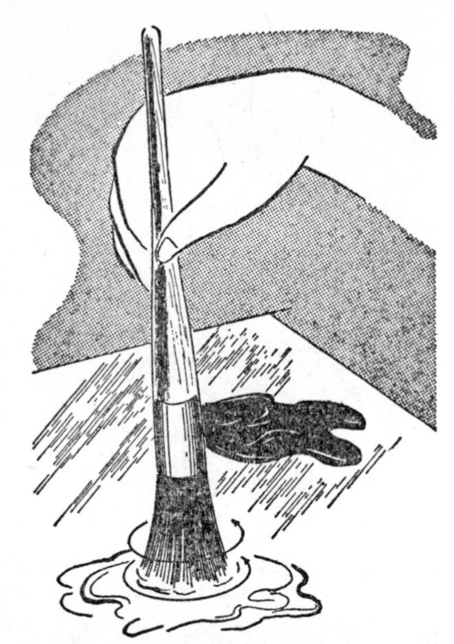

Fig. 21. Correct method of loading a stencil brush with paint.

hand, apply the paint through the openings in the stencil until it is filled.

Turn the stencil over and gently wipe off any paint which has crept under the edges. Load the brush, locate the stencil for the next design, using the repeat keys, and proceed.

If you do not have a stencil brush, you can tie a sash tool so that it will do the job perfectly. Use a well-worn brush because the chisel on a new one gives too small a brush to work with.

You can also use a spray gun for stenciling. If you do, make the over-all dimensions of the stencil paper big enough to catch all extra paint.

Wipe the back of the stencil frequently. Apply an adhesive coating to the back of the stencil similar to the adhesive coating on cellophane tape. It keeps the stencil from spreading.

GLAZING

Glazing is the application of a translucent color coating, which may enrich the underlying color. Most glazing is done on a painted surface. This surface must be dry, hard, and free from suction spots or cracks.

Glazing Liquids

There are so many fine glazing liquids on the market that it is no longer necessary to mix your own. Simply add the color-in-oil that you are going to use and stir thoroughly. If the color is old, with skins in it, strain the colored glaze.

Do not attempt to use ordinary manufactured wall flats for glazing. They make poor grounds because they are too absorbent.

Fig. 22. Spraying a stencil. Be sure to make the stencil big enough.

Follow this formula for approximately one gallon of paint upon which to glaze:

White lead (soft paste)	20 lbs
Mixing varnish	8 oz
Turpentine	1 qt, 12 oz
Japan drier	2 oz

Adjust with turpentine to the proper brushing consistency, which is average. Brush this paint out evenly. If you don't want brush marks to show, lightly stipple the paint to an even surface. Do not stipple the woodwork. Instead, be careful to brush evenly in its natural direction.

Application of Glaze

Brush glaze on the properly prepared ground. Work in sections. You cannot brush in a whole wall and wipe it out. The part you put on first will have begun to set. For the longest stretches get some help.

Wiping. If you wish a wiped finish, which generally improves the effect, bunch up about two yards of cheesecloth. Make the bunch loose. Do not roll it into a tight handful. Alternately pounce and wipe in circles. Try to even out the glaze as much as possible. If you wish to leave the glaze a little darker in the moulding, wipe more lightly. This wiping of the walls and woodwork can be followed immediately with stippling to further even it out.

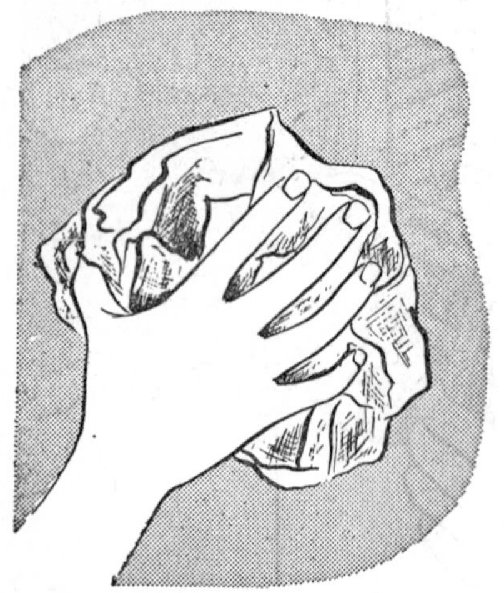

Fig. 23. For a wiped finish to glaze, bunch up loosely about two yards of cheesecloth.

Fig. 24. The dangers of spontaneous combustion cannot be overemphasized.

Safety Warning. Wiping rags used for glazing can catch fire from spontaneous combustion. To prove this, bunch one up tightly in your hand for three or four minutes and feel the heat begin to rise. Always spread the rags out completely and hang them like wash on a line. This way stray rags left lying around cannot build up enough heat to catch fire through combustion.

Stippling. You can brush the glaze on and immediately stipple it without

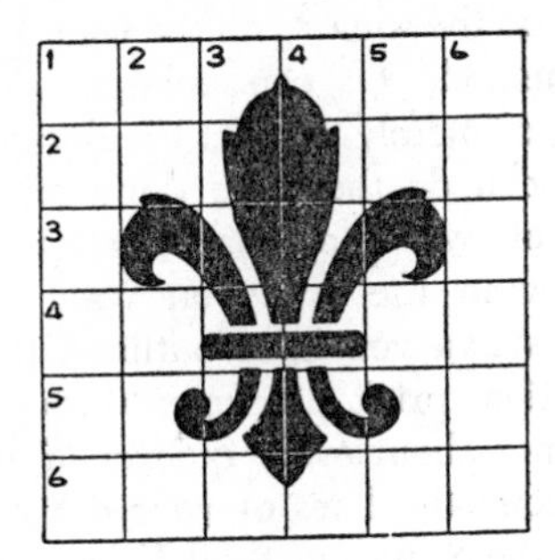

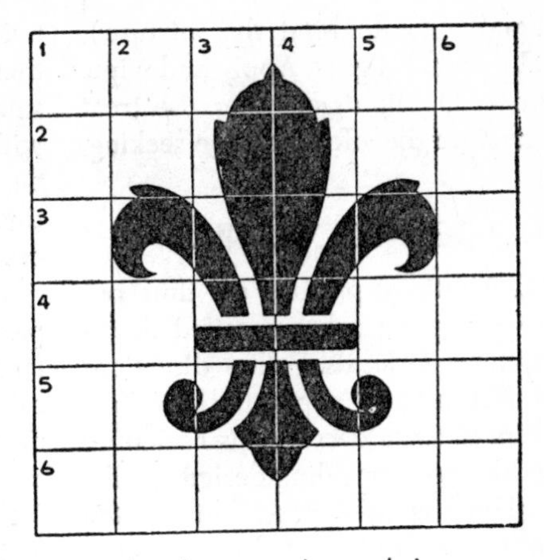

Fig. 25. By the use of squares you can easily enlarge or reduce a design.

wiping to a heavier finish. If you wish high lights on the centers of panels or on the mouldings, finish by a light wiping with cheesecloth.

Rolled and Novelty Finishes. Roll up a newspaper, cheesecloth, or a piece of chamois and roll it down the surface of a newly glazed wall to obtain an unusual texture.

Antiquing. As stated in Chapter 9, on color, one of the charms of old paint can be its faded appearance. Only glaze can duplicate this closely. Glaze used for this must be more opaque than most glazes. To attain this effect, use dry zinc, whiting, or ground pipe clay. Add the necessary amount to colored glaze, brush on, wipe, and stipple.

Protective Coatings

Coat the surface with a flat varnish made for the purpose. This is not the same as the matte varnish made for imitation rubbed finishes on stained wood. A flat varnish is thinner, less yellow, and dries to a really flat finish.

An old fashioned method of protection was to coat the dry glazed walls with a starch solution. Mix starch to a thin paste. Brush it on the wall and stipple it. You can wash this off every year or so. All of the accumulated dirt will come with it. Then recoat the walls and woodwork with fresh starch for another year.

Water Glazes

For very difficult matching problems requiring dull and matte surfaces, for which oil glazes will not suffice, use water glazes. Use any appropriate dry pigments, water (just

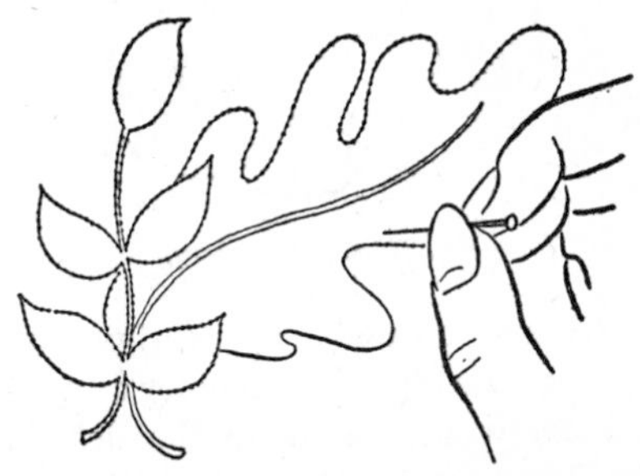

Fig. 26. Making a pounce pattern.

enough glue to bind the mixture), and mix thoroughly. Apply and wipe. Rub in highlights or otherwise treat to achieve the effect you are seeking.

DECALCOMANIAS

Decorations printed on thin but strong paper stock are called decalcomanias or decals. Follow directions for wetting and applying. Manufacturers of these decorations now offer modern and appealing designs. Some of them, as in Pennsylvania Dutch motifs, resemble peasant art. Old-fashioned ones of floral decorations were so obviously beyond the ability of amateurs that they looked false when used.

FREEHAND DECORATION

Little can be said about this because it is so personal. You will select, use, and carry out what is within your ability. Basic information follows, however.

Fig. 27. A pounce bag.

Choose or make the design you wish to use. Sketch it in color or pencil. Draw squares upon the design. Measure the space in which you intend to use the decoration. Divide that space into the same number of squares. Lightly draw the squares with charcoal or chalk. Outline your design on the squares on the wall. By this method you can enlarge, decrease, or merely transfer the design.

You can do the same thing on a piece of wrapping paper slightly larger than the area you want to cover. When you have outlined the decoration, prick pin holes through the paper about every quarter of an inch along the lines of your design. This is the pounce method. When finished, attach the pounce sheet to the wall with some cellophane tape. Make a small bag about as big as an egg out of five or six layers of cheesecloth. Place several sticks of crushed charcoal in the bag and tie it with a string. Tap this bag over the pin holes so that some of the charcoal goes through. The design will appear on the wall when you remove the paper. If the painted surface is not rough enough to hold the charcoal, make it stickier by wiping it over with a rag moistened in linseed oil.

Color

To achieve an easy variation of freehand decoration in colors, first outline the decoration in charcoal. Mix a batch of paint in a color midway between the highlights and the shadows. Paint in the areas with this color and allow it to dry. Then brush in highlights in the appropriate light color and shadow areas in the proper dark color.

With flowers, use the characteristic color as the middle color. Paint leaves medium green and stems medium brown. When dry, proceed with highlighting and shading as above.

More experienced artists can do all these steps while the paint is wet but this is not recommended for the beginner. If your hand proves shaky, make a hand rest by tying a ball of rags to the end of a two-foot stick. Rest your hand on this while painting.

Use artist's bristle brushes, and learn to turn the brush from the narrow edge to the flat side in order to broaden a line.

Fig. 28. After applying the "middle" color brush in the highlights and the shadows in their appropriate colors.

CHAPTER 11

DECORATION: PERIOD AND MODERN

This chapter treats of forms, materials, and colors typical of the most noteworthy periods and of modern decoration. To help you evaluate them it tells why, as well as how, these features originated.

The number of home-owners familiar with the fundamentals of period and modern decoration mounts every year. Some knowledge of this subject is vital for planning any intelligent scheme of interior decoration. And of course, the more you know, the greater will be the range of possibilities open to you, the more striking the effects you can achieve, and the more noticeable the charm and taste of your home.

The earliest period borrowed from frequently is English Tudor; the latest, Victorian. We first turned to what we now call modern decoration in the early 1900's but did not explore its possibilities broadly before 1940 or so. In all periods of decoration, three common factors stand out. Let us review them before discussing individual periods.

Common Factors

First, each period produced styles of architecture, furniture, fabrics, and paint color resulting from contemporary circumstance. In this sense the styles were functional. With the development of half-timbered construction for houses, for instance, arose a need for warmer interiors. Wood planks or panels partially answered this need. With the development of wood floors, lighter but equally durable pieces replaced stone and log-hewn furniture. Wood walls in time gave way to plaster. As more tools and power-driven machinery evolved, workmanship became more intricate.

Secondly, each of the period styles expressed a culture. After English architects made the pilgrimage to Italy and Greece early in the 18th century, they adapted the ideas they had found in a manner related to their native cultural climate. When Napoleon's army marched into Egypt, France acquired a lavish but short-lived mode of decoration which symbolized her domination of Europe.

American Colonial decoration sprang almost entirely from English workbooks and drawings. But, using comparatively primitive tools, the colonists simplified these designs and turned them to their own uses. The resulting tables, chairs, and woodwork stand distinctly apart from contemporary English pieces.

The third common factor of all period decoration is that colors were bright and clear when first applied. Many ignore this in judging reproductions of period pieces. Generally, however, the patina of the old colors is preferred to the relatively bold effect intended originally. In painting you must nearly always strive for the faded color rather than the original intensity.

New decoration ideas of any age seek an outlet in bold, vigorous colors. Today's functionalism features colors emphatic enough to convey definite moods. Of course, strong colors must be combined harmoniously. Cloaking colors in heavy, faded glazes does not achieve color harmony. The basic colors must be right.

See tables on page 176. They set forth the characteristics of furniture and decoration according to periods.

HISTORICAL PERIODS

Gothic (about 1100-1453)

Churches show the clearest marks of this period. Oak was the wood most commonly used. The finish was fairly light originally but has darkened considerably with time. Most of the decoration was carved, and fre-

Fig. 1. Gothic halls and churches show most clearly the effects of decoration in the Gothic period (about 1100-1453).

quently outlined in strong colors. Examples of this polychrome coloring have come down to us but are rarely copied today.

To match the lighter original finish of the oak, employ fuming as described in Chapter 13. To duplicate the present dark finish, use a water stain and glaze with a wiped effect. A well rubbed wax finish will complete the job. Plaster and masonry walls of the Gothic period were generally whitewashed. They are not white now, however, and you can duplicate their present color with a glaze of rottenstone.

Renaissance (about 1453-1560)

In this period Europe awakened after the "Dark Ages." Decorations took ornate and massive shapes. Walnut became one of the most popular woods and was used for almost everything. The many types of walnut and the various cuts provided numerous colors and effects. No doubt many of the original pieces were stained; all have darkened. To match their colors you must stain. Follow the directions in Chapter 12, page 179.

Walls were painted in the Renaissance period; heavy colors and mural decorations predominated. Stencils came into common use. Examples of this kind of work can be seen in many of our older public buildings. It was high-style at the turn of this century.

ENGLISH PERIODS

Tudor, Elizabethan, Jacobean (about 1600-1688)

The earlier Tudor and Elizabethan periods in England corresponded to the Renaissance on the continent. Furniture was of heavy oak and similar woods, such as chestnut. The simple finish, usually wax, has since become quite dark. Duplicating it calls for a good stain and even a glaze.

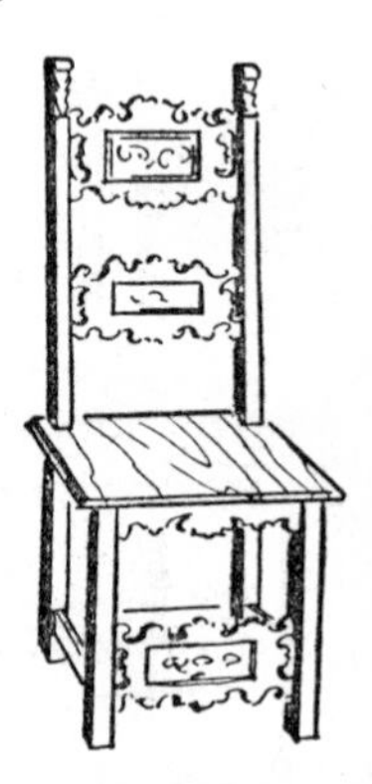

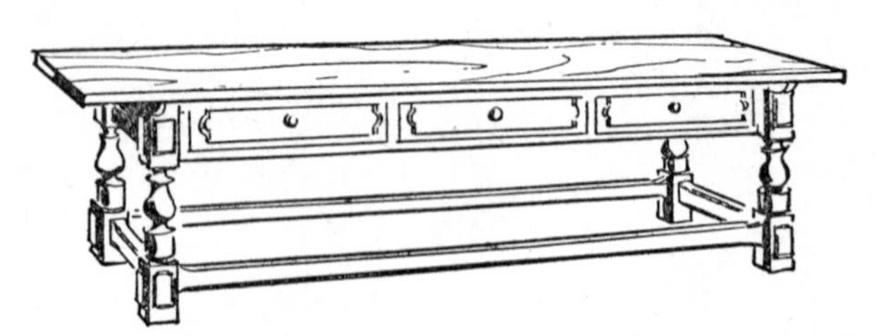

Fig. 2. The renaissance, which marked a reawakening of European architecture, art, and literature, emphasized massive shapes done mostly in walnut.

Fig. 3. Early Tudor and Elizabethan interiors bear the influences of the renaissance on English decoration.

Fillers were never used; the pores of the grain still show. The English rarely used color, other than stain, in decorating furniture. The natural deep brown of English oak is difficult to copy in other oaks. You can come closest to it by using the fuming process suggested in Chapter 12, page 187. You may also have to glaze lightly to match the richness of English oak.

Later in this period much furniture was fashioned of walnut. This wood is so dark naturally that stains were rarely used. You need them today to match the effects of time, however. After applying stain, rub it off the parts of the piece receiving most wear. The less accessible parts should be glazed after a very dark stain has been applied.

Walls were rarely painted, but the plaster was textured. Time, grime, and smoke have endowed these textured walls with mellow tones no new paint can match. To imitate them you must use glaze. Combine rottenstone with raw umber to copy the color. Wipe the walls to make them look as if they were old walls wiped clean.

Fig. 4. During the reign of William and Mary (about 1689-1714) we find liberal use of veneers for paneling and fine fabrics.

William and Mary (about 1689-1714)

During the reign of William and Mary, English decoration began to acquire continental refinements. Veneers and fine fabrics were used on furniture. Rooms were paneled extensively, many in pine instead of oak. Some were painted. Many of these rooms have been dismantled and reassembled in the United States. Some have been stripped of paint and refinished with a simple waxing. Matching the old finish on new pine is described in Chapter 12, page 179.

Georgian (about 1714-1800)

Decoration reached an apex in this period. The combined interest of the nobility and of a new merchant class able to afford luxuries stimulated the arts. Design and decoration became established professions. Furniture became more stylized and highly intricate in construction. Fine veneering and inlaying distinguished it. Use of imported woods and of new treatments for native woods became common. Mahogany, from the West Indies, became so popular that today it is almost impossible to get wide planks of the wood. Fruitwoods of all types were introduced, as well as some exotic tropical woods. The finishes for these woods were just as varied. Chapter 12 describes them.

Varnishing, French polishing, lacquering, and hand decoration developed into fine arts in the Georgian period. The painting of homes in flat colors as well as glazes became commonplace. Murals were used with discrimination. Formal decoration of walls and ceiling, in plaster as well as paint, flowered into an art. At the same time fabrics and upholstery became more intricate and diversified. Machine weaving made possible the widespread use of a great many new fabrics.

Famous Designers

By the end of the 19th century some designers' names had become household words. Chippendale, Sheraton, Hepplewhite, and the Adam

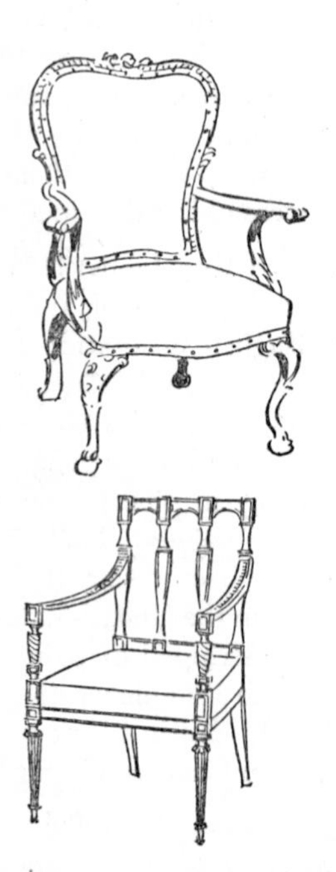

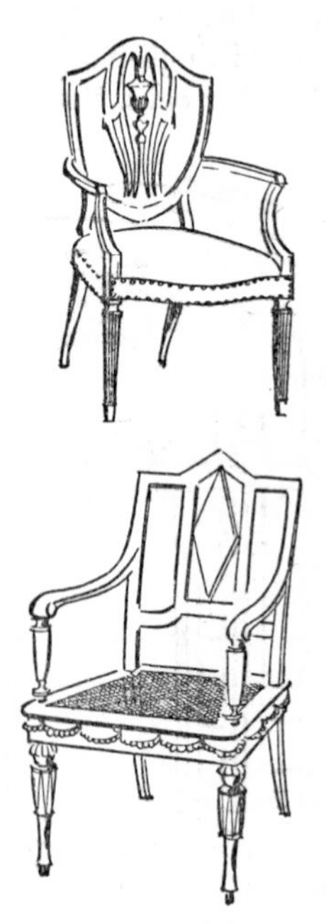

Fig. 5. Big "names" appeared in furniture decoration in the 18th century as the merchant class became interested in design and decoration. These chairs show the styles of: Chippendale (upper left), Hepplewhite (upper right), Sheraton (lower left), and the Adam brothers.

Fig. 6. A fastidious French nobility insisted on luxurious interiors. The result was elaborate carvings in walls and furniture overlayed with gilding and glazes.

brothers contributed designs which are still copied assiduously.

The early part of the century was characterized by fairly strong colors on walls. Colors used later in the century, by men like the Adam brothers, were more delicate. Early Georgian colors glowed with a vigor not seen otherwise before the advent of modern decoration. Samuel Pepys, among others, describes the clear peacock blues, vermilion reds, and rich jade greens used on walls. In reproducing them, however, decorators usually try to capture their present soft, faded tones rather than their original strength.

You may approximate the patina of early Georgian colors by first preparing a ground color somewhat lighter than the original would have been. Glaze it with a dulling wash composed chiefly of raw umber. See Chapter 10 for further instructions.

Victorian

Later English periods contributed little. The English did not imitate many French Empire period styles (see below). In the 19th century Victorian styles dominated all new decoration. Little of the period besides some furniture remains in favor today. Colors were too heavy to enhance any part of period or modern decorations.

You may want to remove some of the dark mahogany stain so freely used on Victorian furniture. Although called Bismarck brown, the stain is a murky purple red. It is penetrating and difficult to remove. Painting over it requires application of metal leaf to seal in the old color. Refinishing in a wood finish requires very cautious use of shellacs. Highly soluble in alcohol, the stain will rise up to plague you if given the slightest opportunity. It is better to use a simple wax finish if this duller finish is acceptable. With repeated applications you may also apply an oil finish with a polish of wax.

Golden oak finishes became very popular late in the Victorian period. They should present no serious problem because they were for the most part simply stains on fillers. Many pieces have been pleasingly refinished by removing the old finish with combination remover and bleach. This is easy to use, being water soluble and presenting no danger of fire or noxious fumes. Simply follow directions on the label. The resulting finish, called wheat or Cordovan, approximates the color of cigarette tobacco.

FRENCH PERIODS

Louis XIV (1643-1715)

Before this period decoration had been relatively primitive in France. Simple furniture was made from the local woods available. Painting was restricted to public buildings and churches. Decoration came into its own only with the advent of an elaborate formal court for the king and his nobles.

Spacious castles were built and handsomely ornamented. Gilding became a fine art, perhaps never surpassed since. The stains on oak, walnut, and chestnut used for panels and furniture were generally of medium strength. Oil and wax ordinarily served as the finish. The technique of French polishing was to flourish later. However, no hesitation was shown in the use of polychrome coloring on stained furniture to bring out the beauty of the framing or carving. You can see examples of this furniture in museums.

Louis XV (1715-1774)

In contrast with the Louis XIV period, in which the straight line predominated, this period utilized the curved line extravagantly. Painting, enameling, glazing, striping—all developed into complex arts. Artists of national repute lent their talent to embellishment of furniture and interiors. It was not considered beneath the dignity of a highly qualified artist to decorate panels on furniture or walls.

Fig. 7. The Louis XV period utilized the curved line in interiors with a subtle extravagance

The basic wall colors were rich grays, soft greens, powdery blues, and mellow tans. Stripes were of all colors but were generally vivid and balanced for intensity. French artisans employed accent color with a skill no others have approached. When you examine their work, note that the colors all agree with the rules for color harmony given in Chapter 9. Fabrics woven to go with this splendid furniture were equally charming. Many of their patterns are still copied by fabric manufacturers.

The staining and finishing of furniture passed through as much of a transition. Staining was used as it should be—to heighten the beauty of the wood and not conceal the grain or make it look like something else. Stains were very light; bleaching was seldom resorted to. Separate pieces of wood to be fitted together were painstakingly matched for color. Some furniture fashioned in this way looks as if it had been formed of one solid piece of wood. Many types of wood were used, including exotic varieties from the Orient. Marquetry, the making of designs or pictures in furniture with separate pieces of wood, attained near-perfection.

Fig. 8. French furniture and room paneling highlighted simpler and lighter effects during the reign of Louis XVI.

The final culmination of the finisher's art, French polishing, also developed in the Louis XV period. This is a method of applying shellac to a wood finish with a cloth pad. It requires diligent practice. To apply French polishing, pick up either pure shellac or a mixture of shellac and oil in a cloth pad. Gently but firmly rub the pad over the surface, depositing the shellac. If successful, the finish will be the clearest, deepest, and shiniest attainable. (See also Chapter 12, Staining and Finishing Wood.)

Louis XVI (1774-1793)

The inevitable reaction to the ebullience of the previous age set in during this period. Furniture and room paneling became simpler and lighter. Heavy and richly ornamented cabriole legs became straight and sometimes fluted. Wall panels lost their heavily scrolled head-rails and ornate corner decorations. Restraint was exercised in hand-decorated panels on walls and furniture. The prevailing caution and delicacy stamped this as the feminine period of French decoration.

Basic colors used on walls, mouldings, and furniture were the same, but accent colors and striping dimmed. Furniture staining continued on the same high plane. Exotic woods, metals, and such materials as tortoise shell diminished in popularity. Furniture was either painted delicately or stained with nice respect for the particular type of wood. Varnishes found wider favor but never supplanted French polishing for the finest furniture finishing.

Empire (about 1795-1815)

Napoleon introduced this brief period. Based on the classic styles of Egypt, it was more of a fad than a sound new style for France. Furniture became heavy and ponderous again and colors lost the subtlety of preceding periods. Clear reds and yellows dominated color schemes. Mahogany was stained a strong red and heavily ornamented with gold leaf. We see little of this today.

Fig. 10. Simplicity to the extent of using natural woods and whitewashed ceilings and walls express the French Provincial style.

Fig. 9. The Napoleonic period was short-lived. Heavy gold-leaf ornamentation and ponderous furniture was reintroduced.

French Provincial

In the outlying parts of France furniture resembled court styles slightly, but for the most part they reflected the earlier Gothic style of the Middle Ages. Local woods were used along with a great deal of fruit wood. There was rarely any stain used and the finish was generally oil or wax. Fabrics were simpler, usually of linen or cotton. Many of these materials were hand-block printed. Painting was primitive. Most walls and ceilings were simply white washed. These styles expressed natural dignity, however, and can be used to advantage in our homes today.

AMERICAN PERIODS

Our own heritage in decoration stemmed entirely from European styles. The country of origin of the settlers determined their modes of decoration and furniture. Early settlers of the southern states built houses of the William and Mary period; later settlers erected Georgian homes. Our stately southern mansions of the east coast are almost without exception one of these two styles English settlers of the northeastern states built houses in the Elizabethan style and put stiff upright furniture in them. Georgian types followed. The Dutch of the Hudson River Valley and New Jersey lined their village streets with brick dwellings resembling those they had left behind them in Holland.

In each case, furniture bore similar resemblances to the home product. This made for an interesting variety, which complicates classification by exact periods. Consequently American Colonial periods are usually divided by dates, rather than by styles.

Fig. 11. Much of today's furniture is patterned after the early Colonial period (about 1620 to 1725).

Fig. 12. The fashionable mansions of the south encouraged the introduction of finer woods in the Later Colonial period.

Early Colonial (about 1620-1725)

Liberal use of maple and pine characterized this period. New England produced these woods in abundance. Fabrics used with this furniture were generally homespun and either vat-dyed or left their natural hue. As for painting, all painting materials had to be imported from Europe and had to compete for ship space with more essential cargo. It was not until the introduction of canned paint by American manufacturers around 1845 that it became the widespread practice to paint exteriors.

Today's maple furniture, imitating early American maple, should be stained very lightly. The originals were rarely stained. You stain reproductions merely to copy the darkening of antiques. In general the colors vary from a very light honey to a medium dark amber. It is common to wipe the worn parts of the piece and wipe out or lighten the center of panels.

Later Colonial (about 1725-1780)

This period saw the introduction of finer woods, such as mahogany, walnut, and cherry, in furniture making. In this most notable of American periods most of the large mansions of the south and the stately town houses of the north were built. Cabinet-making advanced in the States, although fabrics and wallpapers continued to be imported. Indentured artisans brought skills they had learned as apprentices in Europe. Lacking the equipment available in Europe, they simplified most designs.

Stains and varnishes came to be widely used. Varnish makers frequently peddled their wares from door to door. People awoke to the fact that furniture and wall paneling were much easier to keep clean when varnished. They also utilized more paint on interiors for both cleanliness and decoration.

As for colors, the Williamsburg restoration in Virginia shows us some of the truest examples of the period. Most museums in large cities contain samples of Later Colonial colors in the "old" rooms on exhibit. Usually these colors were simple and soft. The cost of imported tinting pigments partly accounted for this. We find few natural tinting pigments in this country, and these are principally dull earth colors. Sample cards of Colonial colors will help you to judge reproductions of your own.

Fig. 13. Furniture design in the United States during the Federal period bears marks once popular during the Empire period in France.

Federal (about 1780-1847)

In this period we see the first authentically American styles. This applies more to architecture, however, than to decoration or to painting and staining colors. Duncan Phyfe (1784-1854), the furniture designer, stands out among individuals of the period.

Most of his middle and later work bears marks of the Empire style then popular in France. In the American version we lost much of the color intensity and gained thereby. Furniture was stained darker. Mahogany became more red, suggesting the later deep red of the Victorian period.

Victorian (about 1847-1915)

The Victorian period, which followed the Federal, has only recently been dignified by the term antique. It was characterized by expense without taste. Fine fabrics and meticulous workmanship availed nothing. Much of the furniture was fashioned of fine woods, however, worth cleaning and refinishing to reveal their natural beauty.

When it became possible to buy factory paint cheaply in America, Victorian decorators took too-full advantage. They painted walls deep and dark, in maroons, midnight blues, or gaudy purples. Fine but depressingly dark silk damasks frequently swathed the walls. Rococo designs in plaster garnished the ceilings.

However bad the taste, the craftsmanship was generally superb. Some rubbed enamel and varnish finishes exist today in nearly original condition. The famous piano finish was developed. To attain this, as many as eight coats of varnish were applied to a wood surface and then scraped off. This varnishing and scraping was for filling the pores of the wood only. The finishing and rubbing varnishes were applied next, rubbed to a very high lustre with the palm of the hand. Unfortunately this finish was applied on a stain so dark, generally, that the wood could not be distinguished.

The popularity of Golden Oak merely extended the Victorian period. Oak succeeded mahogany as the favorite wood. Designs became even less meaningful.

Fig. 14. Though the craftsmanship of the Victorian period is generally considered excellent, the decorators are nowadays accused of bad taste in the selection of color schemes and designs.

Fig. 15. Modern interior decoration aims at combining utility and beauty.

MODERN DECORATION

Present modern architecture and decoration rest upon the concept of functionalism. This means that all parts of a building, including furniture, should indicate their function in their form. A wall should look as if it supports the roof and shuts off the weather. A window should leave no doubt that it is intended to admit light. A chair should look as if it holds up a person comfortably and a table should look as if it provides space and support for eating or working. Once explained in these terms, modern decoration begins to make sense.

In the normally confused development of this new concept, however, some designers forgot we are human beings. They talked of a home as a "machine for living." Some drew plans for homes and furniture not unlike the ugly factories of the 1890's. Today the human yearning for aesthetic satisfaction is recognized. It is conceded that flat wall surfaces without texture or color can be depressing, that the natural colors of wood are not necessarily the most attractive.

As a painter, you haye at your command a thousand and one possibilities for modern decoration. You can apply textures to walls to lend them solidity. You can color others to focus attention on important features. You can finish furniture to appeal to the enjoyment of natural color. Keeping functionalism in mind, you can bring out the best in modern decoration.

Living Room

You must think all this through, of course. There are no simple formulas as for most period decoration. You must look at a room and think in terms of its use as well as its form. If it is a "living room," consider all the activities it can conceivably provide for. Consider also the shape of the room and the view through the windows. Bear in mind how it will look at night with incandescent or flucrescent lighting.

Walls separating this room from others probably offer the most convenient locations for high pieces of furniture. Unless a wide expanse of these walls will show, it would be foolish to spend much time or money on them. A simple color to provide a harmonious background for the furniture placed against it will suffice. A window wall will probably be more window and curtain than wall and will need no elaborate finish.

A fireplace wall or entertainment wall is another story. As the center of interest it warrants special treatment. Before we had reliable heating systems the fireplace was of necessity the center of interest in a room. The trend now is to install radios, television sets, and phonographs near the focal wall. This wall requires a distinctive texture or a vivid coloring. Many architects and decorators are using brick, stone, or novelty-finish wood. But these are expensive. To achieve comparable results at less cost, use methods suggested in Chapters 10, 13, and 14 for graining, marbling, stone-texturing, or glazing, or adapt your paperhanging or stencilling.

Ceiling and Floor

Ceilings and floors are best treated as nature treats ground and sky, the floor relatively dark and the ceiling light. The color of the floor depends largely upon the material. Ready-made materials like asphalt tile or linoleum will, of course, be self-colored. But wood floors allow considerable freedom in selecting hues. Recognize the purpose of a floor and remember the maintenance problem.

The widespread use of indirect lighting makes light ceiling color almost mandatory. Even the clearest white paint reflects only 88 per cent of the light which strikes it. From this clear white to dull black the percentage drops to 4. A medium-strength color reflects between 40 per cent and 60 per cent of the light. This rather low efficiency adds to the cost of illumination.

Bedrooms are usually decorated around the bedhead wall or the storage wall. Whichever is chosen, it should be treated as the focal side. Varieties of color, texture, or wood finish offer numerous possibilities.

Color Harmony

In each case use correct color harmony. Chapter 9 tells you how. Don't be timid. The harmonies work; they are psychologically sound. If you use weak, faded colors you will defeat the purpose and possibilities of modern decoration. On the other hand, do not try to imitate the colors of an amusement park. Those colors are there to arrest your attention.

A house should provide both restfulness and stimulation, but neither to an extreme. Express your own personality or that of the person for whom you may be doing the work. If you feel uncertain about color schemes, study those illustrated in home-decoration magazines. Check color harmonies and note the textures of building materials or fabrics. If they agree with the standards given in this book and please your taste, they will satisfy in the end. Don't be afraid of imitating some room colors. With a room of different dimensions from your original guide, you cannot avoid making changes which will give it individuality.

Decorator's Methods

A conscientious decorator or architect studies the tastes of his client. Building or decorating conservatively would not likely do for a sophisticated young couple. Modern treatment of a home for a tradition-minded older couple, could be as bad. Once the decorator has determined the type of decoration to use, he thinks of materials available under the budget. After making a rough estimate, he assembles samples. After deciding upon fabrics, rugs, wood finishes, and upholstery, he considers paint and wallpaper.

Paint and wallpaper are the most variable of the factors. They should be adjusted to the others. It is true that you can have fabrics custom-dyed, but the expense is usually too high to be considered.

Comparing Samples

In comparing samples, place the carpet sample on a floor similar to the one you intend to install. Do the same for any flooring material such as asphalt tile, rubber, or linoleum. Next take a small chair or table finished in the typical wood color to be used. On this drape the upholstery and drapery fabrics. Study them for color harmony and texture in both daylight and electric light. Use the same type of electric light which will be used in the finished room.

Next consider paint colors. Using the color wheel, determine which general colors can best be used. Think in terms of intensity and values. Make

Fig. 16. The average home decorator has become increasingly aware of the importance of simple, tasteful decoration towards achieving pleasant living areas. Study the combined effect of furnishings and drapes before you make a final decision.

up a small sample on a piece of cardboard or prepared wood. Place it near enough to your other samples to see how well it harmonizes or matches. Make the necessary additions of tinting colors or white, and paint in a sample about 2x2 feet. Let this dry and recheck your color scheme in both day and electric light. When satisfied that the color scheme is right, you can go ahead safely with mixing enough paint for the room.

Beware of placing paint samples on either bare white walls or previously painted walls. The whiteness of a new wall intensifies any color, while the present color of a painted wall usually alters the effect of a new sample. It is wiser to study colors with a minimum of distraction. As suggested in the chapter on color, Chapter 9, use a white card with a window cut in it. Look through this at your assembled samples. The true colors and their relationships will show forth unmistakably.

When the color scheme has been worked out, do the entire job without pausing to weigh the color scheme again. Don't falter if the colors look intense in contrast to the white plaster, unfinished ceiling, or uncurtained windows. Your comparison of samples will have given you the surest chance of satisfaction when the room is finished and with curtains and furniture in place.

Decorator's Colors

The following list will guide your choice of pigments for mixing. Most of the names given paint colors vary from time to time and from place to place. One man's seal brown may be another's nut brown and a third's tobacco brown. The list is short to minimize confusion. Quantities of tinting colors to add to white have not been stated because the strength of commercial tints varies. White paint is always the base. Add the tinting colors in the order given.

PERIOD AND MODERN FURNITURE

Period	Date	Woods	Finishes	Fabrics
English:				
Jacobean	1600–1688	Oak, some walnut	Dark brown stain, thin shellac, wax	Needlepoint, velvet, leather, brocades
William and Mary, Queen Anne	1689–1714	Walnut	Medium dark stain, shellac, rubbed, waxed, polished	Needlework, chintzes, damasks, leather
Georgian, Chippendale	1714–1800 d.1779	Mahogany	Natural to medium, brown stain, shellacked and rubbed smooth	Brocades, needle-point, leather
Hepplewhite	d.1786	Mahogany, satinwood, rosewood, inlays	Natural to medium brown stain, highly rubbed and polished finishes	Brocades, damasks
Sheraton	1751–1806	Satinwood, mahogany, rare woods	Natural to lightly stained, highly rubbed finish	Brocades, damasks
Adam Bros.	1728–1792	Mahogany, maple or pine	Mahogany, natural finish; pine, painted or gilded	Brocades, moiré
French:				
Louis XIV	1643–1715	Oak, walnut, chestnut	Medium stain, thin shellac, waxed, polychrome colors	Tapestries, velvets
Louis XV	1715–1774	Oak, rosewood, mahogany, walnut, beech	Medium stain or natural, shellacked, rubbed and polished, gilded	Needlepoint, damasks, velvets, prints
Louis XVI	1774–1793	Beech, mahogany, walnut, rosewood, satin-wood	Natural, lightly stained, gilded or painted	Damasks, brocades, silks, satins
Empire	1795–1815	Mahogany, ebony, rosewood	Clear, light, red stains, highly rubbed finish	Heavy fabrics, leather
American:				
Early Colonial	1620–1725	Pine, oak, maple, ash, fruitwoods	Natural to medium brown stains, wax-rubbed finishes	Rush, chintz, homespun
Later Colonial	1726–1780	Mahogany, walnut, maple, fruitwoods	Natural to medium brown stains, varnished, rubbed	Chintz, linens, haircloth
Federal	1780–1847	Mahogany	Medium brown to deep red stains, varnished and rubbed	Brocades, satins, damasks
Victorian	1847–1915	Mahogany, oak, rosewood, ebony, black walnut	Purple-red stain, golden oak stain, rubbed enamel, varnished	Damasks, horsehair, heavy satin, rep, needlework
Modern	1915–	All woods, plywoods	Natural, rubbed	Textured

Period and Modern Decoration

Period	*Date*	*Walls*	*Trim or Paneling*	*Effect*
English:				
Jacobean	1600–1688	Textured plaster smoked finish	Oak, dark wax finish	Dark, heavy, quiet
William and Mary, Queen Anne	1689–1714	Painted in rich vigorous colors	Painted in harmony with walls	Warm, colorful, livable, simple
Georgian	1714–1800	Painted in rich colors	Painted, detail sometimes picked out in separate colors	Rich, full, formal
Chippendale	d.1779			
Hepplewhite	d.1786	Painted in lighter colors	Painted, artists' panels	Lighter, formal
Sheraton	1751–1806	Painted in strong pastel colors	Painted, detail picked out in separate colors, artists' panels	Light, delicate, fresh, and formal
Adam Bros.	1728–1792	Painted in pastel colors, decorated plaster in various colors	Painted, striped, artists' panels	Very light, delicate, effeminate
French:				
Louis XIV	1643–1715	Painted in rich vigorous colors	Painted, picked out in separate colors	Heavy, ornate, impressive
Louis XV	1715–1774	Painted in rich vigorous colors, ornamental plaster in separate colors	Painted, free use of color on details, gilded, artists' panels	Heavily ornamental, formal, imposing
Louis XVI	1774–1793	Painted, soft but rich colors	Painted, striped, gilded, artists' panels	Profusely but delicately ornamented, light, formal
Empire	1795–1815	Painted, clear primary colors	Painted or stained finishes, gilded	Restrained, formalized
American:				
Early Colonial	1620–1725	Smoked finish	Oiled or waxed	Simple, and primitive
Later Colonial	1725–1780	Painted in vigorous colors	Painted or stained, varnished	Refined, dignified
Federal	1780–1847	Painted in clear primary colors	Painted or stained, varnished	Elegant but lacking in vigor
Victorian	1847–1915	Panels, drapes, ornamental plaster, maroon, deep blue, purple	Gilded, ornate carving and wallpaper, maroon, magenta	Ornate, fussy, elegant, heavy, depressing
Modern	1915–	Painted in vigorous colors	Painted or varnished	Striking, simple

Table of Decorators Colors

Paint Colors	Tinting Colors (Pigments)
Blue:	
Azure blue	Prussian blue
Misty blue	Ultramarine blue
Sky blue	Cobalt blue
Brown:	
Tobacco brown: light	Burnt umber, yellow ochre
dark	Burnt umber, raw sienna, lamp black
Fawn	Burnt umber, raw umber, yellow ochre
Café-au-lait	Burnt umber, raw sienna, Venetian red
Gray:	
Light gray	Lamp black, ochre or orange chrome yellow
French gray	Lamp black, cobalt blue, orange chrome yellow
Slate gray	Lamp black, Prussian blue
Green:	
Apple Green	Medium chrome green, orange chrome yellow
Gray green	Ultramarine blue, lemon chrome yellow, lamp black
Sea green	Prussian blue, raw sienna
Purple:	
Orchid	Ultramarine blue, vermilion or madder lake
Lavender	Ultramarine blue, rose pink
Red:	
Brick red	Venetian red, burnt umber
Pink	Madder lake, vermilion or Venetian red
Yellow:	
Apricot	Medium chrome yellow, Venetian red, carmine lake
Buttercup	Medium chrome yellow
Canary	Lemon chrome yellow
Cream	Raw sienna, medium chrome yellow
Ivory	Raw sienna, burnt umber, orange chrome yellow
Peach	Venetian red, orange chrome yellow

CHAPTER 12

STAINING AND FINISHING WOOD

Wood is such a widely available material and so easily adapted to man's use that he learned how to preserve it and incidentally beautify it long before the advent of written history. Paradoxically, as wood comes from nature, so it must be protected from nature. Climate and insects both take toll of wood. In general, wood must be preserved from three things. Fungus and insects attack it, drill it full of holes, reduce it to sponge, or turn it into a powder. The treatment for these is an application of copper naphthenate. Water or moisture also harms wood. In order to prevent this damage, wood is either painted or a waterproof surface, called a finish, is applied to it. If, in applying a protective surface, you can also improve the appearance of the wood, why not do so? This chapter tells you about finishes and finishing.

Much of the beauty of wood lies in its color and in its markings, which are also called grain and figure. Many woods, especially the fancy tropical woods, have a color that is not improved by staining. Yet even these woods do not reveal their real beauty until they have been smoothed, coated, and polished. If this is true of these naturally beautiful woods, it is even more so of the paler and less vigorously figured woods of our temperate zone.

Staining and Finishing

The art in staining and finishing lies in good judgment. The color must be strong enough to enhance the beauty of the wood without being too strong. Very dark staining obscures the delicate markings of the wood, toning down instead of emphasizing the natural textures. Stained wood is dull and does not brighten until the finish has been applied. The finish clears and gives contrast to the grain and the stained wood. Different finishes can be gotten from a variety of materials. These materials include oils, waxes, shellacs, varnishes, and lacquers. In the order listed they will provide a gloss from almost dull to very bright.

By carefully selecting the stain and the finish and just as carefully applying them, you should obtain satisfactory results. The instructions that follow will cover all the usual woods with which you will probably work. When you have become proficient in handling them, you can confidently try some of the more unusual woods.

In addition to so-called brown staining, there is a blonde finish, which is popular with designers of

Woods Used in Finishing

Type	*Characteristics*
American Woods	
Hard:	
Birch	Takes all kinds of stains well; no filler required; used for veneers, to imitate other woods, for trim, interior finishings, furniture; good for blonde finishes
Cherry	Takes light reddish stain; generally no filler needed unless lacquered; will not bleach; used for furniture, to imitate mahogany
Hickory	Takes water stain best; takes fine polish after sanding; generally a heavy filler needed; used for furniture, to imitate mahogany and walnut
Maple	Stains well in lighter colors; takes fine finish; no filler needed; widely used for furniture, veneers, floors
Oak	Takes many kinds of stains; heavy filler generally needed, but not for many period effects; widely used, especially for floors and heavier pieces of furniture
Walnut	Takes many stains well; bleaches well; heavy filler generally needed, except for old English effect; used for furniture, veneers
Soft:	
Cypress	Takes oil and water stains well; close, even grain; used for interior and exterior trim, garden furniture
Fir	Takes oil stains well; has very strong figure; used for interior trim; doors, flooring, also shelves, cupboards
Pine, yellow	Takes oil stain well; prominent grain; resinous; widely used for bedroom and kitchen furniture, closets, bookcases, floors
Pine, white	Takes oil and water stains well; no filler needed generally; straight grained; when finished is generally used to imitate maple
Redwood	Takes red stain well; does not readily bleach or take lighter stains; filler sometimes used; used for veneers
Imported Woods	
Avodire	Natural finish preferable; takes light stain; requires filler; bleaches well
Circassian Walnut	Stains well; bleaches well; requires filler; has very fancy figure; used mostly for veneers
Mahogany, Philippine	Takes all stains well; needs heavy filler; has very beautiful grain; used for furniture, trim, floors, to imitate walnut and true mahogany; may fade if not properly finished
Mahogany, true	Takes all stains well; generally needs filler; excellent color and figure; used for furniture; often called the finest of all woods
Rosewood	Requires "washing" before finishing; needs filler; will not bleach; used mostly for veneers
Satinwood	Takes light stains; often finished naturally; needs filler; will not bleach; used mostly for veneer and inlay

modern furniture. Then, too, there is the processing of less expensive woods to resemble the more valuable types. A good finisher can do amazing things with stain, glaze, shellac, varnish, and lacquer.

Hard and Soft Woods

Woods are commonly classified as hard and soft. This classification is of concern in finishing as indicating the powers of absorption of the wood. In general, soft woods absorb the stain more readily and consequently require a lighter mixture. A list of woods frequently used in finishing is shown in the accompanying table.

PREPARATIONS

General Preparations

Some general instructions apply to the preliminary treatment of all woods. The surface must be clean. There should be no finger marks, oil stains, or other smudges. To remove them, apply a little benzine, alcohol, or turpentine. If the marks are deeply ingrained, use a little paint remover and rinse with benzine or turpentine.

Fig. 1. You can raise grain by merely sponging the surface with water. A little glue added to the water will do a more thorough job.

The wood should be free of machine markings or scratches. These markings come from the ribbed rollers which push the planks through the milling machine. Often they must be removed by hand or machine planing.

Other marks, more widely spaced, generally come from blades that are poorly set in the machines. These also must be removed by hand planing. Scratches are also generally too deep to be removed with sandpaper.

When your wood surface is perfectly clean and smooth you are then ready to proceed in one of two ways—by water staining or by oil staining.

Preparation for Water Staining

If you intend to use water stain and want a very fine finish, the best practice is to raise the grain and sand it smooth. By raising the grain at this point and sandpapering, you prevent the grain from rising later when you apply the water stain. You can achieve this by sponging the surface with water and sandpapering it when dry. This, however, does only a partial job. To do it thoroughly, mix one or two tablespoons of glue with a quart of water, and use this for sponging. Sponge it on but do not leave any puddles. When dry, the glue will hold up the fibers of the wood. Thus your sandpaper will remove them rather than push many of them back down again. Use a #2/0 sandpaper for this work. If you wish a particularly fine job, finish sanding with #5/0. Always sandpaper in the direction of the grain. It will take ten strokes with the grain to remove scratches made by one stroke across the grain. Use a cork sanding-block or a sandpaper holder sold in paint stores. While a soft wood block is usually satisfactory, it can dent or bruise the surface you are trying to make smooth if you're not careful.

Raising Dents. For dents, you can frequently raise the dented portion by carefully wetting it with water. Do this with a small brush and do not bring the water to the very edges of the dent. The absorption of the wood will take care of the least dented, outer ring. You may have to repeat the wetting to raise the deepest part. If the dent or bruise is too deep to be raised, you will have to resort to one of the materials made for repairing this kind of damage, a hardening cellulose compound. Be certain the wood is dry, and then apply according to directions. When the applied material is dry, sandpaper to the same smooth surface as the surrounding wood. Although this material will not take the stain the same as the wood, a little touching-up will take care of the difference.

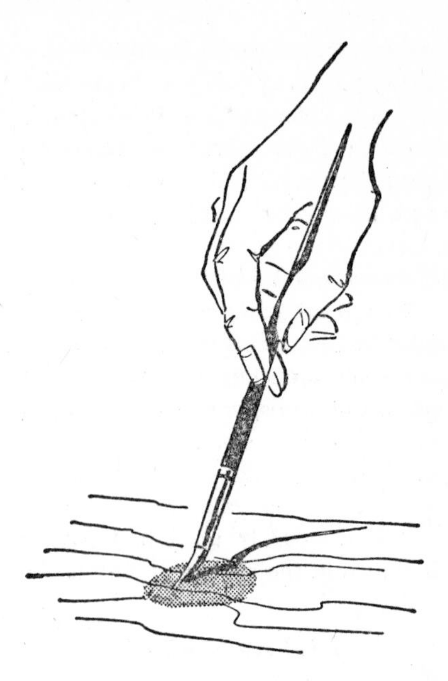

Fig. 3. To raise a dent, wet it carefully with a small brush, as shown above, but do not brush the edges of the dent.

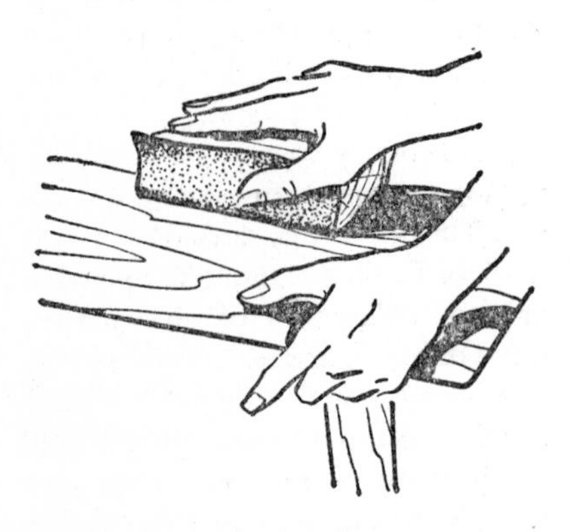

Fig. 2. Use sanding paper and a soft wood block, and always stroke with the grain.

Preparation for Oil Staining

Oil stains do not raise the grain, consequently there is nothing to be gained in wetting the surface before sanding. Carefully check the surface for markings. Remove any marks you find, and sandpaper. Use the medium or fine grades of sandpaper, depending on the smoothness you desire.

Special Preparations for Staining

Scraping. Hard woods, such as oak, are much improved by scraping rather than sanding. This scraping operation leaves the surface of the wood clearer and more brilliant. It is essentially a planing process, but it is done with a steel blade slanting in the direction of the stroke. This direction must be the same as the grain. If you do not have a scraper and your job is a small one, a small piece of newly cut, flat glass will do. Needless to say, be careful. You can get a bad cut. If you use glass, rub a file along the last quarter inch of the cutting edge. Then your scraping will not show tool marks.

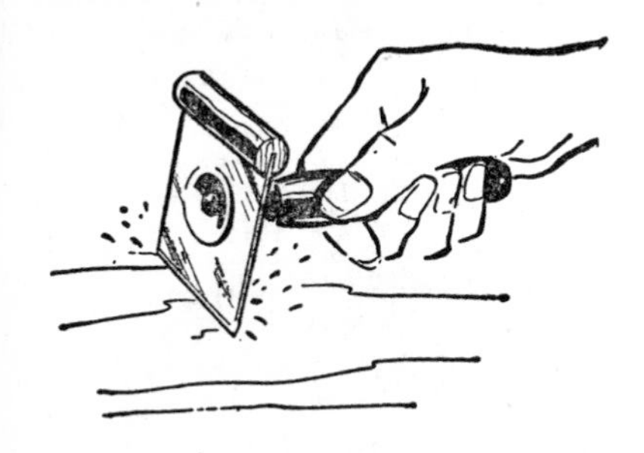

Fig. 4. Hard woods are often scraped instead of sanded. The steel blade of the scraper should slant in the direction of the stroke.

Removing Discolorations. Occasionally you will have to work with wood which has natural dark streaks. It is best to remove as much of this darkness as possible before staining. This is accomplished in the same way as bleaching for blonde finishes, which is described more fully on page 190. For this touch-up work, confine the solutions to the dark areas and follow the directions for blonde finishes. Frequently a slight discoloration can be cleared up with an application of any common brand of sodium hypochlorite preparation. After the bleach is dry, sandpaper to remove salt from the surface of the wood. The wood is then ready for staining.

Removing Sap Stains. Sap stains frequently occur in the soft woods, such as the pines. It takes two forms: a brown color caused by a fungus, or a blue color caused chemically. There are other brown discolorations caused by high temperatures in the kiln-drying process or machine burns. These are readily removed by planing. The fungus brown stains, however, usually go deeper – even through the wood. Try to remove the stains by planing. If they are only surface deep, you are fortunate. If they penetrate through the wood, it is best to replace the wood, if possible. The growing fungus has weakened the cells of the wood and, under the right conditions of humidity and temperature, may continue to grow. Bleaching the surface and treating the wood with a colorless preservative such as a copper napthenate may be helpful.

Blue sap stains are less harmful to the strength of the wood but are very discouraging to the finisher. Almost nothing will restore the wood to its normal light color. Even if the bleach does accomplish this on the surface, the stains will generally recur.

Neutralizing Sap. Some woods with a high oily sap content are frequently improved for staining if they are treated with a strong alkali. To do this, wear rubber gloves and a rubber apron. Make a solution of ½ pound of sodium hydroxide or potassium hydroxide to one gallon of water. Use a wooden or enamel pail. Common lye is not recommended as it contains too many impurities. Using handfuls of cotton waste, thoroughly wet the surface. Let the solution soak in for about twenty minutes, then rinse down with plain water or a weak solution of oxalic acid or vinegar and water. The plain water will leave the wood a lemon yellow, and the acid or vinegar solution will make it more neutral. When the wood has dried, you can sandpaper it. Then it is ready for staining. This process is commonly used to effect an antique finish on white pine.

Equalizing Wood Color. On stained wood, differences in color between heartwood and recent growth are most easily taken care of after staining. The lighter outside growth can be given a light glaze to equalize the color. If the finish is to be blonde, it is better to bleach the heartwood a second time.

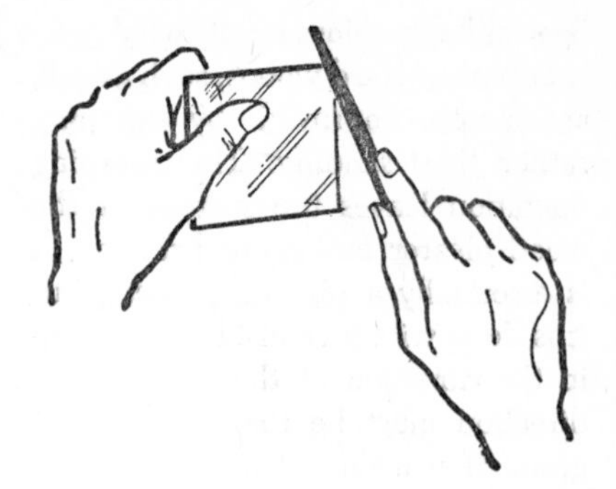

Fig. 5. You can make your own scraper from a piece of glass. File the corners to prevent making tool marks on the wood.

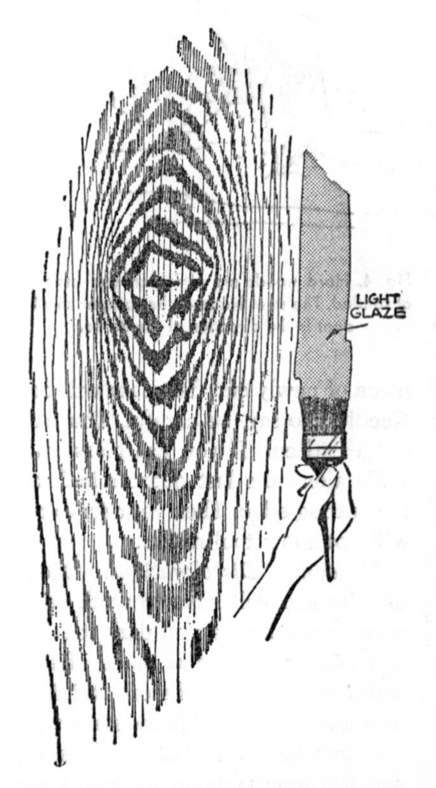

Fig. 6. After staining, a light glaze on the outside growth of wood will equalize the color between it and the heart growth.

STAINS AND STAINING

Water Stains

If you are dissatisfied with the clarity of oil stains and you have noticed that oil stains fade, you may want to try water stains. As you have probably noted in the discussion of the preparation of the surface, water is one of the most penetrating liquids you can put on wood. The deeper you can make the water stain penetrate, the better the color. All paint stores carry small envelopes of water-soluble aniline stains. These will make about one quart of stain, enough to stain more than 100 square feet of surface. Follow directions on the envelope for mixing and applying.

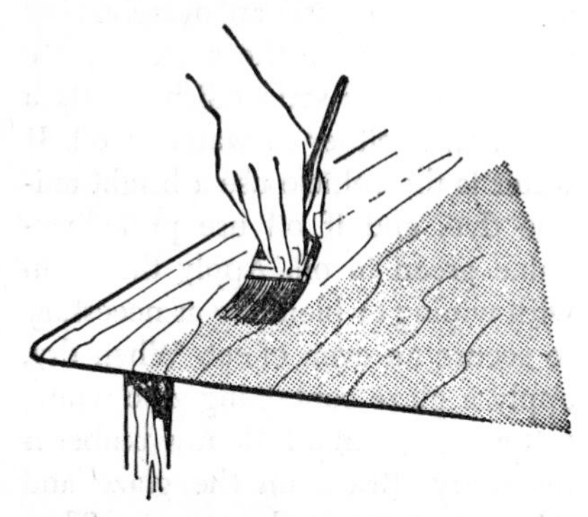

Fig. 7. Use a medium-soft bristle brush to apply water stain, but do not saturate it.

Water-Soluble Anilines. The water-soluble anilines are also available in quantity If you wish to stock the basic colors to mix your own stains, the following will make almost any stain color.

1. Walnut extract
2. Crimson Red
3. Auramine Yellow
4. Nigrosine Black
5. Malachite Green

Walnut extract should be mixed with water and placed in a covered stone crock or wide-necked bottle. It will thoroughly dissolve overnight and is then readily soluble in water. It is the stain you will use most. One pound will make a quart of highly concentrated stain. A pound of any of the other colors will last you a lifetime.

Most woods are stained some shade of brown. The best approach is to mix a walnut stain of nearly the required shade, and then change the tone by the addition of one or more of the other anilines.

Water stain is best applied with a medium-soft black bristle brush. Do not saturate the brush. Drops that fall on unstained wood will show as dark spots. Apply the brush with the grain, along the full length of the piece of wood. Breaks or laps will show as darker patches. Always stain panels first, then mouldings, and finally, stiles and rails. The stain should be dry within an hour, if the humidity is not too high. If you wish to highlight the panels or mouldings, you can wipe lightly with a damp cloth. Wring the cloth well and shake any water off your hands or you will have light spots on your wood that you won't be able to touch up. This wiping, or highlighting, can be done while the stain is still damp. You can also use this procedure to remove stain from naturally dark areas of wood.

Oil Stains

Oil stain has the advantage of being more easily applied than water stain. An oil stain is a simple mixture consisting of a pigment, raw linseed oil, turpentine, and drier. You can readily make your own stain with these ordinary materials. For one gallon of brown oak stain use:

½ lb burnt umber in oil
3½ qts turpentine
1 pt raw linseed oil
½ oz Japan driers

This stain is easy to apply, simple to wipe out, and it dries hard. This kind of stain can be brushed or sprayed. After the stain has had time to soak into the surface, you must wipe off the excess. The time for soaking in will vary from about three minutes to twenty minutes. The shorter time will be for the softer woods like pine. Hard woods, such as oak, take longer.

Brown Stains can be made with the following pigments:

burnt umber
Vandyke brown
burnt sienna
or
chrome yellow medium
chrome yellow orange
lamp black

Warm Brown Stain:
burnt umber
burnt sienna

Gray Stain:
burnt umber
lamp black

Mahogany Red Stain:
burnt sienna
or
rose pink
burnt umber

Green Stain: Phthalocyanine Green

An improved form of this stain is "penetrating oil stain." You will probably have to buy this material. It is now available in a wide range of colors, and the colors are clearer than the stains you can make. It is made with oil aniline stains. If you can obtain these colors, you can make the stain. Add the necessary color to a mixture of 40 parts solvent naptha and 1 part gloss oil. This stain can also be brushed or sprayed. After soaking in, it should be wiped to clear the surface.

Another finish which is popular is a clear green with an overglaze of soft gray. Prepare the wood surface as for all other stain finishes. Mix a green stain either in water or oil. If water is the vehicle use a bright aniline dye, and if oil use phthalocyanine green in oil. Apply this stain with wiping or blending as necessary to secure an even effect. When dry, apply a glaze containing zinc white, rottenstone, and a little raw umber if necessary. Brush on the glaze and wipe to remove the excess. Then blend the still wet glaze to an even finish with an almost dry brush. When this two-stage staining operation is complete, you can apply any one of the standard finishes, shellac, varnish, or wax.

Spirit Stains

These are similar to water stains except for the thinning liquid, which is denatured alcohol. The extremely rapid rate of evaporation makes this stain almost impossible to brush on a large surface, but it can be sprayed by a good operator. In fact, it is one of the preferred materials for shaded panels. You have probably seen furniture whose panels are very light in the center and blended darker into the corners. Sprayed spirit stain is an ideal material for this process. Unless you have the equipment or intend to do production work, it is not recommended that you struggle with this type of stain. If you are going into production work, the large furniture-finishing supply houses will be glad to make up batches of stain and give you specific instructions for their use.

Chemical Stains

These are the most interesting stains and the most difficult to use. Industry has generally given up manufacturing them because of their inherent difficulties. Yet for the person interested in the very finest colors obtainable, and willing to take the time to check and test at every step, no finer stain can be found.

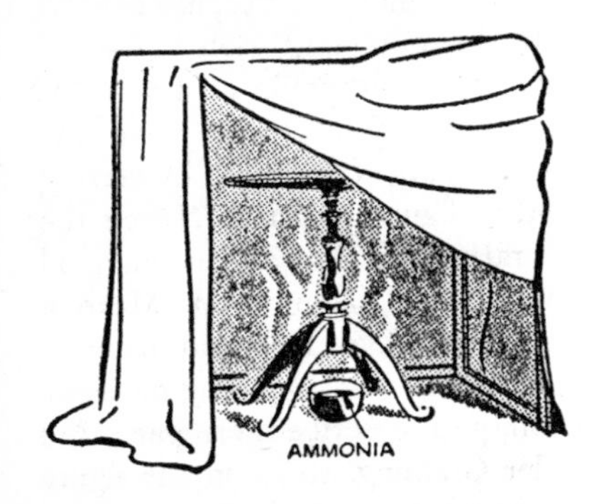

Fig. 8. A simple fuming enclosure for fuming oak. One side is drawn back to show the proper arrangement. During actual fuming, the enclosure should be completely enclosed.

The most commonly used of these stains is potassium bichromate on mahogany. You can start with one ounce in a quart of water. This will give you a medium-dark brown on genuine mahogany. Brush the solution on, being careful not to make laps. If you wish a darker and purpler color on your mahogany, dissolve from one to two ounces of potassium permanganate in one quart of water and apply. Test these colors on a sample board of the same wood, or on the under side of the wood if no sample is available. They will give your mahogany the rich color of a good antique. All the best in the figure of the wood will be brought out. Chemical stains do not coat the wood with a dye or pigment. They actually change the color of the wood.

Fuming Oak. Oak can be fumed to a rich brown with 28 per cent ammonia. Make a frame big enough to enclose the piece of furniture. Cover the frame with heavy paper, tar paper, or the new crêpe paper dropcloths. Place the piece of furniture inside and put a glass or china bowl of this strong ammonia on the floor under the piece of furniture. Close the opening in the enclosure and let the fumes go to work on the oak. In one or two days the oak will have darkened and is then ready for further finishing. The grain will not have been raised and the wood will be a rich warm brown. Use a minimum of finish on fumed oak. One good coat of shellac and several coats of a fine polishing wax will do justice to the color.

Sulphate of iron in water solution will make some woods black and others gray. This is an excellent base for black finishes with white filler in the pores, but you had better check with a sample of the same wood.

You can use either potassium bichromate or potassium permanganate on oak for either orange or purplish browns, and potassium hydroxide will give you a very reddish brown on oak. A spoonful of this caustic will make a very strong stain.

Nitric, sulphuric, and picric acids have also been used. In weak solutions these acids produce yellowish colors on most woods.

Caution. All these stains are caustic chemicals. You should handle all of them excepting the potassium permanganate and potassium bichromate with caution. Wear rubber gloves. Place them in containers of glass or china. If your hands stain purple after using the potassium permanganate, dip them in an oxalic acid solution. Then wash immediately, as oxalic is a strong poison. Care *must* be exercised in using chemical stains. Read carefully the instruction on the container.

Varnish Stains

These are simply varnishes to which some pigment or oil-soluble aniline has been added. They are available in a variety of colors. You will find that it requires considerable skill to spread these colored varnishes evenly. They are effective for simple, quick work which will not be criticized for having a false look of stained or finished wood.

Staining

Blending Out. More often than not you will find that your stain has not taken evenly. There will be some areas too light and others too dark. If you used an oil stain, you can carefully brush a second coat over the light area. For this purpose, make a cloth pad about the size of an egg, moisten the pad with turpentine, and pad off the right amount of stain to even the color. If the stain was water or chemical, darkening a light area is best left until the first coat of shellac has been applied. Make up a glaze (see page 155) and carefully darken the area. Areas that are too dark in chemical or water stains are reduced by padding with a water-moistened pad. Spirit stains are best reduced by rubbing with fine steel wool, preferably #3/0. Build up light areas as with water or chemical stains.

Veining. Occasionally, in the interest of economy or because of difficulty in obtaining richly figured wood, a simple grade of a wood is substituted. You can improve the natural figure of this piece by glazing another figure on to it. Notice the natural color of the veining of a good piece of the same wood. Make a glaze (see page 155) and color it to match the veining. Using the same techniques described on page 214 under Graining, strike in the figure and blend it in to make it seem natural. It is best to do this work on the first coat of shellac, so that you have maximum control of the process. Ribbon mahogany is probably the wood most often so treated. Whitewood and gum are frequently used as substitutes for mahogany and walnut. Good imitations of fine woods can be made this way.

Fillers

Many open-pored woods such as oak, ash, chestnut, mahogany, and walnut are treated with a filler. The purpose of this is to fill the pores flush with the surface of the wood. The filler can be lighter, the same color, or darker than the stained wood. The most commonly used form of filler is made of silica (sand), raw linseed oil, turpentine, and Japan drier. It is obtainable in a natural shade (almost white), or tinted with a variety of colors to match most stains. It is not recommended that you make your own filler, as it should be properly ground in a mill.

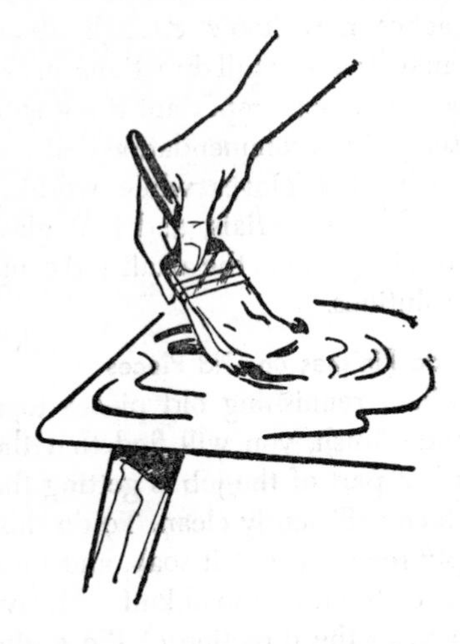

Fig. 9. In applying filler, brush with the grain, then across it, and finish with a light stroke along the grain again.

Applying Fillers. The application of a filler is relatively simple. Most labels carry specific instructions on the amount of turpentine to add for various woods. The larger the pores in the wood, the less thinning of the filler is a good general rule. In blonde finishes the filler may be applied to the raw wood after bleaching. On stained wood, it is best applied after the stain. Use color to match the stain.

Stir the filler well and continue to stir it as you apply. The filler settles rapidly and will not fill the pores unless it is of an even consistency. Brush the filler on, using a partly worn brush with stiff bristles. Brush with the grain and then across it to force the paste into every pore. Finish with a light stroke along the grain. After the filler has dried for the time indicated on the label, generally 15 to 30 minutes, it is ready for wiping. You can check when it is ready by the appearance of light or dull areas. The filler is ready for wiping when nearly all the thinners have evaporated.

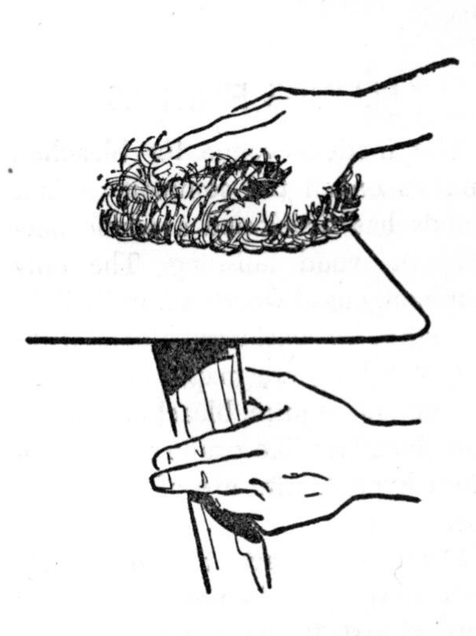

Fig. 10. After the filler has dried sufficiently, wipe it—excelsior will do nicely—first across the grain and then with the grain, but not too hard.

The wiping operation is generally done with excelsior or burlap. Start the wiping by going across the grain. This will remove most of the excess filler but will leave the surface streaked. Complete the wiping by going with the grain. Be careful not to use too much pressure on these strokes or you will pull the moist filler out of the pores. Allow 24 hours for drying.

Tinting Fillers. To tint fillers, it is the common practice to buy natural filler and add any of the common colors ground-in-oil. This way you can match your stain color more closely.

BLONDE FINISHES

The modern vogue for bleached finishes on all the common cabinet woods has developed a whole new field of wood finishing. The only commonly used woods naturally light enough to be considered blonde without bleaching are maple and birch. All others require bleaching. Ordinary bleaches like oxalic acid or sodium hypochlorite are of very little use.

Strong two-part bleaches have been developed. In use the alkali is applied first. It dissolves the coloring matter in the wood. Then a strong bleach is applied which bleaches the dissolved color. When this second coat is dry, the surface is sanded to remove the salt crust which accumulates. In general, one application of the #1 and #2 parts of the bleach are sufficient. If not, a second application of the #2 solution is enough.

For partial bleaching action to make the "wheat" finishes, two variations on the blonde finish are used. One is to apply the #1 solution only. Follow this by sanding. The other is to apply both solutions and to lightly sponge water over the #2 solution before it has dried.

Most of the manufacturers of these bleaches now know enough about them to give you full directions on the label. The most important thing is to observe the recommendation that you wear rubber gloves while working with these materials, and that glass be used to contain the alkali and caustic solutions.

Blonde Finishes on Old Pieces

When refinishing old pieces to a blonde finish, you will find that the hardest part of the job is getting the surface sufficiently clean. To do this, apply remover. Let it soak, and then scrape off with a broad knife. Always scrape in the direction of the grain. One application is seldom enough. Two or three are better. If most of the finish came off with the first coat, scrub the second with steel wool. Have a can of benzine handy. Dip the steel wool into it as soon as it is saturated with remover and old finish. Finish up with a thorough scrubbing, using naphtha, benzine, or alcohol. Any of these solvents will remove the wax and sludge. You will find that an ordinary scrubbing brush will be helpful, especially if the wood is one of the open-grain varieties. Remember, it is almost impossible to get the wood as clean as new wood. For restaining, a good cleaning is sufficient, but for bleaching the cleaning must be perfect. The finishes to follow bleaching will be described under "Other Finishes," just below.

Care in Using Remover and Solvents

You cannot be cautioned too much about the danger of fire or an attack of nausea from the use of removers and the rinsing solvents. Work in a well-ventilated place. Step outside for a breath of fresh air while the remover is soaking in. Above all, avoid having matches around. Do not work in a cellar where there is a furnace or any open flame. The fumes of the remover are particularly inflammable. Unfortunately, you cannot work out of doors with these removers, except on a warm, still day. Even then you must work in the shade or the solvents will evaporate too rapidly to soften the old finish. In factories using these materials, the work area is always under a hood and forced ventilation is continuously provided.

OTHER FINISHES

The purpose of applying a finish to wood is basic. It protects the wood from moisture and dirt. We have taken advantage of the fact that wood needs this finish, to preserve and beautify the appearance. We use a variety of materials for the purpose, the simplest being a drying oil, and the most complex, a sprayed lacquer. Those most commonly used, and their application, will be treated in this section. You can apply all of these finishes over the stains previously described.

Linseed Oil Finish

Boiled linseed oil makes an excellent finish if you have the time and patience to apply it. A high-gloss finish may require seven or eight coats. Brush a coat of oil on the surface, let it soak in for about a half hour, then wipe off the excess, and allow to dry at least one, and preferably two, days. Repeat this process until you have built up the desired finish. Do not apply a new coat if the previous one is at all soft. There are other finishing oils on the market and you may find one which exactly suits your purpose. It is unlikely that it will contain anything harmful. If you are satisfied with the finish, do not hesitate to use it.

Wax Finish

A simple finish similar to oil is wax. If placed on raw or stained wood, it is best to use the liquid type of wax for the first and possibly the second coats. Apply the liquid wax with a brush, let it soak in, wipe off the excess, and allow to dry overnight. When you have built up a good body and it is thoroughly dry, apply a coat of very hard drying wax containing some carnauba wax and vigorously polish to a good lustre. A scrubbing brush makes an excellent polishing tool on the harder woods.

Shellac Finish

Shellac is probably the commonest material used for finishing. It has many qualities that contribute to its usefulness. It is relatively inexpensive, simple to dilute, flows well if properly brushed, sandpapers or rubs to a good surface, and dries quickly. Its only drawbacks are that it remains alcohol-soluble and blooms, or whitens, under excessively humid conditions.

It is generally purchased in gallon cans marked either 4- or 5-pound cut. This means that the manufacturer dissolved 4 or 5 pounds of dried shellac in one gallon of denatured alcohol. If you are not going to use all the shellac within several weeks, it is recommended that you transfer it to a glass container. Metal reacts with it and turns it dark. This is so whether it is white or orange shellac. While it is true that you can bleach it back to almost its original color by adding one or two tablespoons of oxalic crystals and allowing these to soak overnight, the glass container saves you this trouble.

Applying Shellac. For use as the first coat, thin the shellac with a little more than the same amount of denatured alcohol. Use only 190 proof denatured alcohol. Anti-freeze alcohol is only 90 proof, the rest being water, which will cause the shellac to bloom. Using a soft bristle brush, flow on the shellac. Start at one end of the surface and stroke to the other end, always going with the grain. Continue this, being careful not to lap the strokes. Shellac of the right consistency will flow to a smooth finish. Brushing it out will roughen up the surface. Later coats can be as heavy as three pounds to the gallon. Anything heavier than this will cause pockmarks. Between each coat you should sandpaper or steel wool the previous coat; #2/0 steel wool is correct for all but the last coat. The last coat should be done with #3/0. You can speed up the polishing by dipping this steel wool (#3/0) into a pan of liquid wax and combining the operations of rubbing and waxing. When the wax is dry, simply polish with a dry rag or scrubbing brush. If you sandpaper between coats to make the surface flatter, use #0 for the first and second coats. Wrap the paper on a soft block, like cork or felt-covered wood. For the final coat use #5/0 or #7/0. This will give you a finish which can be polished by simply waxing.

If you wish a superfine finish, you can apply four coats of the shellac, sanding between coats. Then rub the finish with oil and pumice, and end up with oil and rottenstone. This will be described in detail later in this chapter.

Varnish

Gloss. A waterproof and frequently alcohol-proof finish is made with varnish. Varnish is a cooked mixture of gums, drying oils, thinners, and driers. The proper varnish to use for furniture or woodwork is called "cabinet rubbing." It dries to a hard glossy surface which can readily be sanded and rubbed. The general practice is to put one coat of thin shellac on the stain and follow this with the varnish. Most varnishes take much longer than shellac to dry. Very few, not excepting the fast-drying type, can be sanded before 24 hours have passed. However, varnishes do, almost without exception, have flowing qualities far superior to shellac.

Brush varnishes on with almost the same free stroke as used for shellac. Do not brush over the same area more than three times. Apply with the grain, brush across the grain once, and finish off with a light stroke once more with the grain. If you can flow on an even coat without having to brush across the grain, your work will look better.

Rubbing the final coat can be done with water and pumice if you wish to speed up the job. The water is less lubricating than other mediums, consequently the pumice cuts faster. Check the state of your rubbing by drawing a small rubber squeegee over a patch of the surface. As always, go in the direction of the grain. Using water and a soft rag, wipe all pumice off the surface when finished, dry the surface with a damp chamois, and finish the rubbing with rottenstone and oil. See full directions for rubbing below.

Semi-Matte and Flat Varnishes. If the job does not warrant the time and labor of rubbing it to a smooth finish, you can use a semi-matte or flat varnish. These are varnishes to which a wax or other material has been added to reduce the glossy surface, and they are entirely satisfactory if carefully applied. They provide the protection required, but the clarity of a rubbed finish is missing. This material is best applied with a spray gun although it can be brushed on.

Lacquers

These modern finishes can be applied successfully only with a spray gun. They dry in a matter of minutes, much too fast to brush. Made of nitro-cellulose and thinned with a highly inflammable liquid, these finishes require a spray booth. A wide variety of finishes is available, and you should use a lacquer particularly suited to your job. In addition, you must stain with water and use a special filler which will not rise under the effect of the strong solvents in the lacquer thinner. It is recommended that you consult a dealer who is familiar with this material before proceeding to use it. Most lacquers can be rubbed the same as shellac or varnish. In fact, there are special wax rubbing compounds made for them which are fast and effective.

"Bleaching lacquer" is one of the most useful of modern lacquers. Used on the blonde and wheat finishes so popular today, it contains a bleach which helps to overcome the slight darkening effect of a finish and to keep the finish light. All heavily bleached woods tend to darken in time, and the presence of a bleach helps in part to keep the wood as light as intended.

RUBBING

Rubbing is a simple operation if you use the right materials and tools. Assemble a rubbing block as indicated in the illustration, or one similar to it, and purchase some #2/0 pumice stone and rottenstone in powder form. In addition, buy some crude oil and lemon oil. For checking your work, cut a piece of rubber about 2x2x¼ inches from an old rub-

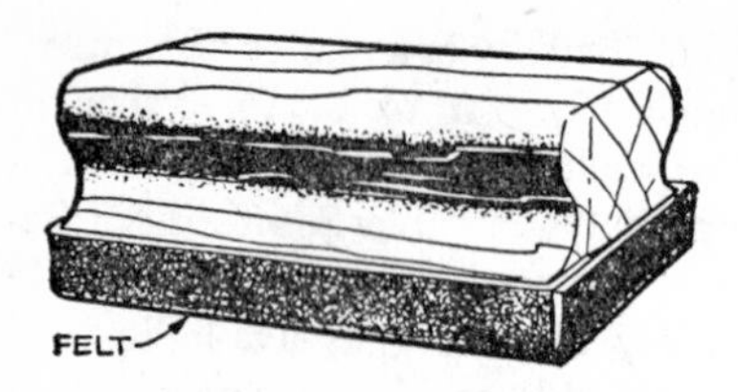

Fig. 11. You can make a rubbing block easily from a piece of wood and a strip of felt. A professional model is shown above.

ber mat or an old rubber heel. (See Figure 12.)

Oil Rubbing

Place about 4 tablespoons of pumice in a saucer or small pie pan and pour in enough crude oil to make a creamy paste. Dab some crude oil over the surface to be rubbed. Use a rag or your fingers. Dip a felt pad into the oil and pumice and start your rubbing. Always rub with the grain, and stop when you see dull spots. Dab some oil on these dull spots and continue rubbing. After fifteen or twenty strokes over any one area, check with the rubber squeegee. If the surface is perfectly flat, move on to unrubbed areas.

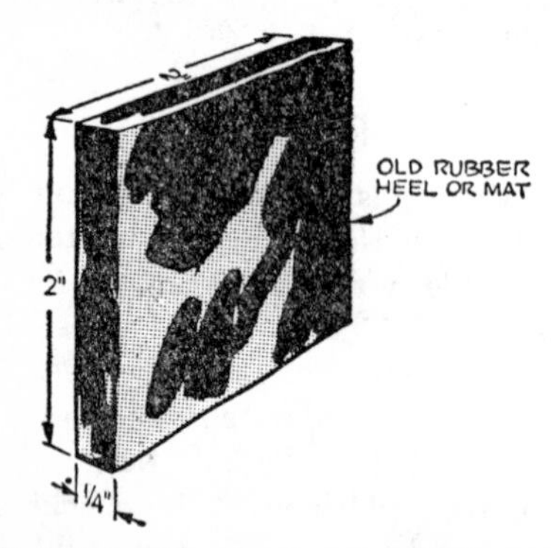

Fig. 12. A rubber squeegee for checking your work can be cut out of old rubber.

When the whole surface is flat, wash off the oil and pumice with benzine or turpentine, and rinse your pad. Now make up a similar dish of

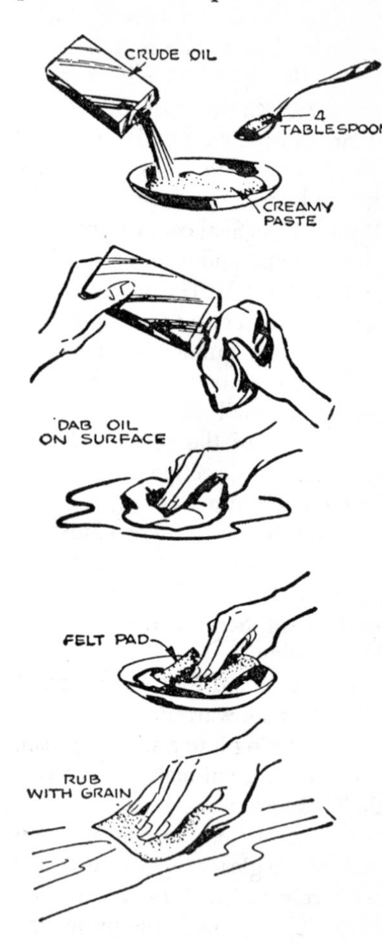

Fig. 13. Successive steps in oil rubbing: Mixing, dabbing oil on surface, picking up mixture, and rubbing it in.

rottenstone and lemon oil and proceed as before. You do not need to test; simply polish a small area with a dry cloth and continue until you have polished the whole surface. If an excess of rottenstone and oil has accumulated in the corners, rinse them off with turpentine, and then complete the polishing. This procedure can give you a mirror-like finish if the steps are followed carefully and done thoroughly. Be careful not to rub through. Frequent testing with your squeegee will tell you when the varnish film is getting too thin.

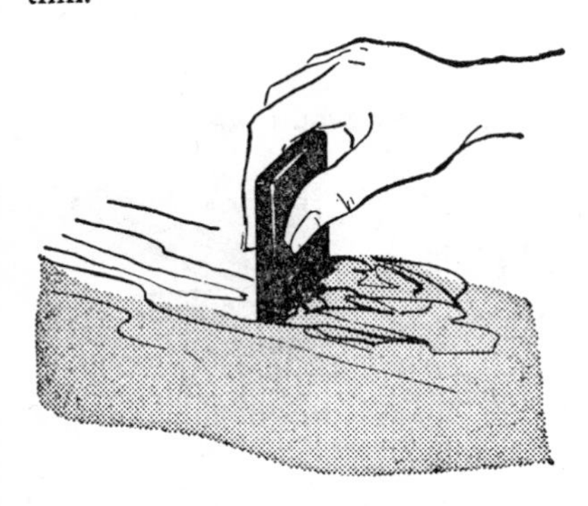

Fig. 14. Testing with a squeegee to determine that the surface is flat or has been rubbed sufficiently.

Rubbing carvings or deep mouldings is best done with a stubby, worn-out sash tool. Use it instead of a pad. All the other steps are the same.

If you are going into production on this type of work, you will want to purchase a machine rubber. It will save you a great deal of time.

Water Rubbing

This is done the same as oil rubbing. Simply substitute water for the crude oil in the rubbing operation. It is not advisable to use this method on shellac due to the possibility of blooming. Water rubbing is somewhat faster than oil, but the difference is only worth considering for a large job, such as paneled walls.

You have a choice in the finishing step. You can use lemon oil and polish as you complete the rubbing, or you can use water. Then wash clean and wax polish.

Rubbing Compound

This material is made for use on lacquers or the new synthetic finishes (used on your auto), and consists of a wax emulsion and an abrasive. To apply it, keep the surface moist with water. Dip a cloth pad into the compound and rub with the grain. You will feel when the abrasive has worn out and can check your finish by polishing with a dry cloth. If not satisfactory, moisten the surface with water again and continue the rubbing. Instructions for use on various materials are available from the manufacturers, if they do not appear on the label.

POLISHING OILS AND WAXES

Oils

Practically every old-fashioned wood finisher has his favorite formula for a polishing oil. Many of them have merit, but it hardly seems worthwhile to try to investigate all of them when there are excellent manufactured ones available at reasonable cost. Most polishing oils are based upon a lemon or linseed oil mixture with other oils, such as camphor, added. If it will polish out dry with a reasonable amount of rubbing and if it has a high lustre, you have about all you can expect of a polishing oil. Test the dryness by dragging your finger across the polished surface. If it marks, the surface is not fully polished or dry. If, after additional polishing, it still marks, find a more suitable oil polish.

Waxes

Rubbing waxes, if properly made, are probably the best materials for giving a finish a high lustre which will not mark. The problem is simply one of spreading it on evenly in the correct amount. When using liquid wax, the tendency is to put too heavy a coat on the surface. It will polish beautifully but will continue to mark until worn down by repeated dry polishings.

Those paste waxes that contain enough carnauba wax to dry the polish to a hard, long-wearing finish, are probably the best. However, they require a great deal more effort to apply and polish.

Self-polishing waxes are satisfactory for large areas which will not be severely criticized, but observe the directions on the can very carefully. The manufacturers, recognizing some of the problems raised by the contents, will warn you not to use them on certain finishes.

PATCHING AND REPAIRING

Scratches

The commonest damage to a finish is a scratch. If it is not deep enough to be described as a tear or bruise, you can repair it by rubbing a colored-wax stick over the mark. These sticks are obtainable from large paint stores and radio supply houses.

Burning-in

If the damage is deeper than a scratch, it will be best for you to call on the services of an expert. However, if you do the repair yourself, buy stick shellac. This is a piece of

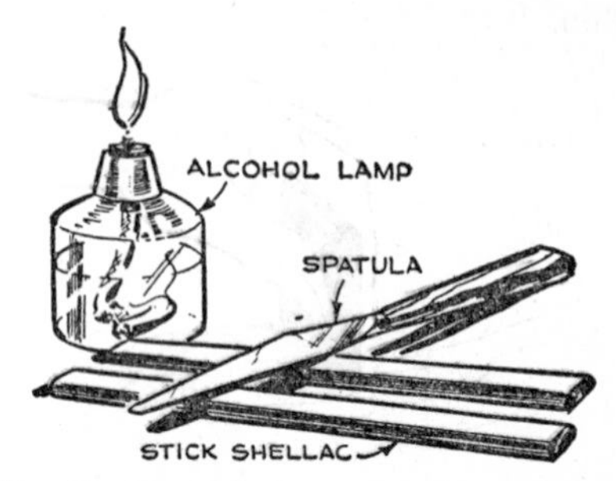

Fig. 15. Materials for repairing tears and bruises in a finish.

hardened shellac. Using an artist's spatula and a small alcohol lamp, heat the spatula blade until it melts the shellac. Drip the shellac into the deepest part of the cut, and very carefully smooth it out flush, using the heated spatula. It is recommended that you practice this before trying it on a good piece of furniture.

Amalgamater

If the scratch is slight but noticeable, you can use a liquid called amalgamater. This will, if properly used, soften the finish on either side of the scratch and flow it over the scratch. Again, practice first. Used carelessly, the solvent action can go farther than you want it to.

Burns

Cigarette burns can only be scraped out, stained, and touched up with a ready-made French polish. You can obtain this from large supply houses.

Bloom

Bloom, which is an all-over milky appearance on a finish, can be removed from a shellacked surface. Dip a soft cheesecloth pad into 190 proof denatured alcohol. Wring it out thoroughly. Shake your hands off well after wringing out the pad as every drip will make a mark which will be almost impossible to get out. With strokes about as fast as you would paint, pass the pad over the finish. If the finish is shellac, the bloom will disappear as if by magic. If it does not, the probability is that the finish was not shellac, after all. In that case, you will have to use the proper amalgamater.

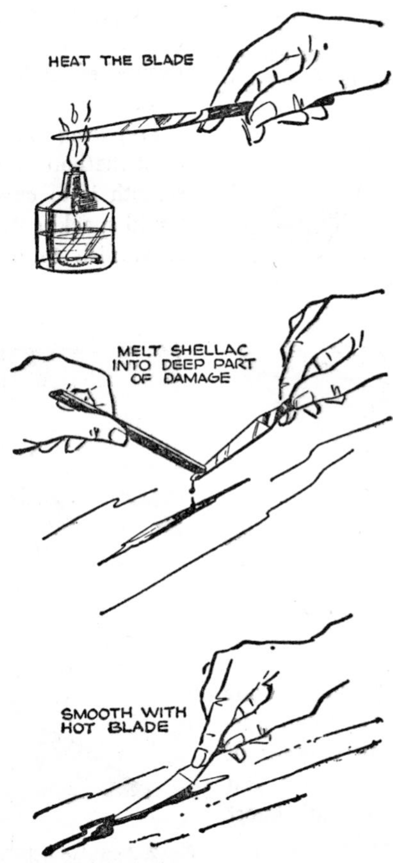

Fig. 16. Procedure in repairing a deep cut.

CHAPTER 13

SPECIAL FINISHES

GILDING

Gilding is a general term referring to the application of metallic powders or leaf on a prepared surface. At one time it meant the use of gold only, but with the development of less expensive substitutes the term came to be used for them as well.

Fig. 1. Gold leaf is used to obtain decorative effects on furniture. It is sold in booklets or rolls and is actually pure gold pounded to 1/200,000 of an inch.

Bronze Powders

The least expensive gilding is done with bronze powders. You can purchase these in different degrees of fineness and in a variety of hues. You have a wide selection, from an almost silver yellow to a brownish antique gold. The finer the particles of bronze, the more finished the job will look and the more closely it will resemble polished metal. The surface upon which the bronze is painted must be perfectly smooth. The finest quality of bronze powder will not give the desired effect if put on a rough surface.

Preparing the Ground. The simplest method of making the ground smooth is to cover it with a warm liquid spackle. Add about one ounce of varnish to one pint of spackle.

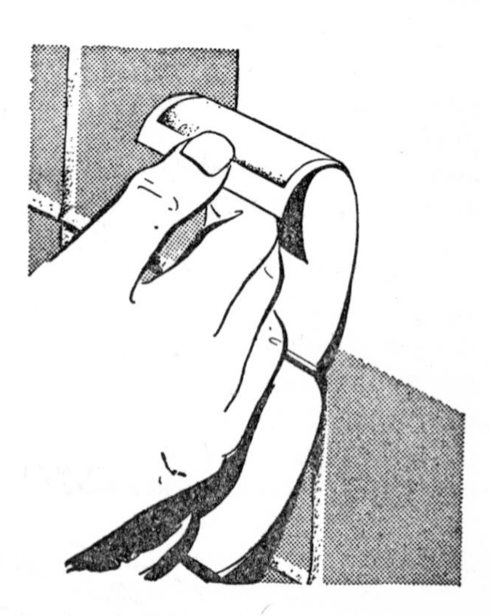

Fig. 2. Applying gold leaf takes a steady hand and extreme care.

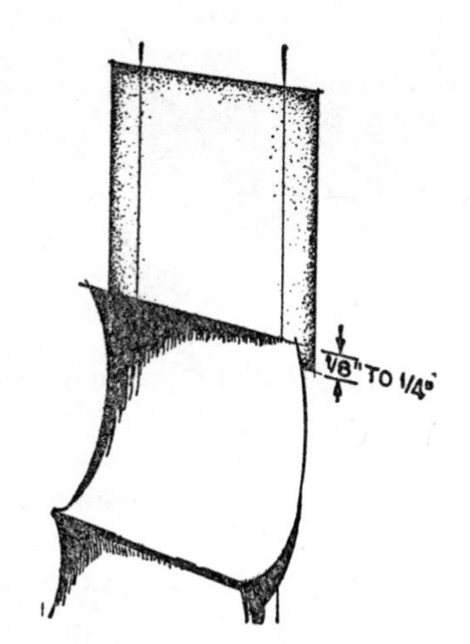

Fig. 3. Overlap sections of gold leaf by one-eighth to one-quarter of an inch.

Place the can of fortified spackle in a pot of hot water. Stir the mixture until smooth and warm. If necessary, strain the mixture to remove any lumps. Using a soft brush, carefully brush over the surfaces to be gilded. When this surface has dried, sandpaper it glass smooth, using a #5/0 grade of sandpaper. Next, apply a very thin coat of shellac (two-pound cut or less), and then the ground is ready to receive the bronze paint.

Applying the Bronze. Mix a small amount of the selected bronze powder with the bronzing liquid. Bronzing liquid is readily obtainable and is far superior to any mixture you can make. Test the mixture until it flows to a smooth and metallic surface. If you have not added enough powder, the paint will not cover, and if you have added too much, it will appear crumbly. When the mixture is right, apply it in single strokes. Do not brush it out. If the mixture is right and your brush is properly loaded, the paint will flow out properly.

Aluminum Powders

These powders—frequently used in imitation of silver—are obtainable as a dry powder, as a paste, and as a ready-mixed paint. Like bronze, they also come in various degrees of fineness. The paste form is probably the most economical. It is sold in a double can. The top, small can contains the aluminum paste, and the larger can at the bottom, the bronzing liquid. Add paste to the liquid until you have a good covering and working consistency. Remember that the full amount of the paste is in the right proportion to the full amount of the bronzing liquid. So, if you wish, you can mix half the paste to half the liquid.

The aluminum powders are the same as you will find in the aluminum

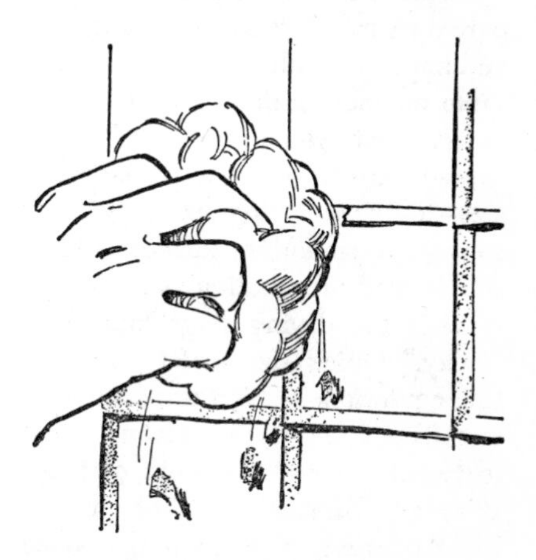

Fig. 4. Rubbing gently with cotton will remove surplus gold, leaving a continuous surface.

paints made for exterior wood priming and tank, roof, and barn paints. The manufacturer simply changes the bronzing liquid to adapt it to each job.

Prepare the ground exactly as you would for bronze paint and apply the aluminum paint just as carefully. The paint will flow to a perfectly smooth, continuous, metallic surface.

Gilding with Leaf

Gold Leaf. Real gold leaf is pure gold beaten out to a thickness of about 1/200,000 of an inch. This extremely thin sheet will completely cover any surface to which it is properly applied.

For reasons of practicability, the leaf is generally cut into squares of about 3¼ inches and sold in booklets of 25 squares, although it is also available in rolls. It comes in various hues, from lemon yellow to a warm reddish gold.

Preparation for Gold Leaf. To prepare the surface, sand the ground well and apply warm liquid spackle in the same manner as directed for bronze paint. Next, you apply a relatively slow-drying oil size or a quick-drying size—the slow-drying size flows to a somewhat smoother surface. Either size is ready for leafing as soon as it reaches the drying stage known as "tacky." Quick size usually reaches this condition in from one-half hour to one hour. Oil size takes from twelve to twenty-four hours. Both of these sizes are brushed on, but do not brush over any place more than once—otherwise the size will not flow to a smooth surface.

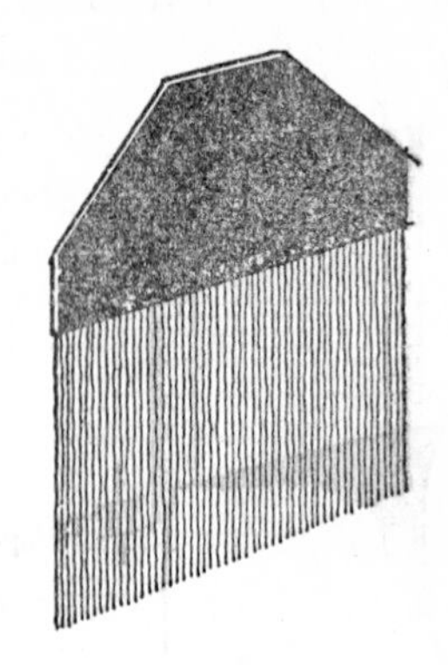

Fig. 5. The gilder's tip picks up sheets of gold leaf.

Application of Gold Leaf. To apply the leaf, open the booklet so that the back edge of one of the gold leaves is still held at the bound edge. Lay the leaf over the tacky size (see illustration). It will stick to the size. Open the page further and all of the leaf will adhere to the surface. Flip to the next page and apply the next gold leaf. Have each leaf overlap the previous one by one eighth to one quarter of an inch. Let the size under the leaf dry overnight. Then, gently rub the gilded surface with a soft piece of cotton. If you have completely covered the surface, the loose gold will come off, leaving a perfectly continuous sheet of gold in place.

Another and more difficult method of application is to use a gilder's tip. This is a simple brush made of single hairs in a row between two pieces of fibre. Stroke the tip over the back of you hand, your face, or your hair and then touch it to the edge of one of the sheets of gold leaf in the booklet. Because of the static electricity now in it, it will pick up the leaf, which you

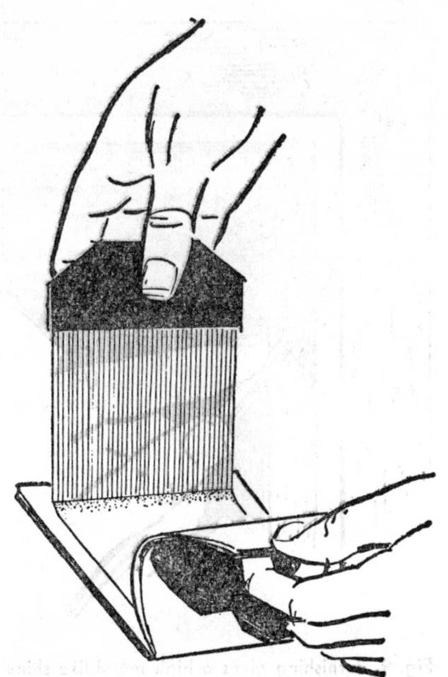

Fig. 6. Touch the charged gilder's tip to the edge of the gold leaf while still in the booklet and lift it out gently.

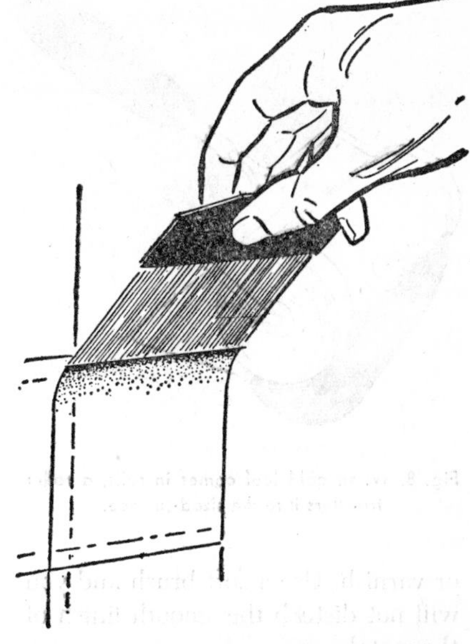

Fig. 7. You should remove the gold leaf from the booklet to the surface in one slow, but steady motion, or else it will crumble. Keep it moving continuously forward.

can transfer to the size. The reason this method is difficult—and it is quite difficult—is that the gold is so light and fragile that it breaks and then floats around in the air. Essentially, the trick is to handle it the way you dry a handkerchief when you wave it in the air. The gold won't stand the same rough motion, but you must keep it in a steady, gentle motion.

Gold leaf in rolls is applied with a simple roller device which unrolls it on to the sized surface, as shown in the accompanying illustration.

Silver Leaf. This can be purchased in the same forms as gold leaf and is applied in exactly the same way. Leaf on rollers is obtainable and is applied with the same simple roller device as described above.

Bronze Leaf. Bronze leaf is generally made in larger sheets than gold. The leaves measure 5 x 5 inches or a little more. It also is obtainable in rolls. It is applied on an oil-sized ground.

Aluminum Leaf. This is made and applied in the same way as bronze leaf.

Protection. Gold leaf requires no protection from tarnish; in fact, the size will deteriorate long before the gold. But all the other forms of powder or leaf require a coating. In order to preserve the color, you use a transparent type of coating such as shellac

Fig. 8. When gold leaf comes in rolls, a roller transfers it to the sized surface.

Fig. 9. Burnishing gives a high metal-like shine to the gilding.

or varnish. Use a soft brush and you will not disturb the smooth finish of the metal.

Burnishing

Bronze powder and all leaf gilding can be burnished. By rubbing a properly gilded job you can increase the luster. The proper preparation is achieved with the warm, liquid spackle. Without this relative soft surface, the agate burnisher would not be able to compress and level the metal. Burnish directly on the metal after the size or bronzing liquid has dried. You will not be able to attain the extremely high luster found on work done by specialists, but you will be able to burnish to a very acceptable luster. Extreme luster is only obtainable by a very complicated process requiring long training and skill. If the metal burnished is not gold, it will be necessary to apply a protective coating to prevent tarnish.

ENAMELING

Ordinary enameling has been described in earlier chapters. This section will describe the application and rubbing of enamel to a perfectly smooth finish. The day when *all* the woodwork in a house was enameled and rubbed is long since past, but a great deal of modern furniture looks very much better with a rubbed enamel finish.

Preparation

To prepare a surface for enameling and rubbing, you should sandpaper it to a smooth finish. Then you should give it a priming coat as described in Chapter 3. When the priming coat is thoroughly dry, sandpaper it lightly, using a #00 grade of sandpaper.

Use of Spackle

Mix a batch of spackle according to the directions on the box; the same quantity as for a coat of paint is enough. Place the container holding the spackle in a pail of hot water. When the mix has become warm, add about one ounce of mixing varnish to each pint of spackle. You will find that the mixture will thin out as it becomes warm. When it is the consistency of paint, it is right. If it does not thin out enough, add a little water. If it is too thin, add a little more spackle powder. Strain this mixture, and it is ready for use. Brush it onto the surfaces, flowing it out well. Do *not* brush it over or you will roughen the surface. When this coat is dry, sandpaper it perfectly smooth. Number 00 sandpaper is the best grade to use. You will find that you have a silky smooth surface when you have finished. Gently dust this to remove all powder, and you are ready for the enamel undercoater.

Undercoater

Buy a good grade of enamel undercoater (it is more trouble than it is worth to try to make and strain your own). Flow this coat on as directed by the manufacturer. If you find that there are dull spots when this has dried (which simply means that you have a generous coat of spackle that is very absorbent) sand lightly and apply a second coat. Sandpaper the final undercoat and the surface is ready for enameling.

Enameling

Using the best grade of rubbing enamel you can buy, tint it to the desired hue, and strain. Using well broken in bristle brush, flow on the enamel. If the enamel is short—that is, sets too quickly—you will have to work quickly to cover an area evenly. If you can, cross-brush the work to further even out the thickness. When this enamel has dried for at least two days, it is ready for rubbing.

Rubbing

Make sure your felt rubbing pad (see page 194) is clean. Mix a paste of #00 pumice stone and water. If there are any lumps in this paste, pick them out; otherwise, they will cause scratches. Sprinkle the surface to be rubbed with water in the same way a woman sprinkles clothing before ironing. Dip your pad into the paste and start rubbing. Stroke back and forth, *always* in the direction of the grain. After a reasonable number of strokes, check your progress by drawing your rubber squeegee over the rubbed area. This will remove the pumice paste. If the surface is flat and smooth, it is finished and you can move on to another area. When you have finished the rubbing to your satisfaction, wash down the whole surface with water. Dry it with a clean piece of chamois. If you have done a good job, you will find that you have a glass-smooth, semi-matte finish. It is a hard, durable finish that will not hold dirt and that is readily cleaned with a damp rag. The extra work is well worth while and does not require any unusual or expensive equipment.

LACQUER

If you have spray painting equipment and are able to operate it satisfactorily, you can use lacquers. These new paints are so fast-drying that they are not suitable for brush painting. When properly applied and rubbed, they make a beautiful finish. Lacquers are obtainable in a wide variety of colors as well as clear, and if you wish you can tint them with colors ground in Japan.

Preparation

Put on a priming coat as in the preparation for enamel. Then apply warm, thin spackle as for enamel. Sandpaper to a smooth surface. Next apply one thin coat of shellac (two-pound cut). This is done to prevent the lacquer from softening the varnish in the spackle. Lacquer thinners act like a paint remover on oil or varnish paints. Finally, you must use lacquer undercoater. Each coat is sprayed on and sandpapered before putting on the next coat.

Application

The lacquer is sprayed on. Rubbing can be done with one of the rubbing compounds made for that purpose or with pumice and water. See instructions for spraying in page 87.

FLOCKING

This is a method for making a finish which resembles suede leather. It is perfectly matte and is useful for lining drawers, metal cabinets, or other places where the deadening of

Fig. 10. Apply shredded felt to surfaces treated with adhesive to get a suede-leather texture. The strainer distributes the felt evenly.

sound is desirable. Flock is simply extremely small pieces of felt. You purchase it loose, by the pound, and in a wide variety of colors. Manufacturers who sell it also carry the adhesive for it. The adhesive is painted over the surface. Then the flock is applied by any one of several methods.

Application

The simplest method of application is to put a good handful of the loose flock in a wire strainer—a kitchen strainer will do. Shake this over the adhesive-coated surface. If you spread newspaper around the surface, you will be able to recover most of the excess flock. When all the flock that will stick has done so and the adhesive is dry, gently brush the remainder of the flock off and the job is finished.

If you have a number of articles to do, construct a box large enough to

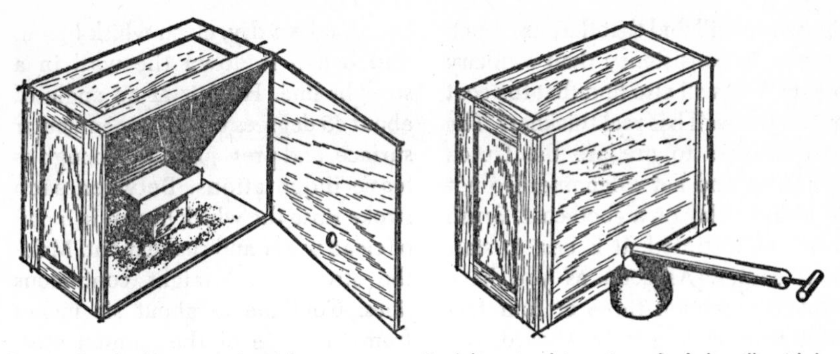

Fig. 11. For flocking several articles, construct a flock box. Applying air to the hole will swirl the felt around the objects to be painted.

hold one or more of the articles. Make an opening in the box so that you can insert a hose with a dusting tip attached. The other end of the hose can be attached to a spray gun or the "reverse" end of a vacuum cleaner. Put a plate with a generous amount of flock on it in the box. When you have coated the articles with adhesive, place them in the box. Then close the box and turn on the current of air. The air pressure will send the flock swirling. Stop the stream of air and the flock will settle on the adhesive. When all the flock has settled, you can open the box. Dust the excess flock off the finished articles, remove them, and recover the remaining flock.

If you are going to do flock work on a production basis, purchase one of the flocking guns made for the purpose.

TEXTURE PAINTING

The subject of texture painting is approached with caution. So much distasteful texture painting has been done that an aversion for it has developed. However, properly applied and textured, the effect can be a credit to painter and decorator. With the development of modern styles in decoration that emphasize texture in fabrics and broad flat surfaces, smoothly painted walls are frequently out of place. The use of checkerboard patterns of wire-brushed plywood is an example of this trend. And you can make similar finishes. Just remember, as a good general rule, that you should not texture trim.

Ready-made texture paints are available. Most of them are water-mixed and can be applied over a size coat on either plaster or wallboard. Some of these paints contain crushed mica; others, crushed oyster shell; and still others, marble dust. Frequently, texture paints are simply applied and left without further treatment. In this case, the cost of those containing the oyster shell, mica, or marble dust is well worth while.

Application

Texture paints should be mixed according to the manufacturer's directions. You will find that they are much heavier in consistency than ordinary paints. You will also find that the coat put on the wall has real thickness. The best brushes to use are the Dutch calcimine and flat calcimine. Do not be afraid to lay on a good coat. Brush it on as illustrated. It is best to start in a corner. As soon as you have applied a section three or four feet wide from ceiling to baseboard, you should texture it. If you wait until you have painted a larger area, the paint will begin to set and will resist further manipulation.

Whisk Broom Texture

As soon as you have applied a section of paint from ceiling to baseboard, take a dry, clean whisk broom and brush it down the wall in a straight line. Hold it at an angle of about 45 degrees to the perpendicular surface, and press just hard enough to leave indentations. Between each stroke rinse the whisk broom in a pail of clean water and shake it out. Make the strokes in straight continuous lines. Continue to about six inches from the edge of the painted area. Then brush in another three-foot section and continue the texturing.

A variation of this method is to do it checker-board fashion—one square of strokes running horizontally, the next, vertically.

When the texture paint is dry, you can paint over it or size and glaze it.

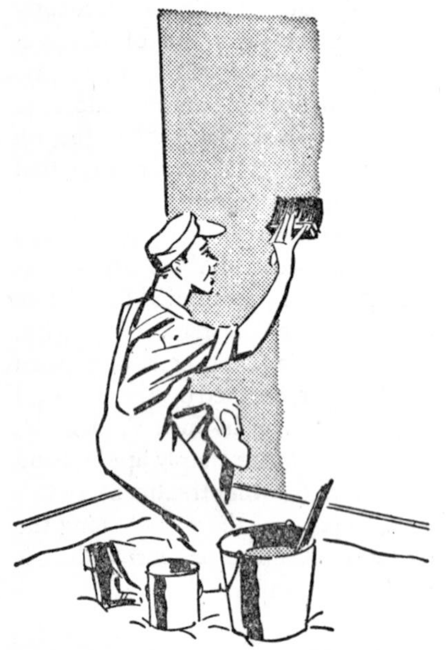

Fig. 12. Don't be afraid to lay on a good coat of texture paint. Use a calcimine brush, starting in a corner. Texture each section before it sets.

Fig. 13. A clean whisk-broom drawn straight down the wall gives an interesting texture.

Fig. 14. Checker-board and other patterns can be devised, using the whisk-broom as a basic tool for texturing.

Glaze will emphasize the texture of it is wiped; the darker coloration will come off the ridges and remain in the indentations made by the whisk broom.

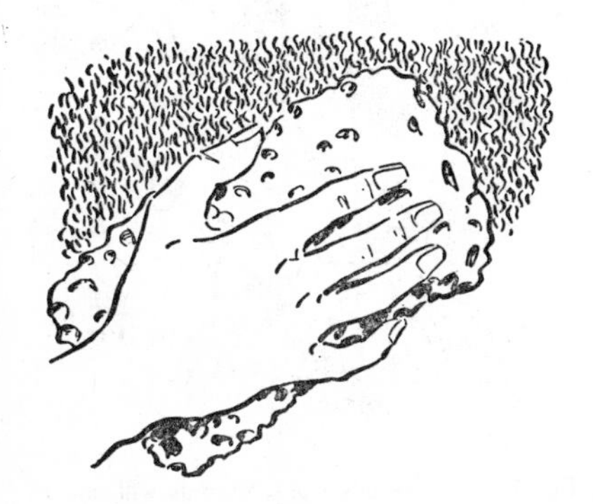

Fig. 15. The effect of Caen stone can be gotten by stippling texture paint.

Other Textures

Combs, worn paint brushes, draftsman's celluloid triangles, plasterer's pointing trowels, pieces of carpet—all these and many other things can be used to create textures. It is suggested that you make up samples of paint and explore the possibilities. In the interests of good taste, keep the texture simple and the glaze light and dull. Excessively rough textures and dark and shiny glazes are what gives texturing its bad reputation.

Caen Stone

This is a texture which is frequently found in public buildings. It is an imitation of a natural stone. The color is a beautiful soft grayish tan. To produce it, apply one of the texture paints containing crushed oyster shell. Lightly stipple it and gently touch it here and there with a damp sponge. Using a stick about one-quarter inch in diameter, score lines representing the joints between stones. When the texture paint is dry, make up a watercolor glaze with a little dry raw sienna. Brush this on each block. As the glaze begins to set, go over it gently with a moist sponge to make the color a little uneven. This will make the work look like stone. Then make up a watercolor glaze in the color of cement—a little raw umber and drop black will do it—and paint in the joints. Sometimes the joints are painted almost white in imitation of Keene's cement.

Travertine

Travertine is an Italian building stone. It is imitated in very much the

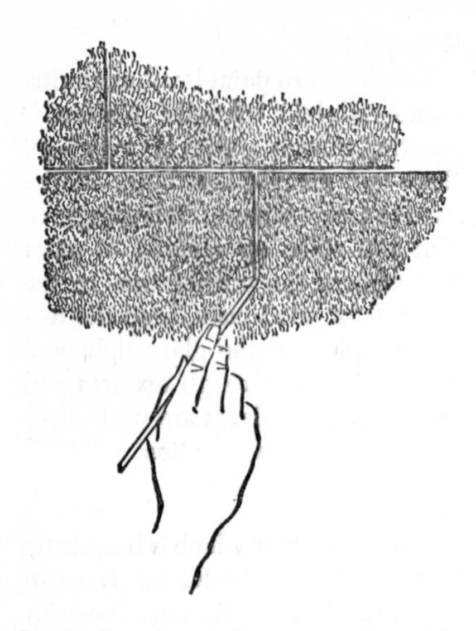

Fig. 16. Score lines in Caen stone with a stick.

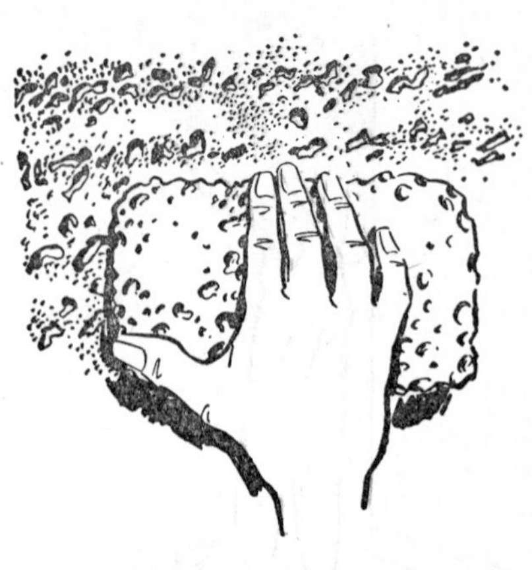

Fig. 17. Reproductions of hollows in travertine, an Italian building stone, are achieved by using textured paint, and later dappling with a sponge (see next figure).

same way as Caen stone. Do not stipple, however; simply dapple with a moist sponge so that you make obvious indentations. And keep these indentations in almost horizontal lines. Then draw a draftsman's celluloid triangle gently across the surface to make it smooth above the indentations. Use the small stick to score out the joints between the blocks. When the texture paint is dry, make up four water-color glazes, the first with a little raw sienna, the second with a little burnt sienna, the third with a little burnt umber, and the fourth with a little raw umber. Use a separate brush for each glaze and apply each color separately, letting some of them overlap. With a damp sponge and a moist stippler work them out to look like natural stone. When you have finished glazing, paint in the joints to resemble cement.

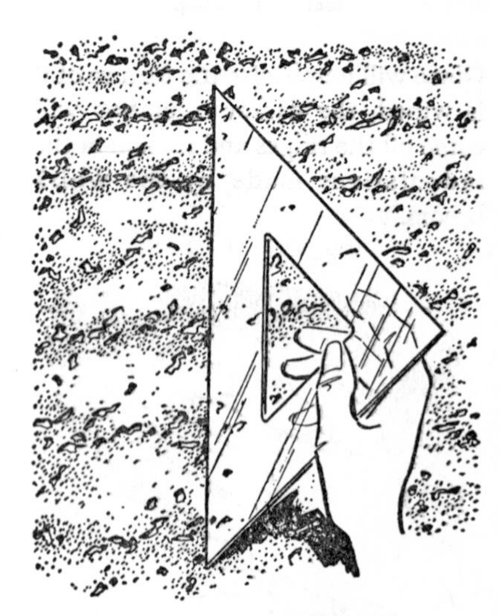

Fig. 18. The flat edge of a triangle will smooth the surface over the dappled paint to complete the travertine finish.

CHAPTER 14

GRAINING AND MARBLING

GRAINING

You may someday want to imitate the grain of wood in a piece of furniture or paneling. The first and obvious step is to examine the piece of wood to be imitated. You will find a grain, that is, dark lines separated by lighter areas. Your problem is to paint in these lines so that they resemble the natural wood. Painting each of the lines separately would be an almost endless task. Consequently, many methods and tools have been developed to hasten and simplify the job of graining. To describe all of the methods would take more than a book. Let's limit ourselves to the commonest and easiest ones.

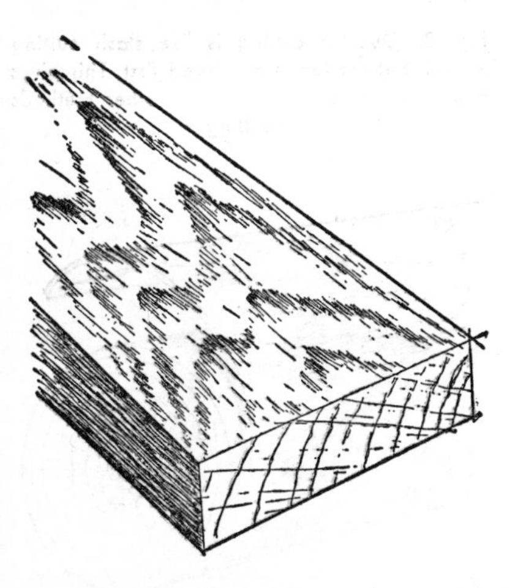

Fig. 1. Each kind of wood has its characteristic grain, which results principally from the contrast of light and dark areas.

Grain Formation

Grain is first formed by nature in the living wood. It is the result of the cells, fibers, and pores of the wood's structure, of the rings, streaks, veins, and density of the wood's growth, depending on species, age, season, food, and climate, and of the twists and turns the wood develops, whether they arise from outside forces or from the meeting of trunk and branch and the formation of crotches.

While no two pieces of wood will be identical in their graining, each type has its own recognizable character. Douglas Fir, for instance, has a very strong figure, which results from alternating bands of soft and hard wood; so strong is this figure, in fact, that this wood is not thought of as a "cabinet" wood. You are probably familiar with the warm color and close grain of cherry. And as an example of an exotic wood with an intricate pattern, there is Circassian walnut, which is vigorously gnarled and twisted by the weather of the Caucasus.

Grain in wood varies principally in the type of pore. The hard woods—oak, ash, hickory, and chestnut—resemble one another in the large open pore characteristic of their grain. Soft woods — white pine, white wood, cedar, redwood, cypress, and maple—resemble one another in the close, almost invisible pores of the grain marking. Medium-sized pores are found in mahogany, walnut, and cherry. Each of these groups is grained differently.

Often when we speak of the formation of grain, we are referring to the way in which the wood is cut. Wood is cut in one of three ways. The commonest is called slash cut. Plank after plank is cut, starting on one side of the log and continuing to the other side. In quarter cutting, the log is cut into four equal wedge-shaped pieces. Then these wedges are cut into planks as shown in the illustration. Veneers can be cut the same as planks. They are simply cut very much thinner. The third method of cutting is used exclusively for veneer. It is called rotary cutting. The log is trued up and set on a massive machine resembling a lathe. A large knife is set against the revolving log, and a thin sheet of wood is cut off. The method resembles pulling wrapping paper off a roll.

A different figure on the wood is made by each method of cutting. If you wish to become very proficient in graining, you should familiarize yourself with as many different samples of wood as you can. Study them well for the characteristic grain and figure.

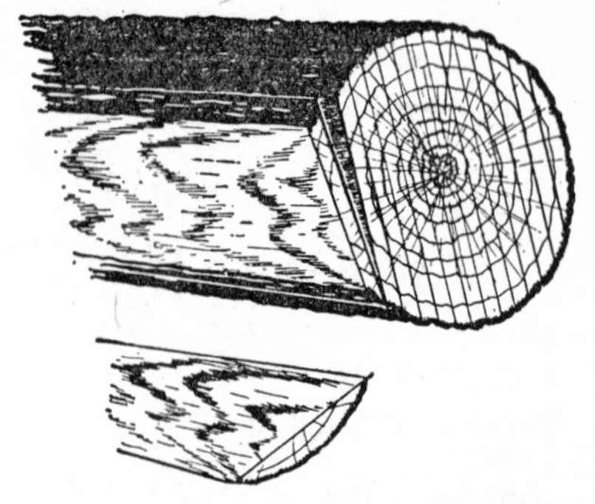

Fig. 2. Slash cutting proceeds straight across the log. This results in one kind of figure in the wood.

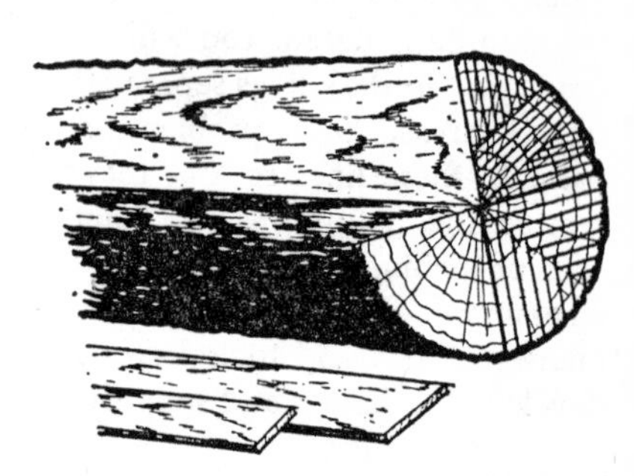

Fig. 3. Quarter cutting is like slash cutting except that the log is quartered first. This gives a different kind of figure from other methods of cutting.

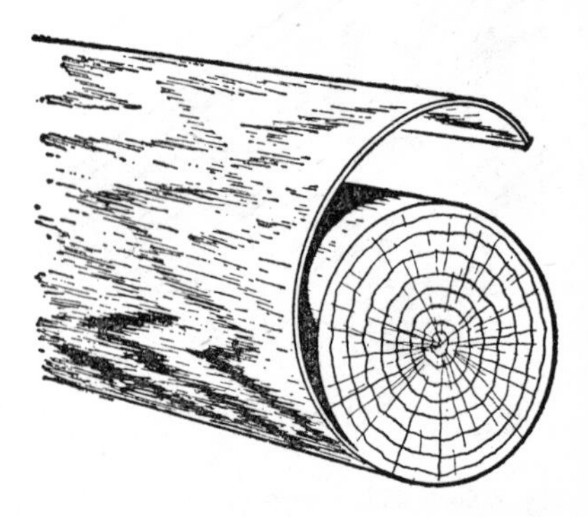

Fig. 4. Rotary cutting, used to produce veneers, gives still another kind of figure.

Preparation

Paint in the surface to be grained, using a medium-hard drying formula. This is done to stop absorption of the ground color. White lead paint with mixing varnish, as suggested for glazing on page 155, is ideal. Tint this paint to a color resembling the lightest part of the raw, unfinished, sandpapered wood. For instance, a touch of raw sienna in the white paint is right for oak. A little burnt sienna is correct for mahogany or cherry. A very little ochre is enough for white pine. Always keep your ground color light. It is easy to glaze later to darken the job. Also flow and brush out your ground paint well so that you have a minimum of brush marks. With the ground paint thoroughly dry, you are ready to start graining. This graining you are going to do will accomplish the same thing as staining and finishing do.

Fig. 5. A whisk broom used in a glaze achieves a simple but satisfactory grain.

Straight Graining

For straight-grained, small-pored woods you can make an oil glaze or buy one of the glazing liquids (see page 155). Color it to a hue resembling the darkest part of the grain. Burnt umber is usually the best color to start with. For oak add a little raw sienna. For yellow pine add a generous amount of burnt sienna. Again look closely at the darkest part of the grain and match your glaze accordingly. Brush the glaze over the surface, spreading it in the direction in which the grain will run. Let it set for four or five minutes or it may wipe too clean.

Probably the simplest tool for turning this glaze into a grain-like appearance is an ordinary whisk broom. Just drag the broom in the direction in which you wish to have the grain run. Wipe off the glaze which has collected on the whisk broom and again drag it over the glazed surface, slightly overlapping the first stroke. Continue this stroking and cleaning until you have completed graining a section or panel. This method will give you a strong and relatively heavy grain. After it dries, protect your graining with a coat of shellac and wax or, for a one-coat job, use one of the semi-matte or matte varnishes used in wood finishing (see page 193).

A second quick method for straight-grained woods is to hold a piece of burlap over a large-toothed hair

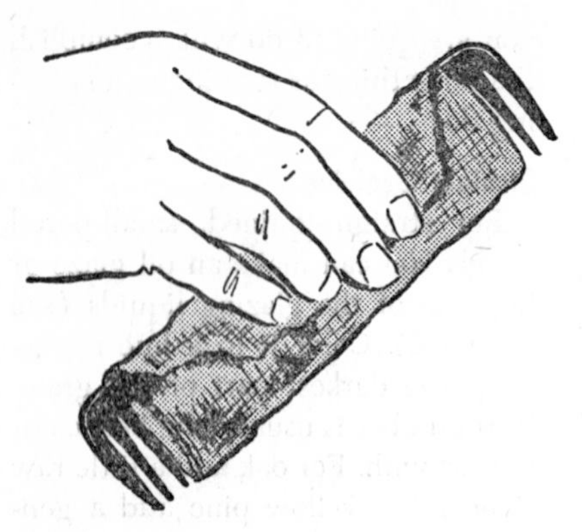

Fig. 6. A hair comb wrapped in burlap can be used to imitate grain.

comb. Drag this over your glaze as you did the whisk broom. Each time you make a stroke you should move the burlap on the comb as it becomes saturated with glaze. This method will make a softer and more blended grain. Protect with shellac or wax as in whisk-broom graining.

It is not recommended that you add knots or other characteristic markings to either of these two types of graining. If you examine your samples of real wood, you will find that the grain swirls around a knot. In the two previously mentioned examples your graining is all straight. Under the circumstances, the addition of knots would not look natural.

Imitating Large-Pored Woods

Straight-grained woods with large and open pores, like oak, are best imitated by the use of a serrated-edged rubber graining tool and a fine-toothed steel grainer's comb. You can make the rubber graining tool by first cutting a straight edge on an old rubber heel, and then cutting teeth

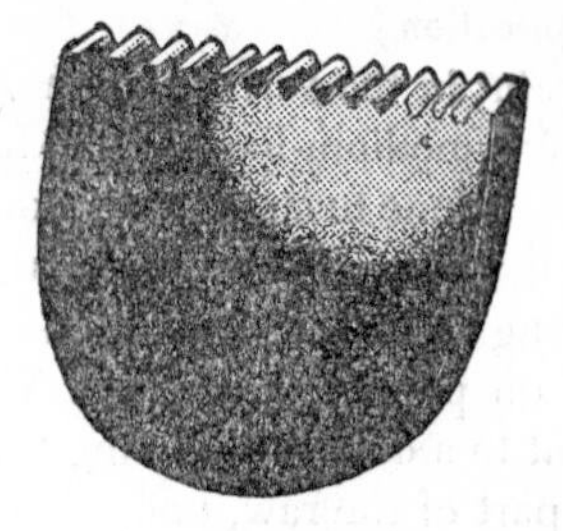

Fig. 7. A rubber graining comb. It can be made out of an old heel.

of irregular width in the straight edge.

Glaze in the ground, painted surface. Wrap a piece of cheesecloth over the teeth of your rubber graining tool, and drag this across the glaze. It will leave ridges of glaze like a natural grain. If you let the glaze in these ridges set for a few minutes, the second operation will be easier. The second operation is done to break these glaze lines into small, short

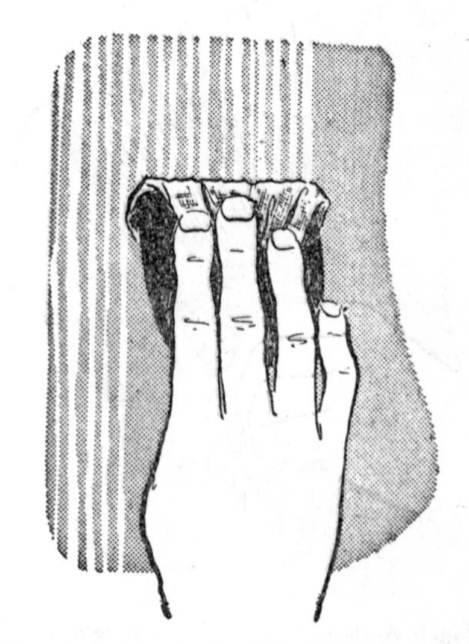

Fig. 8. How to use the rubber graining comb.

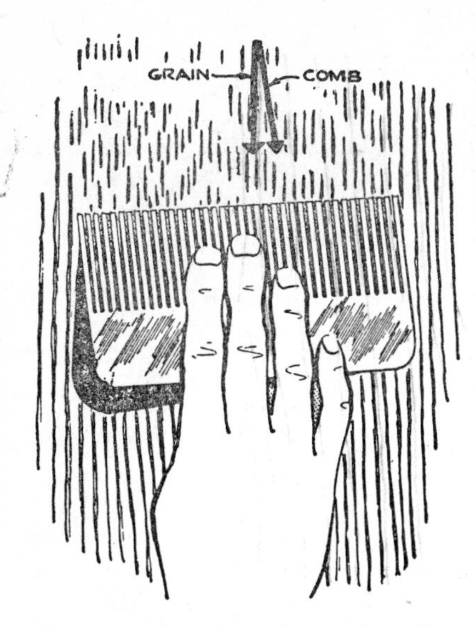

Fig. 9. Draw down the steel grainer's comb at an angle of about 10 degrees from the direction of the grain.

lines resembling the dark pores of the wood. Drag the fine-toothed steel comb over the glaze lines almost in the same direction. An angle of about 10 or 15 degrees from the original lines is right. After each stroke wipe off the glaze which has collected on the comb. Your comb must always be clean. Otherwise you will simply change the direction of the original glazed lines.

Overglazing. When this grain figure composed of pores has dried, the work is ready for overglazing. This overglazing is similar to staining on raw wood. Use a ready-made glazing liquid and add colors ground in oil, just as you would for oil staining. The basic color is generally burnt umber, and you add raw sienna, burnt sienna, or a touch of green to give the work the desired hue. Brush this overglaze on the grained surface. Make it heavier or lighter in various areas to give the work a more natural appearance. When the overglaze is dry, the work should be protected with a flat varnish.

Imitating Medium-Pored Woods

Wood with medium size, open pores, like mahogany and walnut, requires a special method of stippling. The larger paint stores carry a long-bristled, flat, thin brush called a walnut stippler. To use this special brush, apply a glaze to the correct ground. The glaze should be the dark color of the pores of the wood. Hold the flat side of the brush parallel to

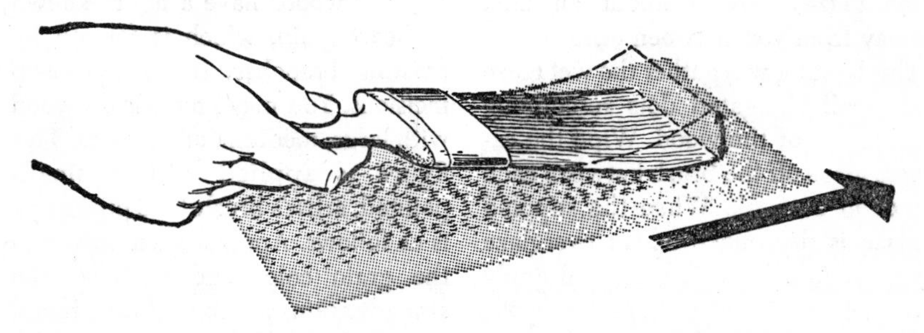

Fig. 10. How to use a walnut stippler to produce a grain in a glaze.

Fig. 11. Tools and materials for overglazing.

the glazed surface. Beat it rapidly on the glaze, moving about an inch away from you between each stroke. This beating will gather the wet glaze in small elongated dots resembling the pores of the wood. Wipe the excess glaze off the brush between each section of work. When the stippled glaze is dry, make up an overglaze similar in color to a stain and apply it. When this is dry, protect your work with a coat of flat varnish.

Heart Grain

Many woods have a figure known as heart grain, which is formed by twisting branches, scars, and deep incisions. You may find this on wood with large, medium, or no pores. This figure is applied with a small, pointed, artist's brush. The procedure is as follows. Apply a glaze mixed to the grain color and work in the straight grain, which is always found on either side of the heart grain. The

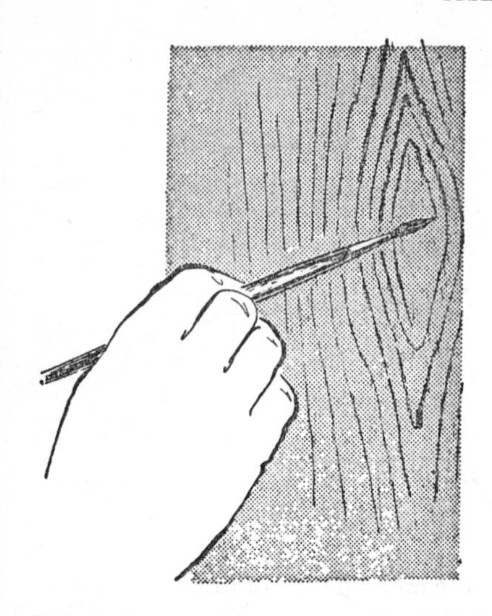

Fig. 12. Painting in heart grain with a small brush.

straight grain is made with the piece of serrated rubber covered with a piece of cheesecloth (see page 212). The center section, where the heart grain will be, is then wiped nearly clean with a bunched-up piece of cheesecloth. Then, using the same glaze, paint in the imitation of the heart figure of the wood. When this has set for a few minutes, very gently blend it with a badger blender or similar soft brush. Always blend toward the center of the loop in the figure. Study the wood sample and note the darker edge toward the center of the loop. When dry, glaze and then flat varnish.

The previous paragraphs described general graining steps for all woods. Now to be more particular. If the wood has large pores, like oak, you will have to run your steel grainer's comb over the graining before it dries to break it into the characteristic pores. If the wood has medium pores, like mahogany or walnut, you should stipple glaze it before you apply the grain. Let the stippling dry before you go ahead with the grain.

Knots

Knots, which are most frequently required in graining pine, are applied amazingly well with your bare thumb. Mix a little drier with some burnt sienna and burnt umber in oil. Dip the pad of your thumb into this thick color. Don't try to pick up too much color. Put your thumb where you want the knot and rotate it nearly a full turn. The twist will give your knot the circular markings. Worn out or stubby brushes can also be used. In fact, you will have to use them for

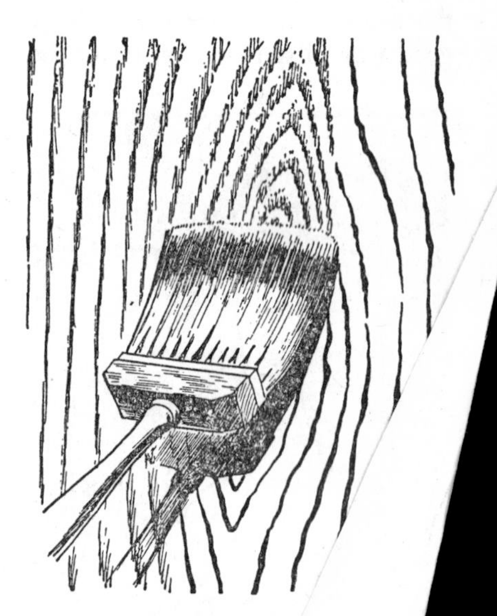

Fig. 13. A badger blender is
grain and achieve a realisti
the heart grain has b

very large knots. But always rotate the brush or finger. And don't forget that the grain has to curve around all knots.

There are many more ways to grain in imitation of wood. You can use water color instead of oil glazes. However, these water-color glazes dry too quickly for the novice. Also, the many special tools used for different methods of graining require the development of special skills. There is no short cut to an exact imitation of wood. You can get very satisfactory effects, but the perfection of the expert is the result of knowledge of wood grains and long skill in using both the materials and the tools.

You can obtain illustrations of many different woods by writing to the associations of lumber mills. A good way to start is to send for the free bibliography of lumber literature published by The National Lumber Manufacturers Association, 1319 Eighteenth St., N.W., Washington, D. C.

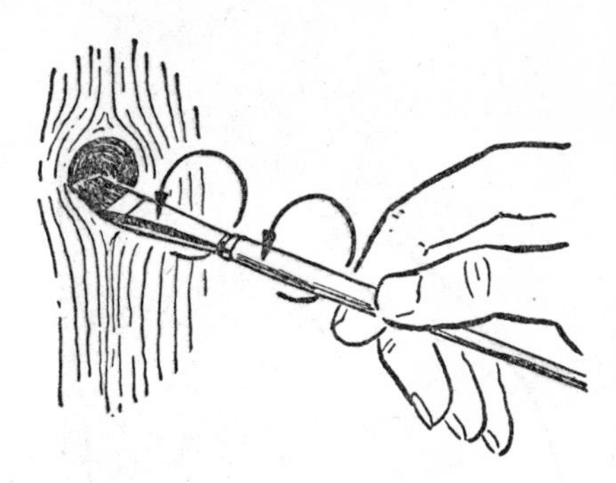

Fig. 15. One use for a worn brush is making large knots.

14. You can make excellent knots with your thumb.

MARBLING

Occasionally you may want to imitate marble. It is not too difficult and requires the use of only three special tools. These are an artist's flat bristle (about a #2), several turkey feathers, and a badger blender. The rest of your tools are regular painter's brushes, and incidentals like rags, cotton waste, and a sponge.

In general, a piece of marble will be one of three types. There is the type with sharp, jagged veins running through it. Then there is the type which looks as though there were a lot of different-colored pebbles scattered through it. And finally, there is the softly blended type with slight color variations drifting into each other.

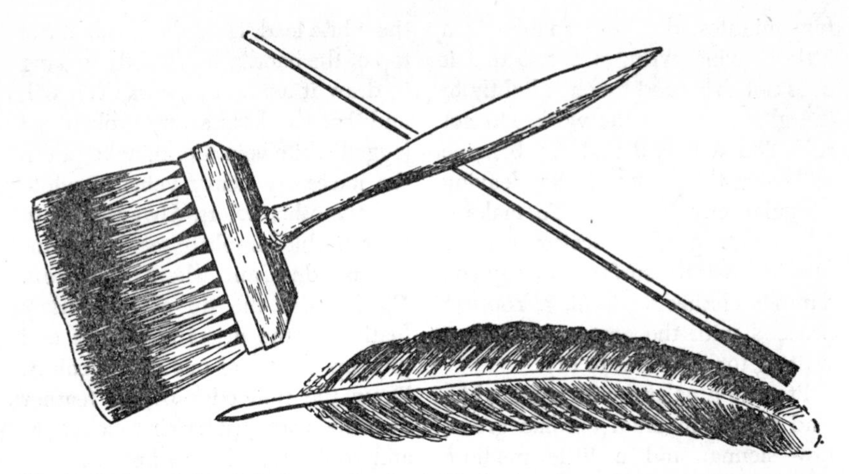

Fig. 16. Tools needed for imitating marble: flat bristle brush, turkey feather, and badger blender.

Jagged Marble

Imitating the sharp, jagged type of veined marble, of which "verte antique" is a good example, takes two steps. The area to be marbled is painted in black. This paint should dry hard and be non-absorbent. You can make it up by adding enough coach black in Japan drier to some mixing varnish to produce a hard matte surface. When this is dry, make up a thin gray-green glaze. A touch of medium chrome green, some dry zinc, and a touch of raw umber in a glazing liquid will be right. Brush this on your work in patches of varying amounts. When this has set for a

Fig. 17. Applying sponge stippling when imitating marble.

Fig. 18. Splattering benzine on the surface by tapping a loaded brush against a stick helps to produce an amazingly natural texture.

few minutes, dip your sponge in a little benzine, wring it out so that it does not drip, and touch it lightly to the glaze all over the work. Do not rub. You will find that the benzine will cause the glaze to gather, leaving irregular clear patches. To make a few larger patches, scatter a little benzine over the surface the way you dampen clothes for ironing. You can proceed with the next step without waiting for the glaze to dry.

Prepare a palette with some white lead in oil, medium chrome green, raw sienna, and a little medium chrome yellow. Make up a small cup of driers and turpentine. Dip your artist's flat bristle brush in the driers and turps and then pick up a little of the white lead. Hold the brush at the top of the handle and, lightly rocking it, draw it across the work. You will find that you have a very broken and jagged white vein. Continue to put in the necessary heavy veins in white and the other colors. Always refer to your marble sample to see what veins are needed and their direction. Finally, dip the tip of the turkey feather in the driers and turps and pick up a little of one of the colors. Draw the thin edge of the feather over the work, just barely touching it, and you will make the fine hair-line veins that add so much to the illusion of reality. When the work is dry, apply shellac or flat varnish for a protective coating.

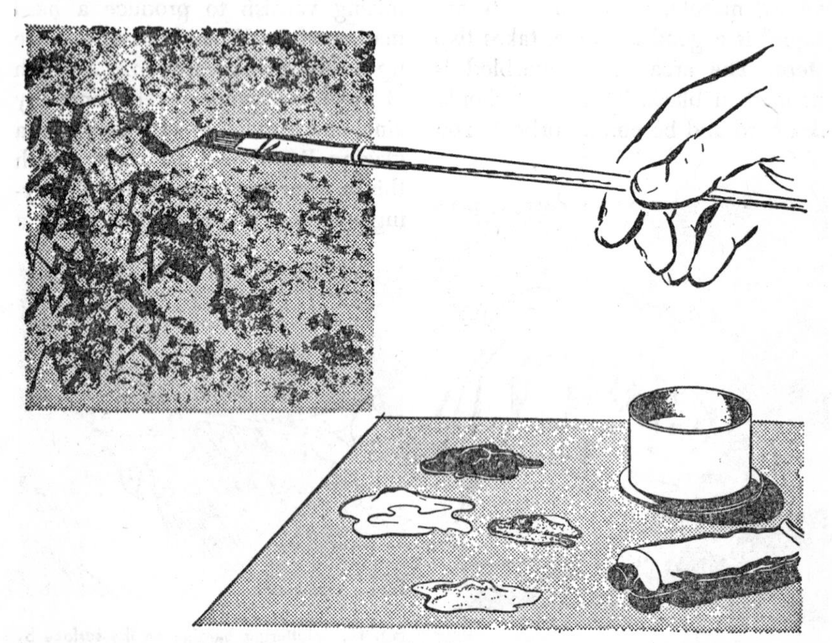

Fig. 19. The veins in marble may be accurately reproduced by painting them in on the glazed surface with a brush.

Pebbly Marble

The pebble type of marble is imitated by preparing a ground as light as the lightest part of the sample. Make up a palette of all the major colors—there may be five or six. Place some glazing liquid in a pot or can. Have a clean sash tool for each color or a handy can of turpentine in which to rinse out your brush between colors. Apply the colors in a pattern roughly like your sample. Do this by dipping your brush into the glaze liquid, then picking up some color. Work this glaze on the ground paint in irregular patches. When the area is entirely covered with patches of glaze, moisten a sponge in benzine and dapple this over the glaze. You will find that the benzine will break up the glaze into irregularly shaped areas. Finish by scattering a few drops of benzine here and there. Finally, touch up and sharpen the colors by using an artist's flat bristle brush or the turkey feather. For this, use the color heavier than when applied with the sash tool. When dry, protect your work with a coat of flat varnish.

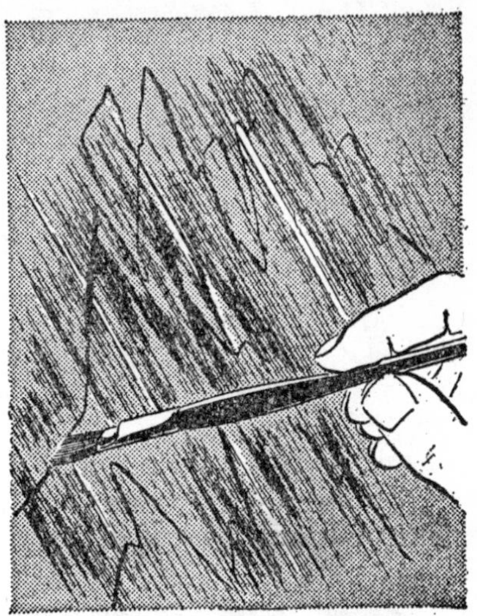

Fig. 21. Sharpening up the appearance of the marble veins with a flat bristle brush.

Fig. 20. Touching up by using the edge of a turkey feather. This must be done very lightly.

Softly Blended Marble

The third, and plainest-looking, marble is perhaps the most difficult

Fig. 22. Stippling blends in the colors to achieve the appearance of the softly colored type of marble.

to duplicate. You will find that the various colors are only faintly different and are smoothly blended into one another. Prepare and apply a ground using the lightest color in the marble sample for a guide. When the ground is thoroughly dry, prepare a palette with the predominant colors. Apply these colors, mixed with a little glazing liquid, in areas. Use the pattern on your sample. Stipple over the whole with a regular wall stippler. This will blend the colors together so that no veins are built up. If necessary, wipe dark areas with a bunched-up piece of cheesecloth. Finish by gently blending over all with the badger blender. When the glazes are thoroughly dry, apply a coat of flat varnish.

Illustrations of marble in good color and with the figure in full size are difficult to find. They are obtainable, however, from large manufac-

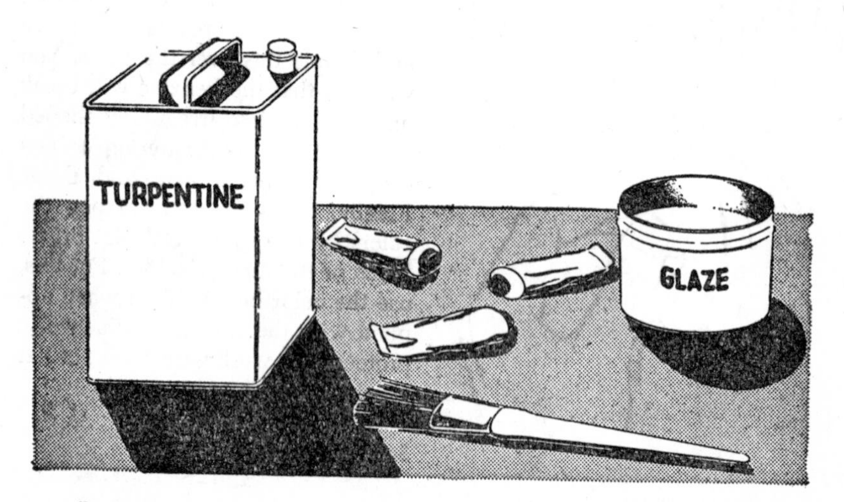

Fig. 23. The simple tools and materials necessary for applying a multi-color glaze.

turers. Look in architectural and decorators' magazines for names and addresses. Second-hand building material companies will frequently have broken and cracked pieces which you can buy for very little.

Fig. 24. A badger blender is also used to blend the colors when marbling.

CHAPTER 15

MARINE PAINTING

Boats confront you with some demands unique in painting. You must contend with vegetable growth, barnacles, and worms in addition to the ravages of sun, salt, and water. Conditions like these force you to stress protection over decoration, without sacrificing appearance, in painting boats.

And as with other structures, in painting small boats your procedures must take into account whether it is old or new work. In general, the painting of a previously painted boat means the complete removal of the old finish and the application of a completely new one, or the thorough preparation of the surface of a sound old finish and the application of new paint or varnish. Painting a boat in the process of construction gives you the opportunity to preserve and seal all hidden or joined surfaces. This will lengthen the useful life of your boat as much as the consistent maintenance of the exposed surfaces. You will find the best and simplest procedures described under the heading to fit your job.

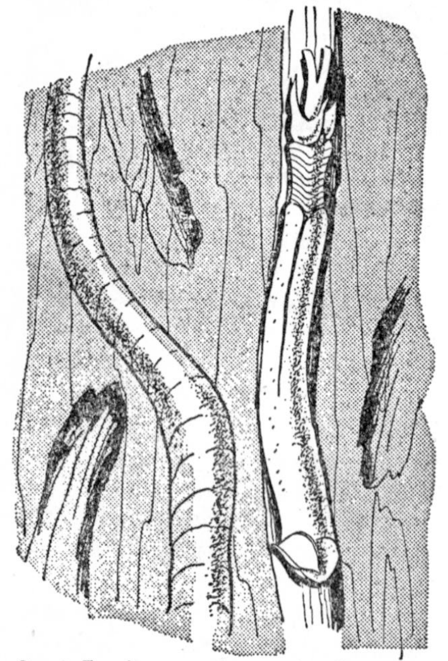

Fig. 1. Teredo worms do extensive damage to boats by boring through hull planking. Here they are shown imbedded in a plank.

Marine Finishes

Paint and varnish completely when fitting out. Do this once or twice a year, depending on whether you use the boat about half a year or all year long. Renew finishes as required throughout the year. *Use only marine finishes.*

Marine finishes should provide extreme moisture resistance, durability, color retention, resistance to foul-water gases, minimum friction, and the ability to withstand sharp temperature changes. These qualities also fit marine finishes for docks, boat houses, floats, and buoys – any objects undergoing the same conditions which affect boats. Ordinary finishes do not stand up under these conditions.

Choose reliable brands of marine finishes, paints, varnishes, and accessories. Nowhere more so than in boats do inferior materials lengthen labor time, multiply expenses, and shorten the life of what you are trying to protect.

Marine paints come in dozens of colors today to meet the increased demand for color. Some colors, however, still do not resist discoloration by foul-water gases as well as do white and black. Your local paint dealers or ship yard painters will usually make reliable recommendations.

Inspection

Begin fitting out with an inspection for painting and varnishing needs. If your craft is not newly constructed, hose it down and let it dry and then examine all painted and varnished surfaces. Check spars, interiors, cabin exterior, deck, deck gear, topsides, and bottom. Determine which finishes need cleaning and restoring only, and which must be refinished from the bare wood.

Starting from the bare wood is best for all surfaces, but is essential only on cracked, peeling, blistered, or stained surfaces. Over doubtful surfaces rub sandpaper several times. If the finish breaks down easily, it should be removed to the bare wood. And if the finish seems sound but is thick, composed of many layers of paint or varnish, it should be removed. These layers will crack, peel, or chip off, ruining the new finish. Too many coats piled on top of each other eventually break down by the shrinking action of the new paint.

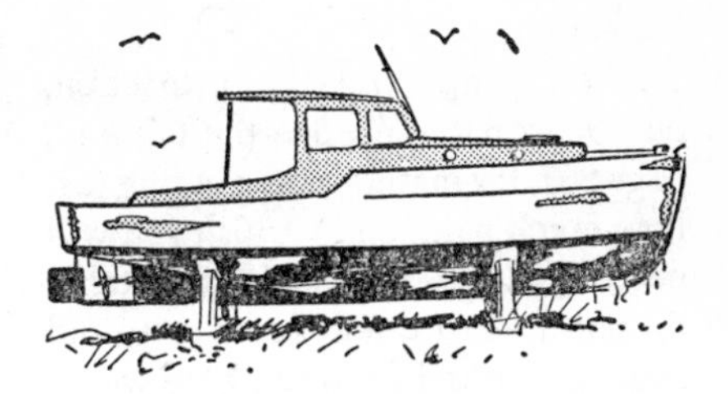

Fig. 2. Damage above and below the waterline by the elements show in the form of blisters and peeling.

Look for dents, gouges, rivet heads, and so on, in metal, wood, and canvas. These must be faired up, above and below the water line. Paint does not obscure such rough spots; it accentuates them. Inspect old caulking to see if it must be replaced or reinforced. If it is black, mushy, or hard, it probably is rotten and should be replaced. Particularly check the often leaky seams at transom, stem, chine, and keel.

Canvas decks which are badly cracked or checked should not be painted over but replaced. Examine the boat cover and tarpaulins for rents and need of waterproofing. Check sails for holes to be patched.

Investigate parts needing preservatives. These include sails, awnings, tarpaulins, ropes, butt-blocks, chines, new planking, and patches. You can attend to this, as well as to surface preparation and caulking, during a winter lay-up.

Materials

After completing the inspection, buy your materials. See the table on page 237, for methods on gauging just how much paint and varnish you will need. Quantities listed by this table do not apply to new boats or to old boats refinished from the bare wood. These require double the quantities listed.

The table below is a basic list of tools and materials (other than paints and varnishes) you will need. Assemble those necessary for the work you are going to do.

PREPARATION

Sequence of Painting

For speed and convenience work on the parts of your boat in this order:

- Preservatives, all parts
- Surface preparation
- Caulking
- Interior
- Spars
- Cabin exterior
- Deck
- Deck gear
- Topsides
- Bottom
- Boottopping and decoration

Keep the weather in mind. You may be able to complete surface preparation and caulking during the time your boat is laid up. When this is done and over-all inspection completed, start on interior surfaces. The weather at this time may be too variable and too wet for outside work. Rain, dusty winds, and quick temperature changes harm newly applied finishes. The ideal temperature for

Tools	*Materials*
Necessary:	Removers:
Caulking mallet or hammer	Paint
Caulking iron	Varnish
Putty knife	Bleach:
Wood scraper	Oxalic acid
Sandpaper blocks	Ready made
Brushes:	Thinners (paint)
4 inch, 1	Cement:
2 inch, 1	Canvas
sashtool, 1	Bedding
Wire brush	Seam
Pots and pails	Trowel
	Preservatives:
	Canvas and rope
Desirable:	Wood
Caulking gun	Primer (metal)
Sanding machine (reciprocating)	Sandpaper, #00 and #1
Blow torch	Steel wool
	Caulking cotton

Fig. 3. Trouble spots on your boat are transom, chine, and keel. A pre-painting inspection should mean double emphasis on these areas.

painting and varnishing is 70 degrees; it is not wise to try to do either at less than 60 degrees.

Beginning with the interior of your boat, you may accomplish a good deal before a stretch of friendly weather lets you work outside. When outside, paint and varnish from the top down. Complete rigging aloft before painting at deck level.

Never paint or varnish a surface that is not entirely dry. Let each coat dry thoroughly before applying the next. All surfaces must be smooth, clean, and free of grease. Apply varnish when the temperature is moderately warm, indoors if possible. Consider applying final coats of varnish and topside paint when afloat, in a quiet mooring sheltered from wind and dust.

Treatment for Preservation

To minimize decay, mold, mildew, blue and black stain, and damage from worms and insects, you must apply preservative to many parts of your craft. Wood, rope, and canvas need this. During construction you would do well to coat all wood, inside and outside, with some brand of zinc naphthenate solution. This comes in green, brown, and clear. It is equally effective for wood, rope, and canvas. It does not stiffen rope. You can mix a little of it with oil-base paints and sealers for extra protection. After its first application, renew copper naphthenate, a wood preservative, every three years.

Brush the solution thoroughly into the wood; the more it soaks in the better it preserves. (The toxic con-

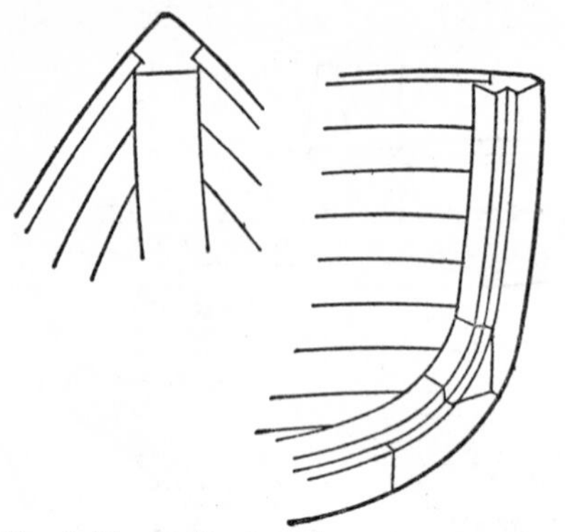

Fig. 4. The application of wood preservatives can save you a lot of headaches in the seasons to come. Care should be taken to cover the inside of the stem and stern.

tent of the solution makes it risky to spray.) Overlook no hidden places in your boat. Particularly cover inside the stem, keel, and stern. Put no paint on any covered and unventilated interior parts; it causes rot. Use copper naphthenate solution instead.

On commercial boats, creosote is sometimes used as a preservative. The two objections to it are that it smells bad and you cannot paint over it.

To check mold and mildew on cabin interiors and exteriors you can use an antiseptic wash. Do not rinse this wash; it leaves an invisible film which wards off fungi and bacteria. When dry, it can be painted over. You can also put a small quantity of antiseptic wash, if oil-soluble, right in the paint you are going to use.

Steel and iron boats need a rust-preventive priming, such as a yellow chromate. This primer prevents most types of corrosion and, being non-conducting, eliminates galvanic action. Steel and iron parts of wooden boats, such as the keel and rudder plate, must have this seam priming of yellow chromate.

Preparing Surface

Fair up dents, gouges, rivet heads, nail holes, and so on in all surfaces. Do this with trowel cement, which comes ready made in cans from ½ pint to gallons. This material remains elastic enough to stay on as the hull twists and strains. First clean, dry, and prime the surface. Using a trowel, apply cement no more than ⅛ inch deep at a time. Allow this to set at least 24 hours before applying more, if necessary; otherwise the cement will shrink and crack in drying.

To fill hairline cracks and holes, use trowel cement thinned to brushing consistency. You can prepare this with turpentine or buy it ready-made. Smooth over crevices, partially filled with regular trowel cement, with thinned trowel cement. You may also use thinned trowel cement as a wood filler and as a hard base (over priming) on any type of surface, as described later in this chapter.

Caulking

Caulking is done on wooden boats to make the seams of the bottom, sides, and decks waterproof. On most wooden boats the seams between the planks of the sides and bottom widen from the inside outward. This space must be caulked, or filled, both above and below the water line.

Boats with lapstrake or clinker-type planks, which overlap tightly, do not require caulking but may benefit from sealing with a seam-filling

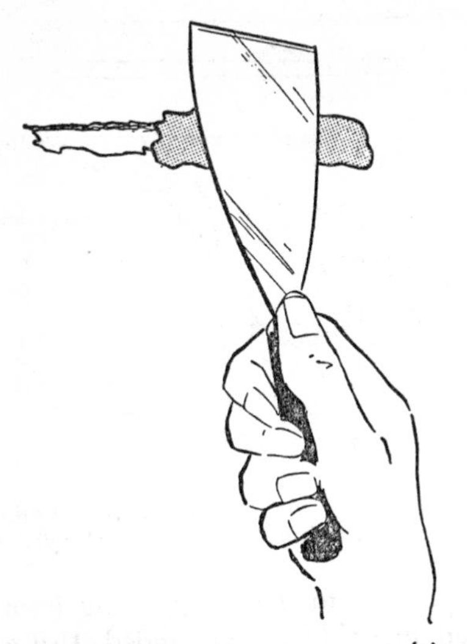

Fig. 5. Use prepared trowel cement to fair up dents, gouges, rivet heads, and nail holes.

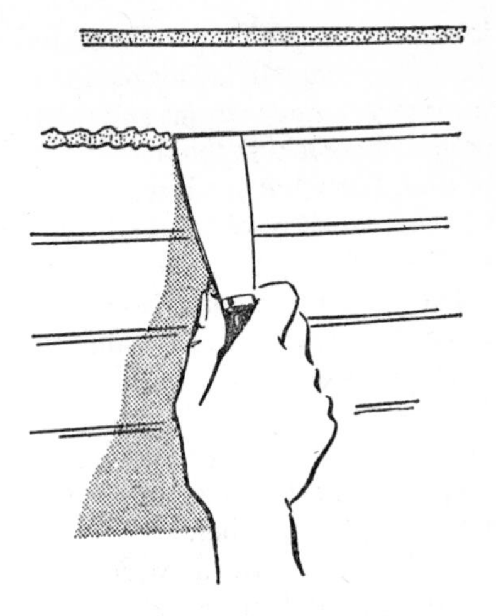

Fig. 6. Caulking is done on wooden boats to make the seams of the bottom, sides and deck waterproof.

compound. Boats with seam-battened planks, the seams of which are backed with a narrow wood strip, require only seam filling compound.

All carvel or smooth-planked boats, except very small ones, require caulking when new and, usually, at least once a year. It is best to caulk the bottom of a new boat after it has been planked to the bilge point, and before it has been turned over to plank the topside.

Very small smooth-planked boats usually require no more than seam-filling. As boats increase in size, with the space between planks widening in proportion, in becomes increasingly necessary to insert caulking material before filling the seams. Deck seams need to be caulked or simply filled, according to their width. If less than about 1/16 inch wide, they need no caulking.

Materials. The caulking material consists of twisted cotton or oakum strands (oakum is made of tarred rope ends). Both are sold in strips or wicking in paint and hardware stores. Bottom seams between planks less than one inch thick require cotton for caulking. Planks between one and two inches thick take either cotton or oakum. With planks over two inches thick, use oakum only. The strip to be inserted should be about as wide as the space between planks at the surface.

For filling seams, or "paying," use a ready-made seam-filling compound or make your own. To do this, mix whiting with white lead to the consistency of putty. On commercial boats a little engine oil is often added to prevent hardening, but this will stain the edges of the surrounding wood. In areas where bottom fouling is excessive, use a prepared anti-fouling seam compound. This compound turns away teredo worms and may be used to fill cracks in the rudder, stem, or keel. For filling deck seams a special compound is sold and it is highly advisable to use it.

Do not underestimate the importance of using the proper seam-filling compound. It has to harden only at the surface to receive paint, and should remain spongy and resilient enough not to be shaken or squeezed loose in heavy weather.

Procedure. With a wide wood chisel or a caulking wheel, which is a free-turning disk resembling a paper cutter's wheel, clean the seams to a uniform width, if necessary. Clean out shavings and sawdust from between the seams and smooth off rough spots on the surface with sandpaper.

With a seam brush or sash tool, apply a coat of white lead between seams and let dry. This helps to hold the caulking firm and make it last. Begin caulking at one end of the boat

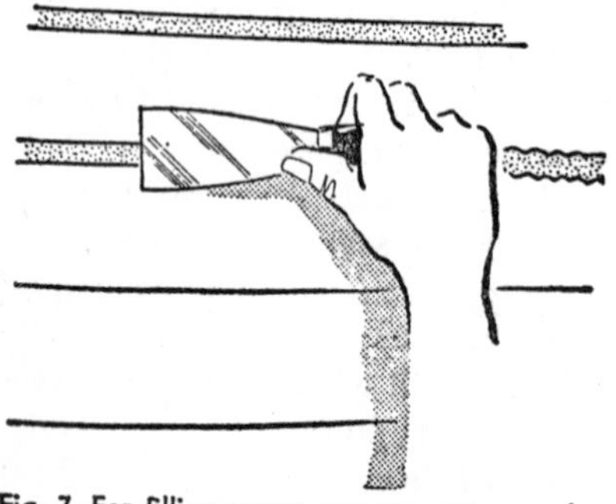

Fig. 7. For filling seams, you can use a ready-made seam-filling compound. You can make your own by mixing whiting with white lead to the consistency of putty.

Fig. 8. If using cotton to fill a seam, tap a strip into the seam in loops of convenient length.

and work to the other, going from left to right if right-handed. Use a caulking mallet or hammer and a caulking iron to drive the strips of caulking material into place, as shown in the illustration.

If using cotton, *tap* a strip into the seam in loops of convenient length or tap in one layer over another. If using oakum, do not make loops unless the continuous strip will not fill the space. Unless the planks are of very hard wood, do not pound with the mallet or hammer. This might cram the strips in so tightly as to loosen the planks and probably pull them right away from the ribs when the caulking swells in water.

Avoid knocking cotton or oakum into the edges of the planking. This causes leaking and rotting. Work slowly at first to get the feel of it. Leave space at the outside of the seams for filling.

After Caulking. Apply a light coat of thick paint over the caulking material to provide a base for filling.

This painting will also limit absorption by the planks of linseed oil from the putty or seam-filling compound. Otherwise the putty would dry out and tend to work loose, and the linseed oil might crack the wood.

Next, fill the space over the caulking material with putty. Use a putty knife or a caulking gun. A caulking gun pumps putty into the seams by hand pressure as you move along them. Depress the putty slightly between the seams. When the planks swell in water they will squeeze the putty out to surface level giving you a watertight hull.

Allow at least 24 hours for the putty to dry, then rub over-all with sandpaper again before painting. If the boat is new or has been out of the water long enough to dry out, let it stand idle in water for several days after caulking and painting. This allows the planks to swell and bind the caulking.

Without this precaution the caulking material might loosen. And whether or not it did so, the boat would not be waterproof until its planks expanded to their normal size in water.

PAINTING AND FINISHING

Interiors of Boat

The engine, though often overlooked, benefits from a coat of enamel. After cleaning it with kerosene, apply heat-resisting, rust-inhibiting primer. Then brush or spray on engine enamel. Use no other enamel. Only engine enamel resists heat, gasoline, and oil adequately. It also dries quickly to a tough, scuff resisting finish which cleans easily.

Protect the bilge against absorption of water and oils with red lead or bilge paint. This lessens decay and guards against fire. When fitting out each year or whenever it is necessary to reapply bilge paint, first clean out the bilge with one of the reliable alkali cleaners in common use. Put the cleaner in the bilge before draining it and let it stay there for a couple of days. Then drain and rinse the bilge. After it has dried out, you can brush on the new coat of bilge paint.

Wire insulation, ducts, pipes, and other spongy or uneven surfaces may show through or discolor ordinary finishes. Use a sealer made for such surfaces before painting over them.

Fig. 9. Using a putty knife, fill the space over the caulking material with putty.

Cabin Interior

Preparation. If you are replacing an old finish, it is best to remove it with one of the fireproof removers—

not with a blow torch, as the flame will probably scorch the wood. Spread the liquid remover on with an old brush and let it soak in long enough to pucker up the varnish. Then gently scrape it off with the broad knife. If some of the old finish remains, apply the remover again and scrape the softened varnish off. Be careful not to gouge the wood in scraping.

Fig. 10. It is best to remove old finishes with one of the fireproof removers when working on your cabin interior.

Wash off all remover left on the wood with a rag soaked in turpentine or alcohol. This neutralizes the remover. Wipe dry and rub smooth with fine sandpaper. Always rub with the grain. Rub vigorously – a bright finish shows up every flaw. Do not use steel wool here or at any point above the waterline; flecks of it often imbed in the wood and rust or make a black spot in the finish.

To restore varnish in good condition, rub the spars smooth with #00 or finer wet-and-dry sandpaper. Do not dig through or damage the old finish.

Bleaching. To equalize the color of predominantly light wood, bleach dark or discolored areas before varnishing. Also bleach stubbornly dark spots on the darker woods. Preferably use a ready-made bleach, in weak solution. Mix your own, if you wish, by adding one teaspoon of oxalic acid to each pint of water. Sandpaper off the salty crust left by the bleach.

Staining and Filling. To equalize the color of predominantly dark wood, stain before varnishing. Use a manufactured stain for most reliable results. Let it stand long enough to penetrate, then wipe dry with a cloth.

Open-grained woods, such as mahogany or oak, especially need filler to make the open grain less noticeable. You can apply paste filler after applying stain, or you can combine these operations. You can also mix oil stain with filler yourself. Stained fillers are sold for mahogany and oak.

Lay the filler on heavily. Let it set a few minutes. If it gets too dry, brush it lightly with turpentine. Briskly rub across the grain to work in the filler. Then rub with the grain to remove the excess.

If some open joints in the wood are too deep to be leveled with filler, fill them with white lead putty. Mix whiting with this putty to make it harden satisfactorily. Color it with stain, slightly darker than the stained wood. Press the putty in deeply, leaving it high. After it drys, sandpaper it level.

Varnishing. Choose moderately warm, windless days for varnishing.

The varnish should be spar varnish for exterior use and the new water- and alcohol-resistant type for interiors. Thin the first coat of varnish with turpentine. Brush it out to make it spread and penetrate, sealing the filler and putty. Use long, single strokes, brushing toward the area already coated.

Apply two or three more coats, not thinned. You can use special varnish made to dry in a few hours. Otherwise let each coat dry at least 12 hours or the recommended drying time before applying the next. Smooth each coat, after drying, with #2/0 or finer sandpaper, preferably wet-and-dry cabinet sandpaper. Use a portable reciprocating sanding machine if possible, not a rotary sander unless you are highly experienced in its use—it is a *very* rapid cutter.

Flow on the last coat of varnish. After it dries, wipe off any dust that settles on it with a turpentine-soaked rag. Then sand it to a flat surface with #5/0 or finer wet-and-dry sandpaper. To give it a mellow luster, rub it after sanding with rottenstone and crude oil on a pad. For added protection and to reduce the number of coats, yon can try applying one of the plastic finishes. These plastic finishes are a new development and must be applied exactly as directed by the manufacturer.

To refresh the finish, wash, wipe, and, when dry, apply another coat of varnish as needed, generally every few months.

Paint. If replacing an old finish in poor shape, remove it with one of the fireproof removers, scrape clean, wash with turpentine or alcohol, and sandpaper smooth. Apply one coat of primer, thinned as necessary. The thinning will depend principally upon the temperature but somewhat upon the type of wood. Harder woods require thinner primers. When the primer is dry, apply a coat of undercoater, which should be sanded when dry, and then you are ready for the enamel or flat, whichever you are going to use for the finish. Generally one coat will do, but if necessary apply a second.

Fig. 11. Open-grain woods, such as mahogany or oak, especially need filler to make the grain imperfections less noticeable.

If the old finish is sound, simply sand it to a smooth surface and, after dusting, do any necessary puttying or trowel cementing. Then apply one coat of undercoater, sand it, and finish with a coat of either enamel or flat.

Spars

For varnishing, follow the directions above, under *Cabin Interior,* except that you should use spar varnish, which is heavier and more durable than varnish used in the interior. To paint, use a topside deck-and-spar finish, preceded by a primer if you are finishing from the bare wood. Thin it enough to flow freely. This paint drys fast and lasts long. If of good quality, it retains the original color and sheen many months.

Cabin Exterior

If any deck canvasing is to be done, delay cabin-exterior work until it is finished. Canvas-laying is described under *Deck,* below.

To varnish, follow directions above, under *Cabin Interior,* except that you should use spar varnish.

Painting. To paint, remove an old finish in poor condition with a blow torch or, preferably, one of the steam jenny removers, if available. Do not use a wax-base paint remover, as it is almost impossible to remove all the wax before painting. The wax causes the paint to chip later, exposing the raw wood.

Fig. 12. To remove exterior finishes in poor condition, use a blow torch held close to and at right angles with the planking.

After sanding clean and smooth prime a new or burned off cabin exterior with thinned flat deck-and-topside paint. Thin it according to the manufacturer's directions. Next apply one or two coats of flat marine paint un-thinned, or thinned only enough to ease brushing. Use yacht or deck semi-gloss or gloss as the final coat. While painting the cabin exterior or deckhouse, keep a turpentine-soaked rag handy to wipe off spots from the deck.

An old finish which is still smooth and un-cracked may be painted over, after sanding, without priming.

Avoid harsh paint cleaners in washing the cabin exterior. A good-quality finish sheds dirt readily when sponged or brushed with soapy water. To maintain, rinse salt spray from the entire exterior of your craft with fresh water—daily, if possible.

Deck

To varnish, follow instructions above for *Cabin Interior,* except for using spar varnish.

Painting. To paint, follow the procedure given above for the *Cabin Exterior.* Whether the deck is wood or canvas you can make its finish resemble varnish from a distance of a few feet by using some yellow or brown shades of deck paint.

In any case use a deck paint containing non-slip compound. You can buy this ready-mixed in the paint or add it yourself. Use non-slip paint on any part of the superstructure, including metal or canvas, on which you walk. Wet weather or spray makes these places dangerously slippery, otherwise.

Canvas Deck. If the old canvas is split or checked, more paint will only cause more damage by its shrinking when it dries. Remove the old canvas, clean to bare wood, and prepare the wood for new canvas. To do this, first remove all hardware, moldings, and so on which the canvas will not fit around or under. Plane and sand the deck until smooth and even. After puttying all ruts, gouges, and the like, apply a priming coat of deck paint, if necessary. Let this dry.

Then, with help from another person, if possible, cut the canvas to fit with a minimum number of pieces. The best starting point for the canvas is along one gunwhale just below the sheer-plank edge. Do not attempt to cut around the coaming until later, when the canvas has been fastened near the coaming.

Size both sides of canvas before brushing on white lead paint, with drier added, or with waterproof canvas cement. Do not apply either for more than a few feet ahead of the canvas as it unrolls.

While the adhesive is wet, tack the edge of the canvas into place at the middle of the starting end, using flat-headed copper tacks. Roll out the canvas, stretching it tightly in all directions, but do not stretch the warp and fill of the canvas out of woven alignment.

Resume tacking in both directions from the starting point around the sides and transom. Drive in the tacks at close pitch, on alternate sides. Space them an inch or so apart. Do not drive them deeply enough to pinch or pucker the canvas. At the coaming turn up the edge of the canvas and cut it to fit snugly. Tack the canvas down at the angle where it turns and at its upper edge. Trim off excess canvas with a very sharp blade.

When the molding is in place over the canvas, apply a filling coat of glue size or thinned canvas cement (four parts canvas cement to one part benzine or gasoline). Let this filling dry

Fig. 13. Get a friend to help you lay new canvas decking. Start at a point along one gunwhale just below the sheer-plank.

at least 24 hours. Without this protection the linseed oil in the paint would eventually rot the canvas.

Old canvas in good condition needs cleaning and sanding before applying paint.

When ready with new or old canvas, apply two coats of deck paint. Dry each coat for 24 hours and sand lightly between applications. Be sure the paint is thin enough to spread and penetrate thoroughly. The paint should dry hard and not too smooth, to provide sure footing without overloading the fabric.

Steel Deck. Remove rust and scale with steel wool and a wire brush. Inasmuch as many spots are likely to be bared in removing rust, it is best to apply two coats of metal primer on either old or new work. Use galvanized metal primer on galvanized metal. Allow each coat of primer 24 hours to dry. Finish with two coats of topside or deck paint.

Deck Gear

Make canvas articles such as sails, awnings, and canvas anchors mildewproof. Use preparations especially made for canvas, or general purpose preservatives such as copper napthenate solution. Dip or generously brush on the liquid preservative. Wash, dry, and sun-bleach canvas before using this treatment.

For metal surfaces — trim, davits, stanchions, railing, and so on — follow the procedure given above for steel decks. Signal paints may offer more vivid colors than do topside and deck paints.

For any surfaces to be varnished, follow the varnishing directions under *Cabin Exterior,* given above.

Topside

In painting the hull above the waterline, go by the same procedure as given for *Cabin Exterior,* above. Mark the lower level with a pencil line or with masking tape, leaving at least an inch and a half of space for boottopping.

For the sake of appearance some prefer a flat finish topside, instead of gloss, to eliminate shine and shadows. This way, it is said, the entire curved sweep of the hull stands out distinctly from any angle. But glossy paints last longer and may be cleaned more easily. Let the topside dry for at least 24 hours before putting the boat in water to make sure your deck dries to a clear finish.

Bottom

In salt water the bottom of your craft needs copper or bronze anti-fouling paint. Without this the hull is liable to collect cuts opening the way for fungi and shellfish. These damage the hull and cut down speed. Apply anti-fouling paint to the bottom at least twice a year in areas where the toredo worm is common. Most of these paints dry best under water and should be applied immediately before launching.

If you use your boat in fresh water only, you may forego anti-fouling paint. You will need to scrub the bottom several times in a season, however. The temperature of the water also matters; a boat usually fouls more quickly in warm water. Another factor is the proportion of time your craft stands idle. It fouls at a faster rate when idle.

Having attended to surface preparation and caulking, apply the first coat of anti-fouling paint, thinned according to the manufacturer's directions. Mark the upper level with pencil or masking tape. Do not use linseed oil or turpentine in thinning anti-fouling paint. Brush in the first coat to penetrate deeply. Lightly sand this and the second coat, but not the third and final coat.

Do not use ordinary primers under anti-fouling paints. Prime and finish with anti-fouling paint only.

Racing Bottoms. The requirements of speed as well as anti-fouling action enter into the consideration of the finish applied to the bottom of either motor or sail boats intended for racing. The most desirable finish is one as smooth and slick as it is possible to make it. There are available very fine and expensive enamels for this purpose. They should be applied in mild weather and allowed to dry thoroughly between coats. For the last word in smoothness, you can apply a thin coat of trowel cement between each coat from primer to the last coat of undercoater. All coats should be rubbed to a perfectly smooth surface with sandpaper between the intermediate coats and finished with pumice and water rubbing. If you have built up the surface carefully with thinned trowel cement between coats and finished off with a careful but thorough rubbing with pumice and water, you will have a mirror-like finish which will present almost no resistance to the flow of the water over the bottom. However, this is a long tedious process and is usually done only by the most ardent yachtsmen and speed-boat drivers.

Fig. 14. Frequently washing a racing bottom with soap and water helps maintain the sheen and smoothness.

A very satisfactory—and more anti-fouling—finish is racing bronze. This has many of the characteristics of standard anti-fouling paint but it will flow to a much smoother and somewhat harder surface upon drying. Prime with this paint after thinning it with the recommended thinners. When dry, trowel cement the bottom and sand this when dry. Then apply a second coat and let dry. Just before the boat is to be launched apply the final coat. Most brands of this paint dry better under water.

Racing bottoms require more than ordinary care. Enameled bottoms are quite prone to accumulate growth. The boat should be hauled out of the water as often as convenient. While it is out, wash with very mild soap and water and rinse with clear fresh water. This way the sheen and smoothness may last you a whole racing season. If the finish becomes dull or rough, the application of another coat of enamel and a rubbing will restore it. Racing-bronze finishes may need restoring late in the season and this is easily done by hauling out the boat, washing the bottom with fresh water, lightly sanding it, and applying another coat of the finish. Launch again immediately if the manufacturer of the paint recommends it.

These recommendations for bottom finishing are just as good for fast motor boats as they are for sail boats. In fact, the care of speed-boat bottoms is probably more important as they receive more wear due to their greater speed. Many speed-boat drivers who store their boats on trailers finish the bottom with spar varnish. This is a perfectly satisfactory finish if the boat is not moored in the water. The varnish presents an excellent surface, but it is not resistant to the growth of grass or shellfish. Apply the finish as you would for topsides.

Boottopping

For the strip along the waterline between the topsides and the bottom of the hull use only boottopping paint. This paint is toxic to plankton, grass, and minute marine plants at the surface of the water. It dries exceptionally hard, permitting frequent cleaning. To make an even line, paint with masking tape for a boundary.

Attempt decorative painting only after practice has given you a sure hand. Leave all gold-leaf trimming to an expert. Apply bright yellow paint, if you wish, to achieve an effect nearly similar to that of gold leaf.

AVERAGE PAINT REQUIREMENTS FOR VARIOUS TYPES OF BOATS

(Amounts are for two coats for refinishing. If starting from bare wood, quantities should be doubled)

	Dinghies	*Rowboats*	*Outboards*	*Utility*	*Runabouts*	*Cruisers*	*Sailboats*	*Auxiliaries*	*Yachts*
Average length (feet)	10	14	14	24	24	32	20	36	60
Topside paint	1 qt	–	3 pts	2 qts	–	2 gals	2 qts	2 gals	9 gals
Varnish	2 qts	–	3 pts	–	1½ gals	1 gal	1 qt	2 gals	5 gals
Deck paint	–	2 qts	–	1 gal	1 qt	1 gal	1 gal	2 gals	5 gals
Interior enamel	–	–	–	–	–	2 qts	–	3 qts	3 gals
Bottom (anti-fouling)	–	1 qt	1 qt	2 qts	1 gal	1½ gals	3 qts	3 gals	6 gals
Boottopping	–	–	–	–	½ pt	½ pt	½ pt	½ pt	1 pt
Engine enamel	–	–	½ pt	1 pt	1 pt	1 pt	–	1 pt	1 qt

Courtesy "Motor Boating"

APPENDIX

ESTIMATING TABLES

Estimating Time

The following table gives the amount of time that a journeyman painter takes to do the various jobs. In each case, the figure given represents the number of square feet of work which he can do in an hour.

A household painter with fair experience will probably take about twice as long to do a really good job.

TABLE FOR ESTIMATING TIME REQUIRED

Type of Work	*Sq. Ft. per Hour*
Preparatory work.	
Plain siding and trim	200
Trim only	120
Burning off plain surfaces	40
Puttying or glazing sash	45
Exterior painting.	
First coat	100
Second coat	120
Third coat	140
For trim only, deduct 25% from above figures. Sanding and puttying not included.	
Shingle staining	150–200
Painting brick:	
First coat	120
Second coat	160
Third coat	190
Painting interior wood trim:	
First coat	140
Second coat	130
Third coat	130
Preparatory work on interior trim:	
First application	300
Sanding and puttying between first and second coats	200
Sanding and dusting between second and third coats	350
Enameling	80
Staining	220
Filling	75
Shellacking	225
Varnishing	200
Wall finishing (smooth plaster):	
Primer and sealer	200
Flat wall paint	175
Water sizing	470
Stippling	180
Glazing	60
Wall finishing (smooth plaster):	
Gloss or semi-gloss	200
Calcimine	225
Casein paint	225
Wall finishing(sand-finish plaster):	
Primer and sealer	125
Gloss or semi-gloss	130
Flat wall paint	140
Water sizing	460
Glazing	75
Calcimine	220
Casein paint	220
Painting floors:	
First coat	280
Second coat	300
Third coat	320

From "Painting and Decorating Craftsman's Manual and Textbook" by permission of the Painting and Decorating Contractors of America.

Estimating Amount of Paint

The table that follows will help you to estimate the amount of paint you will need for a given surface area under normal conditions. It is always wise to make this calculation before beginning to work. By doing so you avoid waste and annoyance.

There are two external factors which influence the amount of paint you will need for a given area—the thickness of the paint and the roughness or absorbency of the surface. The smoother and less absorbent the surface, the less paint needed. The thicker the paint, the more you need.

TABLE FOR ESTIMATING QUANTITIES OF PAINT

Surface and Type of Paint	First Coat Sq. Ft. per Gal.	Second Coat Sq. Ft. per Gal.	Third Coat Sq. Ft. per Gal.
Wood Siding:			
Exterior house paint	468	540	630
Trim (exterior):			
Exterior trim paint	850	900	972
Porch floors and steps:			
Porch and deck paint	378	540	576
Asbestos wall shingles:			
Exterior house paint	180	400	
Shingle siding:			
Exterior house paint	342	423	
Shingle stain	150	225	
Shingle roof:			
Exterior oil paint	150	250	
Shingle stain	120	200	
Brick (exterior):			
Exterior oil paint	200	400	
Cement water paint	100	150	
Cement floors and steps (exterior):			
Porch and deck paint	450	600	600
Color stain and finish	510	480	
Medium texture stucco:			
Exterior oil paint	153	360	360
Cement water paint	99	135	
Doors and windows (interior):			
Enamel	603	405	504
Floors, hardwood (interior):			
Oil paint	540	450	
Shellac	540	675	765
Varnish	540	540	540
Walls, smooth-finish plaster:			
Flat oil paint	630 (Primer)	540	630
Gloss or semi-gloss oil paint	630 (Primer)	540	540
Calcimine	720 (Size)	240	
Casein water paint	540	700	

From "Painting and Decorating Craftsman's Manual and Textbook" by permission of the Painting and Decorating Contractors of America.

Planning Table for a Room

The accompanying table will enable you to plan carefully and competently for any room in the house. The various parts of the room are listed separately because different materials are usually used for each part. You can prepare a table for each room you have to do, if you want, as well as one for exterior painting.

PLANNING TABLE FOR PAINTING A ROOM

Walls:
- Material__________
- Surface area__________
- Condition__________
- Equipment__________
- Treatment:
  - Preparation:
    - Materials__________
  - Priming:
    - Time__________
    - Quantity of paint__________
    - Cost__________
  - First coat:
    - Time__________
    - Quantity of paint__________
    - Cost__________
  - Second coat:
    - Time__________
    - Quantity of paint__________
    - Cost__________
  - Third coat (if desired):
    - Time__________
    - Quantity of paint__________
    - Cost__________

Woodwork:
- Surface area__________
- Condition__________
- Equipment__________
- Treatment:
  - Preparation:
    - Materials__________
  - Priming:
    - Time__________
    - Quantity of paint__________
    - Cost__________
  - First coat:
    - Time__________
    - Quantity of paint__________
    - Cost__________
  - Second coat:
    - Time__________
    - Quantity of paint__________
    - Cost__________

Ceiling:
- Material__________
- Surface area__________
- Condition__________
- Equipment__________
- Treatment:
  - Preparation:
    - Materials__________
  - Priming:
    - Time__________
    - Quantity of paint__________
    - Cost__________
  - First coat:
    - Time__________
    - Quantity of paint__________
    - Cost__________
  - Second coat:
    - Time__________
    - Quantity of paint__________
    - Cost__________
  - Third coat (if desired):
    - Time__________
    - Quantity of paint__________
    - Cost__________

Floor:
- Surface area__________
- Condition__________
- Equipment__________
- Treatment:
  - Preparation:
    - Materials__________
  - Finishing:
    - Time__________
    - Quantity of material__________
    - Cost__________

Totals for Room:
- Time__________
- Cost__________
- Quantity of materials:
  - Walls__________
  - Ceiling__________
  - Woodwork__________
  - Floor__________

INDEX